Chameleon Readers

Teaching Children to Appreciate All Kinds of Good Stories

Chameleon Readers

Teaching Children to Appreciate All Kinds of Good Stories

Allyssa McCabe, Ph.D.
University of Massachusetts Lowell

IN COLLABORATION WITH

Barbara Burt, Karen Craddock-Willis, Martha D. Crago,
Masahiko Minami, Diane Pesco, Marguerita Jimenez Silva

The McGraw-Hill Companies, Inc.
New York   St. Louis   San Francisco   Auckland   Bogotá   Caracas   Lisbon
London   Madrid   Mexico City   Milan   Montreal   New Delhi
San Juan   Singapore   Sydney   Tokyo   Toronto

McGraw-Hill

A Division of The **McGraw·Hill** Companies

This book was set in Palatino by Graphic World, Inc.

The editor was Michael Clark;

the production supervisor was Elizabeth J. Strange.

The cover was designed by Top Desk Publisher's Group;
illustration by David Flaherty.

Project supervision was done by Hockett Editorial Service.

R. R. Donnelley & Sons Company was printer and binder.

CHAMELEON READERS

Teaching Children to Appreciate All Kinds of Good Stories

This book is printed on acid-free paper.

1 2 3 4 5 6 7 8 9 0 DOC DOC 9 0 9 8 7 6 5

ISBN 0-07-045016-1

Library of Congress Cataloging-in-Publication Data

McCabe, Allyssa.
    Chameleon readers : teaching children to appreciate all kinds of
good stories / Allyssa McCabe in collaboration with Barbara Burt . . .
[et al.].
    p.   cm.
    Includes bibliographical references and index.
    ISBN 0-07-045016-1
    1. Children's literature—Study and teaching (Elementary)
2. Reading (Elementary)   3. Storytelling.   I. Title.
LB1576.M16   1996
372.64'044—dc20   95-38739

About the Author

ALLYSSA McCABE, Ph.D., teaches developmental psychology at the University of Massachusetts, Lowell. She has taught courses in the development of language and narrative structure at the Harvard Graduate School of Education. Dr. McCabe has written, with Carole Peterson, *Developmental Psycholinguistics: Three Ways of Looking at a Child's Narrative.* She and Dr. Peterson edited another volume, *Developing Narrative Structure.* Dr. McCabe founded and continues to edit a scholarly journal, *The Journal of Narrative and Life History.* She has published a number of papers on diverse aspects of the development of narrative talk, and presented at the International Congress for the Study of Child Language, held in Budapest, Hungary, 1990, and Trieste, Italy, 1993. She has a long-standing interest in how to facilitate oral language acquisition and, to this end, published a book for parents called *Language Games to Play with your Child: Enhancing Communication from Infancy through Late Childhood* (New and Revised Edition; Insight/Plenum). Dr. McCabe earned her Ph.D. in psychology from the University of Virginia in 1980, and is the mother of two children.

For my mother, Mary K. McCabe.
Her interest in all kinds of good stories told by individuals from all cultures has always been a staple of my life, and her attention to my own stories is an early, formative memory.

Contents

Preface

WHAT THIS BOOK ATTEMPTS TO ACCOMPLISH

This book is written with the hope of producing chameleon readers: children who can truly understand children who do not share their own cultural heritage, children who can and do read books from other cultures and identify and empathize with heroes and heroines of many different colors and cultures, children who appreciate many forms of storytelling.

Oddly enough, we may more easily find similarities between cultural traditions when we acknowledge, discuss, and come to understand differences than when we simply assert commonalities. In the end, you cannot help but see differences and similarities simultaneously when you examine any kind of cultural construct such as stories.

Chameleon Readers: Teaching Children to Appreciate All Kinds of Good Stories is primarily aimed at kindergarten and elementary school teachers who are interested in multicultural literacy programs, although others may find it useful too. The ideas of this book would be relevant both to programs that emphasize literature-based instruction and to those that rely primarily on basal readers. Information about cultural differences story forms would be critical to the instruction of some stories from various cultures that are included in readers. Such information is equally critical to the instruction of literature written by diverse authors. Instruction regarding cultural differences in story forms could be woven into the kind of preparation teachers are encouraged to do to establish successful *literature discussion groups* (see Raphael & McMahon, 1994, and Routman, 1991, pp. 122-132), where children are encouraged to have a genuine conversation about books instead of simply taking turns answering questions about them. Children's struggles to make sense of stories from different cultures could be one focus of *literature response logs* (see Routman, 1991, pp. 103-117). A literature response log is a journal for recording reactions to literature and is an alternative to requiring students to answer traditional comprehension questions and writing lengthy book reports. In using open-ended questions to evoke thoughtful and/or emotional reflections on literature, teachers can deal directly with students' honest reactions and record progress in getting them to come to appreciate stories from a culture other than their own.

Cultural differences in narrative structure must be factored in by any teacher who adopts a process orientation (see, for example, Routman, 1991) in instructing children of diverse ethnicities. *Process orientation* involves "noticing and valuing what the student . . . does in the process of reading, writing, listening, and speaking . . . For us teachers, this means valuing the process as well as the product, because it is in the process that the learning takes place" (Routman, 1991, p. 16). The product remains important to teachers adopting a process orientation, but emphasis shifts from a focus on correct spelling and mechanics to how the student arrived or is arriving at some final product. Students are encouraged to take risks in such an approach, even if they do not always succeed in accomplishing what they set out to do. The point is that teachers who are unaware of cultural differences in storytelling form do not have the information they need in order to value either the process or products of some children.

Process writing is one example of a process orientation. Graves (1983) and Calkins (1994) have urged teachers to turn their classrooms into writing workshops, where children write almost every day, where they converse with one another to choose topics of interest to them, where they revise their compositions and eventually "publish" them. Such an emphasis on process and group interaction would be very much affected by cultural differences in preferred storytelling form. Teachers seeking to be effective in implementing such programs with diverse children must be aware of such differences. In turn, this book suggests that students not only need to be made aware of different traditions but that they need to be encouraged to value such differences.

The title of this book is emblematic of our ultimate goal, which is to train children (and adults) to read and appreciate deeply stories from their own and other cultures and to identify with individuals of all races. At present such programs are operating without much knowledge of the fact that cultures structure experience quite differently—so differently, in fact, that sometimes stories from one culture literally do not make sense to members of another culture without some translation beyond the level of vocabulary and grammar.

Programs with an interest in multicultural literacy generally fall into two camps. One camp is best summarized by a quote from a person who compiled a list of hundreds of multicultural story books for young children. When asked about the fact that some stories do not at first reading make sense to children from other cultures, she said, "Oh these stories are good stories—they make sense to anyone. But in these books, children are rainbow-colored" (meaning that illustrators included children from various racial backgrounds). A program of multicultural literacy that is based on illustrations is not adequate, as we will show.

Another common approach in elementary school is to compile readers or collections of classroom literature containing stories from other cultures. The idea here is to read a story from, say, Haiti on Monday, a story from China on Thursday, and so on. Without providing any information for teachers or children that would allow them to truly understand these stories, the stories can seem unsatisfying, even bizarre, especially if children read only one story from a culture at a time. In my experience, both teachers and children either tend to avoid such stories or dislike them if they do read them. This approach, while on the right track, can backfire in a potentially disastrous way. Members of other cultures are likely to reject such puzzling stories as being "bad stories, stories that don't make sense," to quote one girl.

Thus, the first goal of this book is to present specific background information about stories and storytelling traditions from various cultures to help teachers understand and translate or extend stories from other cultures that they read to students or that they receive from students with diverse cultural backgrounds. In a way, I am trying to develop a *a tool for translation of discourse* that is equivalent to a foreign language dictionary for vocabulary or grammars for syntax. At present, we understand that phonology, vocabulary, and grammar are aspects of accent or dialect. We do not generally understand differences in narrative style as an aspect of accent or dialect.

Obviously, in such a short space as we will have, we can only begin to tap the immensely rich and complex set of traditions, values, aesthetics, and so on that comprise even one culture. But we have found that certain kinds of information greatly enable understanding.

The storytelling traditions we will discuss in this book reflect the range of traditions found in this country, but are by no means exhaustive of these. Nor is there any systematic means by which particular cultures we have focused on in this book were selected. The cultures detailed here are simply the cultures of people with whom I've had the pleasure of conversing at great length over the years. My coauthors and I take great delight in diverse storytelling traditions. We collected information about each of the kinds of traditions we discuss addressing a similar, but not identical, set of concerns. Because each group of traditions is so different from the others, each of the chapters presenting these traditions will be slightly different from the others.

Another major goal of this book is to examine and expand our current operating definitions of good stories. Resistance to implementing a curriculum that includes a substantial representation of multicultural literature often takes the form of concern for the quality of literature to be included. For example, *The American Society for Curriculum Development* (September, 1993, p. 4) contained the following discussion: "Including diverse voices can conflict with teaching top-quality literature . . . if you teach a work from every group at every grade level, you'll teach some bad literature."

The problem with this argument is that current formal definitions of what makes a good story are based on the European storytelling tradition, as we will see. This is exacerbated by the fact that 86.5% of teachers are "white, non-Hispanic" (hereafter to be referred to as European North American), according to the 1993 figures compiled by the National Center for Education Statistics, and so such teachers would also bring informal notions about what makes a good story from their own European tradition. Thus, this text proposes to expand our definition of a good story to make it more representative of the true range of narrative forms we have in this country at this time.

Of course, a third goal is to advocate the *explicit* instruction of all children about distinctive storytelling traditions of numerous ethnic groups. There are many reasons for this. To communicate with people from other ethnic backgrounds, children need some basic information about one another's language practices. To understand stories in primary grades from different cultures and eventually also great works of literature from many cultures, all children need information about diverse approaches to oral storytelling. All children need to be prepared from early elementary school to read the diverse works of world literature acclaimed by modern critics.

My fourth goal is to heighten *awareness of the importance of narratives* in kindergarten and early elementary school classrooms and to address instructional implications of the information I provide on cultural differences. As part of this goal, my book will provide specific, as well as general, information about published children's stories from many other cultures.

I use a broad but not all-encompassing definition of narrative. Specifically, "*narratives* usually concern real or pretend memories of something that happened, and therefore are often largely in the past tense. However, there are also hypothetical, future-tense narratives and others given in the historical present. Narratives often contain a chronological sequence of events, but one can also find narratives that contain only a single event or those that skip around in time. Narrative is often a kind of language, although there are musical, pictorial, and silently dramatic narratives" (McCabe, 1991, pp. 1-2). As a general rule, I use *narrative* to refer to factual accounts, *story* to refer to fictional ones. However, *story* is the term I often use more broadly in this text, when I wish to refer to both factual and fictional accounts with one term.

Many people avoid discussion of cultural differences out of a sense that only attention to universals of human conditions is nonracist. Some people assume that when you talk about cultural groups or differences of any sort that you are engaging in "sweeping generalizations" or stereotyping. Stereotypes are "simplistic and overexaggerated beliefs about a group, generally acquired secondhand and resistant to change" (Marger, 1994, p. 76). In contrast, the cultural differences in storytelling forms and traditions that we will discuss will be based on analyses of empirical data we or trusted colleagues have collected and, where possible, traditions of which at least one author has first-hand knowledge. We will try very hard not to oversimplify complex traditions, to highlight diversity within traditions, and to present documented changes (when available) in such traditions over time. Moreover, by talking about differences within the framework of aesthetic sensibility, as we intend to do, we hope to make clear that cultural differences are valued, valuable, intricate affairs. Avoidance of such discussion has usually meant that the Western European inheritance is presented as if it were universal and that cultural issues were ignored, invisible. Again , our goal is to steep all children in information about many cultures in order that they may come to identify with many kinds of heroes and heroines and come to appreciate all kinds of stories. Rather than muting the cultural origins of all stories, we seek to emphasize them. The chameleon is never no color at all.

WHAT THIS BOOK WILL NOT ATTEMPT TO ACCOMPLISH

I am an academic psychologist who has worked in the field of education for quite a while now. I have never been an elementary school teacher. Thus there will remain a gap between the information I present here and actual classroom practice. Teachers will need to develop their own specific curriculum mindful of the concerns I address here. In fact, I am convinced that the best curriculum is that developed by teachers themselves. As many (for example, Raphael & McMahon, 1994) have pointed out, teachers are professionals who know their students' needs and interests better than anyone trying to generate a generic curriculum.

In addition, a full provision of specific curriculum suggestions would double the size of this book, making it quite unwieldy and quite beyond the scope my publishers and I intended. Nonetheless, I have been asked repeatedly about how I would envision the ideas advanced in this book being implemented in classrooms. So, to that end, we provide a list of activities or tasks that would be congruent with the concerns we address at the end of each chapter in a section entitled, "Research into Practice." My hope is that teachers will use the ideas in this book to develop curricula and send me reports of what worked and what did not. Perhaps in a few years I will have a large enough collection of such reports to write a second volume.

CAUTIONS

Throughout this book, I have included a number of examples of actual child language. Some of these examples are quite lengthy, and that is not an accident or a mistake. My goal in this practice is to sensitize readers in some cases to the extraordinary storytelling capacities of ordinary children and in other cases to the extraordinary efforts some adults go to lengthen their children's discourse capabilities. I want people to come to appreciate length and elaboration in stories instead of trying to curtail it. Therefore, providing short examples of the "length" I am discussing makes no sense.

What I do recommend is that readers speak the transcriptions of oral language aloud. These words were meant to be heard, not read. Some people are in fact quite alienated by transcriptions of oral language. Voicing such transcriptions restores the stories to the medium for which they were intended.

Of greatest concern to me is the labels we have selected to use in talking about various kinds of groups. We have engaged in considerable discussion with many members of each group referred to in this book and the labels we selected are the ones that offend fewest people in 1995. However, all group labels offend somebody. There is sometimes little consensus among individuals who identify with certain groups about what label is to be preferred. In addition, groups change over time in the labels they identify with. In other words, labels of any sort are inevitable land mines. Nonetheless, we need to get past the level of the noun if we are to reduce the considerable ethnic tensions in this multicultural society of ours. It is in this spirit that the book is written.

ACKNOWLEDGMENTS

I have talked to many people about the ideas in this book and many individuals have made some sort of contribution to this book, but here are some of those (other than the authors of chapters) who have made the biggest contributions: Betty Allen, Chien-Ju Chang, Dr. Richard Ely, Cindy Gimbert, Terri Griffin, Gigliana Meltzi, Rebecca Keebler, Ben Mardell, Dr. Timothy Mount, Carmella Perez, Mignonne Pollard, Ana Maria Rodino, Dr. Elizabeth Taupin, Claudia Vidal, Xiaofang Xu.

McGraw-Hill and I would like to thank the following reviewers for their many helpful comments and suggestions: Nancy Bacharach, St. Cloud State University; Kenneth Cushner, Kent State University; Gayle Flickinger, Illinois State University; Daphne Haddad, University of South Carolina; Robert Kaplan, University of Southern California; Luther Kindall, University of Tennessee; Donald Leu, Syracuse University; Anne Martin, Syracuse University; Roy O'Donnell, University of Georgia; Ileana Seda, Pennsylvania State University; Kay Stickle, Ball State University; and Carl Tomlinson, Northern Illinois University.

Allyssa McCabe

References

Calkins, L.M. (1994). *The art of teaching writing* (new edition). Portsmouth, NH: Heinemann.

Graves, D.H. (1983). *Writing: Teachers and children at work.* Portsmouth, NH: Heinemann.

McCabe, A. (1991). Editorial. *Journal of Narrative and Life History, 1* (1), 1-2.

Marger, M.N. (1994). *Race and ethnic relations* (3rd ed.). Belmont, California: Wadsworth Publishing Co.

Raphael, T., & McMahon, S.I. (1994, April). *'Book club: An alternative framework for reading instruction.* Paper presented at the George Graham Lectures in Reading, Charlottesville, Virginia.

Routman, R. (1991). *Invitations: Changing as teachers and learners K-12.* Portsmouth, NH: Heinemann.

Chameleon Readers

Teaching Children to Appreciate All Kinds of Good Stories

CHAPTER 1

Important Stories

Allyssa McCabe

OVERVIEW

In this chapter, we highlight the pervasive uses of stories, both factual and fictional, in classrooms. We examine formal scholastic and informal social uses of stories. We briefly touch on various recommendations about increasing the use of stories for various instructional purposes. Then we consider the basic functions of personal narrative, functions that seem to be culturally universal so far as we know.

The first function of personal narrative is to make sense of experiences that individuals have had in the past. We focus on children's need to make sense of particularly disturbing experiences, such as death or divorce, and on how books that do not shy away from such strong topics potentially can help a child sort through traumatic incidents. We also address teachers' concerns and fears about possibly stereotypical disturbing content (such as certain kinds of children living in circumstances of poverty) in published stories from various cultures. Narratives derive and transmit important lessons from personal experiences, an analogue of the morals in fictional stories for children.

A second basic function of narratives is to present the narrator as having played particular roles (hero, victim, jokester) during some event. Such roles tap into at least two dimensions: power and moral rectitude. Roles children represent themselves as having played are linked to the roles of protagonists in the fictional stories they hear and read. A third basic function of narrative is to make past experiences (traumatic as well as joyful) vivid or present, accessible to children in a way that more expository, abstract information is not equipped to do. A fourth function achieved through exchanging narratives is to establish relationships with people: teachers with students, students with other students.

Finally, we consider an exemplary instructional program and offer a few specific ideas for translating research into practice.

CULTURAL UNIVERSALS

The Many Uses of Stories in Classrooms

Many people highlight the importance of stories in classrooms (for example, Barton, 1986; Paley, 1990). Stories are the first genre of discourse for children learning to speak publicly in such activities as Sharing Time (Michaels, 1991). Stories are often an early writing form (Calkins, 1986, 1994; Graves, 1983), but one that continues until high school graduation (Freedman, 1987) and sometimes on into college writing classes. Stories are also a time-honored, but recently neglected, means of implementing moral education programs (Ellenwood & Ryan, 1991; Vitz, 1990). Current work in philosophy and cognitive psychology highlights the importance of narrative in developing arguments (MacIntyre, 1981) and thinking in general (Dennett, 1991). Oral history projects (such as the Foxfire series, Wigginton, 1976, 1977) have demonstrated that one of the most effective means of teaching history to children is through the use of familial adults' narratives. Historical projects emphasizing people who made decisions that changed the course of events in the world preclude students' misunderstanding history as a mass of "large, abstract, inaccessible, and uncontrollable forces" (Ellenwood & Ryan, 1991). A teacher in Brookline, Massachusetts has devised an ingenious program to teach science using narratives (Lipke & Lipke, 1992).

Typical curricular uses of narratives include books read to and by children. One study (Flood, Lapp, & Flood, 1984) examined eight leading basal reading programs to determine the types of writing included in the programs from preprimers to second grade readers. Over half (56 percent) of the selections in all readers were narrative materials. Poems accounted for 25 percent and exposition accounted for 15 percent. Few differences between grade levels were discovered. The same study examined three standardized reading tests (the Stanford Achievement Test, Metropolitan Achievement Test, and California Test of Basic Skills) and found that narrative materials were most often used for testing. Another study (Flood, Lapp, and Nagel, 1991) found that 90 percent of the titles on a list of core works selected for students to read in kindergarten through grade six in twenty-four school districts were fictional stories. Unfortunately, that same study also found that the titles did *not* represent a variety of cultures.

Other common curricular uses of narratives include invited performances from professional storytellers, newsletters, story retellings to assess comprehension, dramatic plays, and selected use of videos, movies, and filmstrips. Sometimes classes will recreate field trips together in the form of a narrative about what happened on that trip. Children may be asked to write letters about their experiences to someone as an exercise in imagining a specific audience for their writing. Occasionally, teachers will give children narratives as a kind of mnemonic device. For example, one teacher told his students an elaborate story about ten ants and a wise old spider, all of whom were accustomed to telling the truth about themselves. One day the ants were about to be poisoned if they admitted to being destructive carpenter ants. The spider understood what would happen to them if they told the truth about what kind of pest they were to the human being facing them, so he yelled, "LIE U TEN ANTS!" None of this teacher's young students ever forgot how to spell *lieutenant* again. Another example comes from Suzuki violin teachers, who have children learn a rhyming story, "Henrietta Poppeletta," in order to learn the rhythm and structure of a Suzuki etude.

Informal uses of narratives in classrooms are also numerous. Children tell narratives about what happened to them on buses or during walks to and from school, over lunch, and in the hallways. Young children engage in making narratives during fantasy play, art activities, and even when they are supposed to be quiet during naptime. They use stories to make one another laugh or cry or feel embarrassed and to pass on lessons learned (for example, how bad they felt when they made fun of someone last year and the person heard about it on their birthday). They tattle on one another and use stories as a way of passing on useful retorts they have heard.

Almost as soon as children can write, they also put their narrative skill to subversive uses, such as passing notes containing real and joke narratives among themselves. Even more devious uses of narrative facility involve excuses for late homework and lies about wrongdoing. Eventual confessions for such misdeeds are also forms of narrative.

At the end of the day, children will bring their school experiences home to their parents in the form of narratives. Of course, there is a great deal of frustration on the part of parents (and teachers when they hear about it) when children continually respond to the ubiquitous question, "What did you do in school today?" with the equally ubiquitous answer, "Oh, nothing." If parents are in the habit of not taking "Nothing" for an answer and of drawing their children out, and especially if some unusual curricular event has happened, children will tell a narrative that reveals quite a bit about what happened at school and the sense they have made of it (McCabe & Peterson, 1991).

Not everyone writing in the field of literacy studies is enthusiastic about narrative; there are also those (for example, Newkirk, 1987; Pappas, 1993) who would have teachers de-emphasize the importance of stories in early literacy programs. Of course, stories are not the only important discourse form. (After all, this textbook is expository, not narrative, writing.) However, regardless of what genres are formally part of teachers' curriculum, narratives will continue to be exchanged in their classrooms. As we will see in Chapter 10, cultural differences in narrative traditions will have an impact on social relations among children at the very least.

Furthermore, the issue of the relationship between narrative and exposition is just beginning to be explored, but even these preliminary explorations reveal the interdependence of oral precursors to exposition and narrative. Specifically, there is considerable overlap between early oral explanations to and by children and oral narrative conversation (Beals & Snow, 1994). In other words, the issues highlighted here in the context of storytelling traditions are probably not confined to storytelling. Research to date that has focused on narrative provides a firm base from which to make certain claims, but values concerning narrative discourse are likely to have an impact on other discourse forms. For example, an Asian immigrant child who has been accustomed to succinct narrative exchanges is not likely to produce a lengthy business letter. Nonetheless, this book is about storytelling traditions because that is where most of the research has worked out issues pertaining to cultural differences.

Finally, stories, whether or not they are emphasized in teachers' curricula, have powerful potential for engaging children. The following chapters will highlight the enormous diversity to be found *within* the genre of narrative.

Basic Functions of Stories and Personal Narratives

In their own narratives, children (1) make sense of their experiences as (2) they develop facility in self-presentation, portraying themselves as heroes or victims, clowns or bystanders. Often, children extract lessons from these life experiences. A third, most important, function of narrative is to "make things present" (O'Brien, 1990, p. 204), bringing dead people, historical events, even past personal trauma to life. Another function is to forge relationships; you know someone to the extent that you know the important narratives of their life. In the following sections we will address each of these basic functions.

Making Sense of Experiences

In the ensuing series of transcribed recorded narratives, the reader can hear a little 6-year-old European American boy try to sort out what happened to him when he broke his arm earlier that day. Look at the transformation from a rather garbled account to one that is much more coherent. This series serves as a microcosm that reflects what it means to make sense of experiences in narrative. Please note the conventions of transcription that will be used throughout this text as given in Box 1:

> Version 1 (On phone to uncle right after coming home from hospital) I broke my arm. I did. Well see I went in a branch and it got caught on my baving [sic] suit and then what happened was I falled [sic] on my, I dangled my arm and it got bent. (pause) Now I have my cot, cast on and my . . . Well I went to sleep when it got pulled back and well see afterwards I got pulled in the front with a chair and my mom drived [sic] the car out and I put it in the car. Just, right now I have a cast [for] six weeks.

> Version 2 (On phone to grandmother right after above)
> Hi Grandma. I broke my arm. Well see, I was dangling from a branch, and it
> got bent.
> [GRANDMA replies: "Does it still hurt?"]
> Not really, because it has a cast on.
> [GRANDMA: "How much of your arm is in a cast?"]
> Well upper AND lower.
> [GRANDMA: "How did you know it was broken?"]
> It was BENT. It was bent. That's, it was like [pause] two TRIANGLES.
> [GRANDMA: "How long will you have to have a cast on?"]
> SIX WEEKS.

[GRANDMA: "You know, your uncle just broke his ankle."]

Yeah, Uncle Herb said that that's the same as him.

[GRANDMA: "Which arm did you break?"]

My LEFT. (laughs)

Yep, [it] feels GOOD. Cause I had to have an operation when I was asleep, and they had to bent it [pause] back. [long pause] I got anesthesia.

[GRANDMA: "Did it hurt?"]

What? Oh yes it hurt. It KILLED. All I had to have was a little [long pause] pillow. Why did Richard give Uncle Herb to the farrest hospital?

Version 3 (on phone two days later)

Hi Sue. I broke my arm. I was, well, the day [pause] two days ago. I was climbing the tree and I, Well see, I went towards the LOW branch and I, and I got caught with my baving [sic] suit? I dangled my hands down and they got bent because it was like this hard surface under it? Then they bent like in two triangles. But luckily it was my LEFT arm that broke.

[Was everybody home with you?]

What! NO. Only my MOM was. My mom was in the shower, so I SCREAMED for Jessica, and Jessica goed told my mom.

[Did you go see Dr. Vincent?]

I DON'T have Dr. Vincent. I had to go to the hospital and get mm, It was much more worser than you think because I had to get, go into the operation room and I had to get my, And I had to take anesthesia and I had to fall, fall, fall asleep and they bended my arm back and I have my cast on . . . Do you want to sign my cast?

[I have to have it on for] six weeks.

Disturbing Content. The little boy who broke his arm wanted and needed to go over and over his account of a very traumatic event in his life, which is typical of children's concerns. Egan (1993) criticizes what he calls the "expanding horizons style curriculum" currently popular in early childhood education, a curriculum based on the assumption that what is most accessible, relevant, and thus meaningful to young children is content concerning themselves, their homes, and their families—safe, familiar subjects. This notion needs to be reconsidered, especially as it can devolve into promoting stories about familiar, comforting, and ultimately boring routines (for example, going to bed at night).

Box 1: Transcription Conventions for Oral Language

CAPITALIZED LETTERS signify words or phrases stressed by the child for evaluative purposes.

Repeated letters (for example, "Ohhhh") refer to words elongated by the child for evaluative purposes.

[Words or phrases in brackets are required by readers to make sense of what the child is saying but implied or left out by the actual speaker.]

Italicized words are words or phrases that we are calling attention to but which were not necessarily emphasized by the speakers themselves.

The inclination we have to "protect" children from disturbing content is ironic in view of what we know they themselves choose to talk and read about. In their own subversive oral tradition on playgrounds and behind adults' backs, children are quite strikingly engaged by conventional fictional verses and stories concerned with such supposedly adult topics as alcoholism, violent death, pregnancy and birth, the welfare state, and modern warfare (Lurie, 1990).

Moreover, children's original oral productions, both factual and fictional, are far more likely to concern hurtful or otherwise negative events than positive ones (Ames, 1966; Miller & Sperry, 1988; Pitcher & Prelinger, 1963; Peterson & McCabe, 1983). Over the years, children have shown a keen interest in making sense of painful and frightening incidents. If they are willing or even determined to face these things, it seems unwise for adults to attempt to avert their eyes.

Our adult preoccupation with "safe" content for children is a relatively recent phenomenon. Some older European versions of the Cinderella story deal with the highly unsafe topic of father-daughter incest. "Lawkamercyme" is a traditional English poem for children that tells of highway rape and its profound psychological consequences. Historically, adults structured fairy tales that eventually wound up in the hands of children to reflect the grim realities of physical child abuse and impoverished economic circumstances (Zipes, 1988) or subversively to mock political enemies (Zipes, 1989). That editors have bowdlerized bewitching fairy stories in an effort to make them more safe and appropriately instructional has occasionally been judged reprehensible and counterproductive to engaging children's interest in such stories (Bettelheim, 1975; Lurie, 1990).

Children need to think about and sort through many kinds of experiences. As the broken arm example illustrates, the more traumatic the event, the more compelled children seem to be to talk and to read and reread stories about such experiences with adults.

Death. Of course, the most traumatic event of all is death. Despite the fact that many children face deaths of pets, grandparents, even immediate family members in some cases, and despite our knowledge of children's interest in distressing topics, modern storybooks written by and for European-American children, especially schoolchildren, generally avoid mention of death. Folktales from other cultures, however, are sometimes not so sanitized. Thus teachers who wish to discuss such folktales are faced with the dilemma of how to deal with this disturbing content in light of concern about its developmental propriety. In China, for example, popular fairy tales for children have many adult characters and frequent encounters with death. Would we "improve" such stories by substituting children for the adults in them and by deleting references to deaths, or would we, in fact, gut such stories of their impact in the process? Aren't children really quite curious in general about the world of adults and in particular about what death means?

Teachers who opt for multicultural literature in their classroom will have to consider how they will deal with strong subject matter, such as the death of key characters. I would recommend preparing children before reading the story by discussing the topic with them, perhaps after consultation with parents.

Listening to children tell their own stories about disturbing incidents presents another set of difficult issues. When adults listen to children talking about matters that seem disturbing, they might want to bear in mind that children will not necessarily express feelings the adult expects regarding the incidents, as is shown in the following encounter between a 6-year-old African American girl and her doctor:

> NATALIE: I seen people, I seen amu- ambulance outside lots a times, and uh, they be coming over this way, and uh police and fire trucks be coming over this way too.
>
> DOCTOR: Why do they come over?
>
> NATALIE: Cause some, some people, cause I went, uh, uh . . . a ambulance went down here one day, and uh they parked right there by the street, by her, by the store, and uh, I went down there with my friends that live over there by me. They live uh, over there, and I live this way, and they live that way, and they live just across by me. And they be, and then we ran down there and to see what happened and then my daddy and my mommy came down there, but my, Ma didn't make it cause she was walking too slow. And uh, and then uh then this man—his name is Larry—he looked in the ambulance to see who got hurt. I don't know who got hurt! We just went down there.
>
> DOCTOR: Sounds very exciting, I must say. Did you think it was exciting?
>
> NATALIE: Not to me.
>
> DOCTOR: Not to you. Why?
>
> NATALIE: I seen too much of it that's why.

Or consider the narratives children tell or write about death, narratives in which they are often unexpressive about their feelings for the deceased (Menig-Peterson & McCabe, 1977–78). Although I have never in any way deliberately probed for difficult material, children have spontaneously conversed with me on many occasions about experiences like the following, and often they do so with the kind of flattened affect you see below:

> CARL (European North American boy, aged 7 years): I seed what, I seen what [a hospital] looked like. That's when my dad had a wreck and got killed. Yeah, Friday when I had to go the emergency. When I was waiting in the waiting room, I saw a ambulance pull up and bring the dead woman in . . . It was my cousin [whom I visited in the hospital another time]. See, he was with my dad. And so my dad had a wreck and my dad didn't get killed, and my cousin got killed right at the scene . . . That was before my dad had a wreck and got killed.

It is demanding but also illuminating work really to listen to children and encourage them to describe *in their own words* what it is that they themselves feel and think about troubling events. It is very difficult to refrain from evaluating their experiences for them. However, letting children tell their own stories the way they want to in this respect, at least, is critical.

While all children tend to struggle to make sense of whatever is upsetting to them, some children experience profound tragedy in their personal lives. Again, it is likely and advisable that extensive discussion about how to handle this trauma be held among parents or guardians and school personnel. As a part of this discussion, however, teachers might consider recommending books that deal with the trauma as an option the child could select. Librarians, among others, often have lists of books about divorce, disabilities, and so forth. Children who have experienced a fire in their homes, for example, may be drawn to such stories as *The Black Snowman* (by Phil Mendez, Scholastic, 1989).

Stereotyping. Some teachers may be inclined to avoid multicultural books because they fear that the books in one way or another engage in stereotyping people, a lesson many teachers try very hard to avoid passing on to their students. It goes without saying that teachers will want to avoid all books with any kind of glaring racist stereotypical image. This is not hard to do with books written since the 1960s. But there are more difficult, subtle issues that are of concern. What should one do about the socioeconomic backgrounds of African American characters, for example? To portray many such characters as poor might be considered stereotyping, although to invariably portray such characters as middle-class might be considered counterstereotyping, denying the realities of the lives of nearly one out of two African American children who do live in poverty (Marger, 1994, p. 254). In her review of African American children's literature, Harris (1991) cites African American writers and scholars who argue that there is a real need to help children confront negative aspects of their lives in positive ways.

The advice from teachers with years of experience teaching such books (Harris, 1991) is often to discuss with parents the issues of what experience(s) a young child does or should have in order to appreciate particular stories and to include a range of portrayals of characters of various ethnicities. This recommendation dovetails with our suggestion that numerous examples of stories from various non-European cultures should be included in a curriculum.

Life Lessons. Many stories have morals almost as explicit as those in fables. In a literary moment reminiscent of many parents' cautionary tales to their children, Beatrix Potter's Mrs. Rabbit admonishes her children and rationalizes her proscriptions with a personal narrative: "Now, my dears, . . . you may go into the fields or down the lane, but don't go into Mr. McGregor's garden: your Father had an accident there; he was put in a pie by Mrs. McGregor."

People are not necessarily conscious of the fact that real narratives of personal experiences often contain similar "morals." In the course of making sense of their experiences, disturbing or benign, by themselves or in conversations with others, people extract lessons to live by. We literally teach ourselves lessons from experience, and those lessons are far more memorable than abstract prohibitions or exhortations. Take, for example, the following narrative by a 4-year-old boy (from Peterson & McCabe, 1983, p. 74):

LYLE: I got a big dog. DON'T EVER TRY AND TAKE A LITTLE CAT BY IT. OR DON'T EVER TAKE LITTLE STUFFED ANIMALS. DON'T EVER TAKE LITTLE, BITTLE ANIMALS BY IT 'CAUSE IT WILL EAT THEM UP . . . Somebody took a baby puppy by her, a tan puppy. Then he ate him up. That was stupid. I watched him. And I said, "Don't no eat him," and he just still ate him, ate him up.

Such childhood lessons may be transient ones. That is, college students reminiscing about early childhood experiences sometimes followed narration of a specific, usually traumatic, experience with comments like, "It took me a little while to like horses again, you know, cause I was scared of them for a while," or, "I stopped riding my bike for about a year . . . I guess these two experiences really got me steered away from my bike because it was really dangerous" (McCabe, Capron, & Peterson, 1991, p. 159). Other childhood lessons last a lifetime: "I never rolled in another box again," or "You have old friends, but new friends you always look forward to" (McCabe, Capron, & Peterson, 1991, p. 159).

In fact, the kind of personal narratives most likely to be remembered are ones that relate some sensational event, usually injuries or accidents (McCabe & Peterson, 1990), which by definition involve drastic consequences for certain courses of action. What we will see with cultural differences in narrative structure may be a kind of cultural adaptation to particular environments. Perhaps the human species evolved language at least in part so that we could pass on culturally relevant life lessons in narrative form to our children and to other members of our culture.

Self-Presentation

The second major point of telling any story is to portray the roles that various characters play in some experience. This point is well known with respect to published literary stories, and we may all intuitively be attuned to looking for it in conversational personal stories. However, the point is worth making in some detail here because implications of this self-presentation have generally not been recognized, let alone tapped, when stories are classroom fare. What follows are the kinds of active roles we have found that young children portray themselves as playing in their oral personal narratives. Often children will retell stories of experiences that happened to other people, experiences in which they played no active role because they were not even there. Teachers who are interested in self-roles will want to encourage children to save those secondhand stories for another day. What follows is an initial typology of the common roles children seem to adopt in telling stories of experiences that really happened to them.

These self-roles may be thought of as occupying some position with respect to two critical dimensions of character: the dimension of power and the dimension of morality. The various roles induced from reading thousands of transcripts of children's stories fall roughly as they are depicted in Figure 1. We would not claim this set of categories to be exhaustive, but instead we would urge teachers to think about each child's narrative self as it would fit or extend these categories.

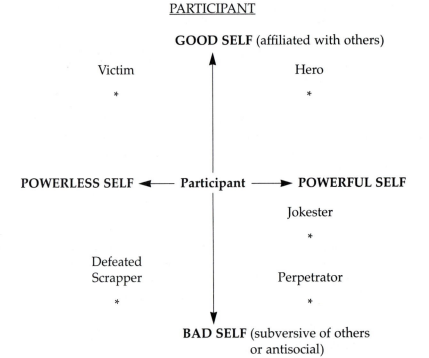

PARTICIPANT

GOOD SELF (affiliated with others)

Victim

*

Hero

*

POWERLESS SELF ◄——— Participant ———► **POWERFUL SELF**

Jokester

*

Defeated
Scrapper

*

Perpetrator

*

BAD SELF (subversive of others
or antisocial)

OBSERVER

UNIMPORTANT EVENT ◄————————► **IMPORTANT EVENT**

Bystander   Reporter

FIGURE 1. Dimensions of self-presentation in young children's oral personal narratives.

Hero. Sometimes a narrator describes an event or activity that required extraordinary bravery or expertise on his or her part. In a story presented in full later on (pages 106-107), an African American girl describes herself: "... And so my cousin, he wanted to take out his tooth, and he didn't know what to do, so I told him, 'I'm a Pullin' Teeth Expert.'" A 7-year-old Japanese girl, Sayaka, articulates her own bravura:

> "I got shots in Japan, well, at school, you know? I was saying, 'It will not hurt, right?' with my friends, you know, with my friends. And in the end, there were some who cried because of pain, you know. I was saying, 'They aren't strong, are they?' with my friends."

Such stoicism and bravery come through in the following stories by a 7-year-old Japanese boy and a 9-year-old European North American boy, respectively:

> Ichiro: It (an injury) hurt a little, but, you know, because everyone was, you know, very scared of bees, you know, we caught a bee, you know, and buried

it under the ground, you know. I, um, held it. I got stung by it, you know. And then nothing happened. My friend got stung too. He got stung two times.

Walter: One time I didn't even know I was handling a poisonous snake, a water snake—they're poison, kind of. Ohh, I picked one up and I thought what could a water snake be and I just had put it in a cage. And I was looking through this snake book and I read that water snakes are poisonous, and I said, thought, "Ohh, I lifted a poison snake up." And my Mom came out there and she said, "What happened?" And I said, "I lifted a poison snake up." She said, "YOU DID! What a surprise." And I showed her that snake. She went, "AHHH! SNAKE! Throw it back in the water." We have a stream in our garden.

Occasionally, efforts to portray themselves as heroes lead narrators into flights of Paul Bunyanesque fantasy, as in the following stories by 5- and 7-year-old boys, respectively:

Paul: Do you know what? Every single tree fell down on our house. Cause there's a snowstorm. I picked them up with one, with my pinky. All of them with my pinky. Do you believe that? I DID.

Ben: And then the deer fell down, slid down the hill. And it, then I slid down the hill. Then I caught the deer. Then Dad shot it. I holded the deer, and Dad was shooting it. And I was holding it. I was holding it right by the front legs, and my dad was shooting it.

Sometimes children portray themselves more modestly as *responsible people,* more unassuming heroes, as does this Latina girl, aged 7:

We saw a car accident in front of our house. Everybody went outside because we heard the accident. Me and Michael were scared, and when we got scared-like, we were hugging each other. We didn't know what it was—like a flat tire around the house. So then we went outside. Then, um, we didn't saw the accident, so then we called the policemen and the ambulance.

As she tells the story, she and her friend were the ones who had enough initiative to call in the proper authorities—no small feat for children. Other young children who have notified authorities have been featured on the evening news, awarded medals, and so forth, as this narrator undoubtedly realizes.

Other children portray themselves as capable of minding their parents' stores, teaching, or helping a person or other living thing—some effort that required exceptional responsibility or was something typically thought of as done by adults. A 9-year-old European North American girl tells us, "I'm the biggest little sister, and then I went downstairs and watched the store for a while. My mom owns it." A boy of the same age reports that, "There was this nest that fell down out of the tree and there were eggs, bird eggs, and the mother had already gone away. So I took them back to our house and hatched them out. I kept them alive. To keep them alive, I put them in a box, and they hatched out, and I put them out there and the mother came back and got them." Another boy of the same age says, "And that Daniel Worth—he's just a scaredy cat. He thought I was gonna hit him. And I just swung my hand down, and I thought, 'I'll have to teach him how to fight.' So I taught him how to fight. When somebody's going to hit him in the head, just duck down and when their arm gets around, just grab it and put it behind your back. That will make them quit. That's what happened to me. I made people quit for doing that twice."

While, as the examples show, heroism is a role adopted by children of both genders, we have found a disturbing tendency for elementary school-age girls to avoid presenting themselves as heroines, due to a fear that they will be seen by their girl friends as "bragging." Perhaps if asked to do so for school assignments, this constraint would fall away.

Encouraged to tell a story in which she was a heroine, a 10-year-old girl resisted for several weeks for fear of alienating her peers, but finally told this story to an assistant teacher:

> Violet: Well see when I got to school, Alice and Angela were carrying Hermie's cage? Hermie was in it, and I go, "Why, why are you DOING that? And they go, "Cause he's DEAD." And I go, "WAIT a minute!" And I run into my classroom and I go, "But he wasn't dead yesterday. He was perfectly FINE when I ran him under the faucet, right?" So I run outside and I catched them just before they were like going to like bury it. "But WAIT a minute. I think he's still alive. Let me check!" "No, no he's dead." I go, "No I REALLY think he's ALIVE." So I go and I put a paper between his pinchers and he pinches it, right. So I hold him and I go, "SEE he's ALIVE." And he PINCHED right here [on her thumb], and he wouldn't let go, and I was like yelling. Anyway cause like he was doing it so hard and he wouldn't let go and I'm like, "Hurry" and so, and so all these people are like, "Here, can you pull him off?" I was like crying, and all, they were going like this [makes back-off gesture]. They were going like this and they were backing away. I'm like, "Can somebody?" They were all backing away. They wouldn't help me. So I had to go into the nurse? And the nurse, she finally got it off. And it was like all red. And everything was fine, you know? And when I got back to my classroom, everybody was like, "oh, oh, oh." And I felt like a hero, because I saved his life and everybody was like talking about it. And so but no, but I had a mixture [of feelings] because I, also, my hand was killing me, though.

Which brings us to the next dramatic role children portray themselves as playing.

Victim. Children suffer many hurts growing up, as the story earlier in this chapter told by a European North American boy who had broken his arm exemplifies (page 5). Children are victims when they report being involved in incidents that evoke specific, unpleasant consequences, physical and emotional. To hear them tell it, children and their families are often unable to do anything but suffer through some miserable experiences. The following story by an African American 8-year-old boy illustrates in some detail the little agonies children frequently experience:

> Larry: And, and I went to the doctor's a lot a times, right, to, to get my ears fixed. Like they was all stuffed up and everything and it hurt, and when I went on a plane it just hurted, right? Yeah, and then my dad took me to the doctor. They had one man. He got some wax in my ears. It was just wax. He got some

out, and he just said, "it's gonna tickle a little bit," and he didn't, he said, like he said that my ears is okay. And then my brother came up because his throat was hurting, and we was both okay, and then we went out to get this thing, like this thing which you would put in your ears, right? And it hurt real, real bad, and I would start crying, right? And then, I went to another doctor, right? And my brother was crying and my dada was crying too . . . I was crying real, real bad 'cause it hurted. And then I went back to the doctor. This lady, she took the big big big big wax out of my ears, and the other one just a little bit. And then the other one was mad, and the other was kind of happy. And then we got this stuff . . . this little tiny weeny stuff—made me cry just a little bit. And then that's it.

On rare occasions, children spontaneously will acknowledge their own contributions to some of their tribulations:

Tatsu (Japanese, aged 7¹/₂ years, a boy): When I got hurt, I had a bone broken, and blood poured out. When I was small, as I was running with a toy, I missed my step on the stairs, "Bashi!" And from here, lots of blood was streaming down, and I had a huge blister on my leg. When I was very small, BECAUSE I WAS SILLY [emphasis mine]. That was not a needle, something to cut here. I touched it. Blood was running down. Blood gushed out. I cut here with a bang of a door. Then when I was sleeping, my bed was full of blood. My nail has turned into this strange, ugly shape, you know. My nail came off, you know. My big nail came off.

While many of their stories concern times when they were victims due to the fact that they were *physically sick or harmed* in some way, there are other kinds of victims in children's stories of their real experiences. For example, there is the case of children who present themselves as *moral victims*, unfairly judged to be culprits, as in the following narrative by a 4-year-old European American boy:

Only Stevie [has been to the hospital] when I hit him with the rake one time, and he hit me with that big broom And she [Mom] didn't take ME to the hospital. Only Steven. He hit me with a sharp broom. He hit me with that, that hard, hard, that hard, ooooohhhhh, I got it in the head. He hit me. I hit him. If he hits me with that once more, that broom once more, I'm going to hit him with the rake once more.

At other times, when victimized by others, children portray themselves fighting back:

Allen (European American boy, aged 9 years): I gave Jeremy Pickford one [bloody nose]. He got me and he went, "Ooohhh." Give me a bear hug, and I went BOOM. I didn't mean to, and he got his nose right in my head. Oooohhh . . . See, my head was in his nose, and he went in the bathroom, and I went in to see what happened. He had a bloody nose.

Bert (European American boy, aged 9 years): [I fought] one guy last week, Bob Tory, when I was in listening. So Alex had come over and he said, "You'd better leave him alone," because I was just new in school. So next day he got mad at me again. And started at me, so he just swung it on around and he hit me in the face, and I thought for sure that I would kill him because I get mad when people hit me. So he came at me and tried to hit me again, so I had to flip him. Because my uncle teaches me a LOT of baseball tricks, a lot of tricks that I shouldn't do.

Scrappers and Other Perpetrators. Sometimes children abandon all efforts at presenting themselves as victims first and foremost. They acknowledge active participation in a fight:

Alena (European North American girl, aged 9 years): Lots of times [I have spilled things]. Well, one time when I was little, my sister wanted something to eat, so we went upstairs. I went upstairs, see. And my sister was only two and I was four, no I was three. And she wanted some pizza. I went downstairs and I got some cream cheese, and we threw it at each other, and we were smashing all over the walls. And when my mom got up the next morning, boy it was a mess to clean up!

Children may even simply acknowledge responsibility for some mishap:

Maura (European North American girl, aged 9 years): At home [I spilled something]. When I was getting a drink with a glass, and I dropped the glass and the water spilled. And there's a whole bunch of little glass. And my mom got REAL mad because it was her good glass.

Jokester. On rare occasions, some children recount times when they played practical jokes on others:

Eric (European North American boy, aged 9): And there was two days later, before we moved, and I was there one more day of school. And Keith, he went down to the store with me, and we was getting bubble gum. And he got that red hot bubble gum, and I got five or six different sticks of this—three sticks of red—and I had two sticks of purple kind of gum. And so we went in there and Keith, he had got mad at his gum because he couldn't chew it, and he threw it right on Teacher's seat. And Teacher sat down, and she got back up and she went, "Ahhh!" and sat back down and went, "Ohhh!" and felt there and there was that gum sticking to her dress! That was funny.

Arnie (European North American boy, aged 9 years): It was one thirty this winter—just two days ago—when we had my sister and brother out. It was snowing, and my Mom was out there building a snowman. I grabbed a bunch of snow and I stuck it down her back. And she was just putting the head on, and she dropped it and I put my foot up and I KICKED it down—the whole snowman down. She ran inside, took her coat off, and she went in the bathroom, took her shirt off and got it out. She had to take a HOT shower.

Reporter. Occasionally, children describe some important, perhaps even traumatic, event they witnessed but did not participate in. The importance of the event and the sense that the child conveys of having something monumental or at least fairly impressive to tell you define this role:

Alice (European North American girl, aged 9 years): I've SEEN one [car wreck]. I don't know where it was, and the car was all tipped over, and the glass was broken out, and the doors was off and everything. I believe it rolled over about twice because, well, no matter how far it was. It wasn't, you know, just part ways or nothing. And it was all, it was in a YARD! I think it tipped over about two times. They said, I THINK, that it KILLED some people. One of them lived.

Participant. Finally, children, especially very young children, often do not present themselves in any distinctive role other than that of a participant in an experience. The relative banality of the event, combined with the child's participation in an undifferentiated way, defines this role. Usually, but not always, there is some dominant affect including the following emotions:

1. *Pride or a sense of accomplishment* may be the primary emotion, as in this oral account by Allie (European North American girl, aged 9): "Know what I did yesterday? I'd been working with [my dog] for a week. Now I trained it to walk on a leash."

2. Children will occasionally tell a story in which the main point is that they were the *center of attention.* Numerous accounts of birthday parties would fall into this category, as would the following narrative by a 7-year-old European North American boy, Larry:

   My mom, when I was just turned SEVEN, she MADE me a angel food cake. THEY'RE HARD to make. It was fun. My grandma got me a wooden soldier. And they're real and nice. They have real nice toys down there too. They're real good name. And Daddy got me [a] Kentucky rifle, play rifle, cork gun. And Daddy and Mommy and Mary got, my sisters got me, my sister, my baby sister, and my sister got me—OH YEAH, there's this little like duck and it was LITTLE and he had like wheels, you just could LIKE A CAR. You could go like that and then let go and it goes [gestures]. And I wanted that so bad. I liked it so much. And then, Mom and Pa got me that for my birthday. And that's all I got—only three things. Uh-oh—FOUR. They sent me some things. Our neighbor, she sent me a Sesame Street book—the sticker ones. But I only got four [presents]. Oh well, it was a nice birthday anyways. We went to see for my birthday, we went to see them blow glass. They didn't tell how they do it, how they blow the glass, but it was real fun. You PROBABLY KNOW they blow it through a pipe and all that. Yeah, I know you know that. And I LIKE it when it comes out. It looks like it's gonna just turn out any old shape and it turns out the shape they want it. But I ALWAYS been thinking HOW DO THEY MAKE it grow the right shape they want it? I thought, I think they just blow the one side, then another, and sometimes straight in on. All that.

3. Often children describe themselves as *amused or entertained:* Theresa (Mexican American girl, aged 8 years, with spellings and punctuation as she wrote it, collected by Bonnar Spring):

   Once I was walking to the washroom. I saw something funny. It was a walking washing machine. I said, "I must be dreaming." Then I rubbed my eyes. I said, "this can't be a walking washing machine." I ran up stairs and woke up my mom and dad. I said, "there is a walking washing machine." My mom and dad said, "stop playing around and go watch something on T.V." Then I thought to myself it is 9:00 I missed Fantastic Max, Richey Rich, Don Ciotey, and that little purple guy. Then I went back downstairs. I turned on the T.V. Then I banged aginst the wall and I woke up. It was just s dream. Then my alarm rung. It was 6:30. I told my mom and dad about my dream. They said, "What a funny dream." It's time fore school mom said [.] get into the car.

4. A favorite topic of both oral and written accounts is *fear*. For example, a story written by a Mexican American girl, aged 8 (with her spellings and punctuation intact):

Once I was fishing with my dad. I felt a tug. I pulled, and pulled, and pulled. It came up. It was a MONSTER! It opened its mouth and reached out for me. It missed me by an inch. I was so scared! My dad was more scared than me. My dad hurried and got the anhor on the MONSTER! My dad was so brave. When I got home I told my mom. She said, "never go fishing again!"

5. A number of funny stories involve the narrator's *embarrassment*. For example, here is an oral story by Bill (European American, aged 9):

When I was with my NEIGHBOR, when we was playing baseball, he HIT one of them in my other neighbor's field. And it was quite a ways back in there. And then when I went to go back over across the fence, I RIPPED my PANTS right in back and they go DDRRIIII—a big old hole. So then, I had that . . . My neighbor and his dad were looking at the fence, so I had to go home and change pants.

6. Once in a while children say they have been *insulted* or their sense of fairness has been *violated* in some way: Eve (a European American girl, aged 9, oral):

You know, only ONE time my Dad lied to me. So he said we had this cat. And the next day it had another cat, and it got the whole side [wounded], and we had to put him away, and we took it to the farm and got rid of him.

7. I have already acknowledged the fact that sometimes children tell about *grieving* the death or loss of a person or pet. A third-grade girl wrote the following account: "One day I took my dog for a walk. His collar came off. He ran away. I called him but he wouldn't come. I miss him[. He] was my favorite dog. I really, really, really, miss him!" A first grader wrote (spellings are as child wrote them): "Mi cat diyd yesttoda I wis sad. that mi cat diyd."

8. Sometimes children tell or write stories that are curiously *lacking in affect*. In a systematic examination of children's stories of grief and loss, we (Menig-Peterson & McCabe, 1977-78) found that children younger than 9 years of age rarely expressed any affect for the deaths of strangers, pets, or relatives. The closer the individual who died, the less likely the child is to tell you anything about how she or he felt. In oral narratives about other kinds of experiences, this lack of emotion is very rare. However, in written narratives, first-graders struggling to produce print of any kind may dispense with telling their feelings in the interest of getting the facts out, as in

this unusually long narrative by a first-grade girl (Here, as elsewhere, many written narratives in this chapter were collected by Bonnar Spring): "Dear mis. Long I was in a wabing [meaning wedding] I was a flar grl. My Setr [= sister] was a flar grl I rod in the lemasen weth the bribd [= bride]. The brid hab beds on hr dras." The beads made enough of an impression to be singled out for mention here, but the difficulty of writing and spelling for this emergent writer was sufficient for her to stick to the important facts themselves. Had she told the story orally, she undoubtedly would have evaluated those facts (for example, "beautiful, sparkly beads . . .")

When a loved one does not die, but merely goes away for a while, children may be quite articulate about their feelings, as in the following story by a European American child, aged 9:

> [I have visited someone in the hospital] just one time. That's when my dad was in there. He had to go there because his leg—it got shot in it. And he never went to the hospital for a long time after it [happened]. And he had to go about a month after it because it was hurting him too much. It wasn't too fun not having Dad around neither. Had to take all my mom's cooking. I like my dad's gravy. Mommy doesn't cook it so good.

The preceding catalogue of emotions is no more complete than the umbrella catalogue of the roles children depict themselves as playing. At other times, children tell stories in which they say they were tired or dizzy, and so forth. Teachers could pick one of these common emotions, use the above examples, or tell stories of their own in which they felt that emotion, and encourage all children in the class to write or tell about a situation in which they felt the same way.

Children progress in the clarity of the roles they portray themselves as playing. In preschool, roles such as hero and victim, while occasionally reported, are less common than those of simple participants with emotions of various sorts. Towards the end of elementary school, children may begin to portray themselves in multiple roles. One may be a hero and a victim at the same time, as the narrative above about saving the hermit crab illustrates; as a 10-year-old, the little girl can articulate the fact that she was hero and victim in the same event. Valor has its price.

Making Past Events Present and Abstract Events Vivid

A third basic function of narrative with implications for instruction involves the way stories "make things present" (O'Brien, 1990, p. 204), involving listeners or readers in a way that expository writing cannot. Egan (1993) is among the growing number of people who argue that despite the prevalence of narrative in classrooms, educators have only begun to tap the potential of narrative in classroom instruction. It is this function of stories to "make things present" that equips them so well for expanded classroom use. For one thing, historical fiction can make past events present and engaging. Far better for a child to read a novel such as *One Foot Ashore* (Greene, 1994) involving imagined characters who struggle with the aftermath of the Portuguese Inquisition than to read a general account of that historical travesty. Liza Murrow's (1987) *West against the Wind* puts faces on specific people who traveled west in the 1850s, drawing young readers into the kinds of experiences and emotions really risked by those who migrated west at that time.

It is far harder to forget a story than it is to forget facts. One study (Bridge & Tierney, 1981) examined the effects of expository and story texts on the explicit and inferred information recalled by both good and poor third-grade readers. All subjects recalled a higher proportion of explicitly stated information from the story than from the expository text. All subjects generated more connections with the story than with the expository text. All subjects were better able to preserve the original order of propositions in the story than in the expository text. Other studies (such as Zabrucky & Ratner, 1992) have also found that students are better able to recall narrative than expository information.

Historical narratives—very specific stories of things that really happened, involving characters who are vividly portrayed—attract many children to a discipline that has in recent years often been presented in an expository manner (Demos, 1994, p. xi). Ann Petry's (1964) *Tituba of Salem Village* enlivens the Salem witch trial horrors, engaging children's sympathies as well as their memories. In a third-grade class in the Boston area, teachers take children on a field trip to Plymouth Plantation, after which the children are given basic factual information about the original Pilgrims. Each child picks a Pilgrim and writes a first-person biography in the form of a journal.

Narratives and stories can make abstract concepts accessible even to young children and more graphic and memorable to all of us. For example, even most 3-year-olds can consider and coordinate at least two different points of view other than their own—a task that is virtually impossible for children this age if presented as an abstraction—so long as they are given the task in story form. Asked to hide a boy from two policemen placed in two different locations, almost all children answered correctly (Hughes, 1975, cited in Donaldson, 1978). Perhaps young children can understand some abstractions directly (Gardner, 1993). Certainly, as noted at the outset of the chapter, narrative is not the only form in which information should be encountered in classrooms for young children. But narrative can be an effective way of presenting concepts some children might otherwise find dull. Stories make things—even remote or distant things—seem immediate to us, present to all our senses.

The *Magic School Bus* series by Joanna Cole is an excellent example of how expository information can be woven into a story format. The books in this series are dense with expository information, but children are pulled along in reading them by a plot. Furthermore, the plot itself imaginatively presents much factual information in a striking fashion. In *Lost in the Solar System* (Cole, 1990), for example, the children's teacher, Ms. Frizzle, gets detached from their school-bus-turned-spaceship, leaving the children to fend for themselves. The children try to land as soon as possible somewhere in the solar system to reconnect with Ms. Frizzle, but find they cannot land on the first planet they pass—Jupiter—because it is made almost entirely of gas.

Forging Relationships and Facilitating Language Skills

Teachers differ in their inclination to exchange personal narratives with children. One teacher resisted asking her preschool students to tell about some home experience because she "didn't know the child well enough yet" (Dickinson, 1991, p. 292). However, other teachers become very familiar with the personal lives of their students. Recordings in preschool classrooms reveal that exchanges of personal narratives in all classrooms studied to date, however, are rare (Dickinson, 1991).

Teachers, especially of preschool and early elementary school-aged children, are in a position to facilitate their students' oral language skills, although they have not necessarily been trained to see this as a possible or valuable professional goal. Oral language skills are a prerequisite for literate ones, and monologic narrative begins in dialogic conversation, a topic we will explore in much more detail in Chapter 2. In particular, talking about past events, future plans, or hypothetical scenarios—nonpresent events, in short—gives children practice in having to make their language stand on its own—decontextualized, explicit in the way that their written compositions are expected to be (Dickinson, 1991).

Teachers can build their students' oral language skills if they put narrative exchanges on their agenda of important things to do during the day. Narrative exchanges seem to happen most naturally in classrooms when the teacher is stationary and when children are engaged in some activity, such as eating lunch or doing artwork, that does not necessarily demand extensive commands to refrain from "outlaw" behavior, commands that compete with conversation about past personal experiences. Several specific strategies are used by teachers who are effective in building the discourse skills of their students. First, they are enthusiastic and playful and unafraid of entering into a child's frame of reference. Second, they ask questions that require elaboration or encourage children to make implicit information more explicit. Third, they elaborate and extend children's contributions (Dickinson, 1991). All of these strategies are at play in the following excerpt from a lunchtime conversation (Dickinson, 1991, pp. 285–286):

TEACHER: What were you talking with Terri (another teacher) about?
JAKE: We were talking about bad things.
TEACHER: Bad things? What bad things?
JAKE: Like kids pushing me and hitting me and punching me.
TEACHER: Kids were pushing you and hitting you and [gap in tape].
TEACHER: How did that make you feel?
JAKE: Mad and angry. Bad.

This teacher was not interested in discipline. It was lunchtime and the children were free to talk. She was unafraid to pursue a topic of somewhat dubious propriety—one can imagine other "bad things" Jake might have talked about. She echoed the child at several points to indicate interest and asked specific questions that required Jake to be explicit about the bad things and about how he felt. Children who ate lunch regularly with this teacher soon learned of her interest in what they had to say. Compared to children who ate with teachers who did not regularly display such interest, these children initiated more diverse topics, engaged in more elaborated talk about personal experiences, and listened to and extended each other's talk (Dickinson, 1991). It is unlikely that either teacher or students realized that they were doing anything that could be considered "academically nutritious." They probably simply, and also accurately, felt they were getting to know each other pretty well.

EXEMPLARY INSTRUCTION

Barbara Lipke is a fifth-grade teacher and storyteller in Brookline, Massachusetts. She developed and disseminated a curriculum that teaches children to be oral storytellers, using gesture, facial expression, body language, and variety in tone of voice to convey a story. She has her students rehearse and revise these oral stories, using audiotapes, in an oral form of process writing exercises. (Her method is available from N.C.T.E. Order Department, 1111 Kenyon Road, Urbana, IL 61801.)

Lipke applied this method to engage students (and teachers intimidated by science) in science activities (Lipke & Lipke, 1992). She encourages teachers to connect storytelling and science in a variety of ways, including telling biographical and historical stories of scientists and their discoveries or asking children to make up a story about some scientific principle they have just learned (for example, pretending they are a tree with rings that tell their own personal histories).

Box 2: Research into Practice

1. Do a unit that focuses on heroes.
   A. Read *The Woman in the Moon and Other Tales of Forgotten Heroines* by James Riordan (Dial, 1985), *The Trouble with Mom* by Babette Cole (Coward-McCann, Inc., 1983), and *Ruby the Red Knight* by Amy Aitken (Bradbury Press, 1983). These books present girls and women as heroines. Riordan's book collects Native American and Aztec tales, as well as some from Lapland, Estonia, Mongolia, Italy, Ireland, Asia, West Africa, Japan, Norway, and Vietnam—all of which feature women as heroines in folktales. The other two books take place in European American settings but with the unusual feature of hero-

ines instead of heroes. Ask children to tell and then write real and pretend stories in which they are the hero. Talk about issues of bragging, because elementary school-age girls, especially, may resist portraying themselves as heroes because they are afraid their friends will accuse them of bragging.
   B. There is no shortage of books that portray European American boys as heroes. The *Nate the Great* series by Marjorie Weinman Sharmat (Dell Yearling) and Roald Dahl's *The Minpins* (Viking, 1991) are only two among many such books. These might be read with discussion centering around the standard secondary characters in

---

Box 2: Research into Practice—cont'd

the Nate the Great Series and the Swan, without whom Little Billy could never have become a hero, in the case of the Dahl book.

2. Do a unit that discusses and identifies other roles people can play in what happens to them, such as are exemplified and discussed above. Take the children's favorite stories and identify the roles played by various characters in these stories. Try revising favorite fairy tales where villains are turned into heroes, and vice versa.

3. Discuss real heroes and heroines like Rosa Parks, who triggered the bus boycott in Montgomery, Alabama, by simply refusing to give up her seat. Talk about how sometimes you may become a hero without setting out deliberately one day to do so. Ask children to identify their own favorite hero or heroine. Ask them to collect pictures, information, and books about this person.

4. News stories: Bring in newspaper stories for children to read. Especially good candidates are stories from a local paper about something that happened at school. Point out that the reporters have to tell readers very specifically about who, what, when, and where something happened.

5. Sharing Time: Many teachers of preschool and early elementary school arrange a regular time during which children can share an object or experience. Teachers interested in highlighting narrative may want to discourage bringing in objects, since that tends to promote informational or demonstrative talk rather than narrative. During or after their contributions, ask children follow-up questions to clarify or identify who, what, when, and where their oral Sharing Time Narratives happened. Be mindful that while less than 2 percent of European American children's narratives happen in more than one place, many children from different cultures will tell stories that did happen on more than one occasion and in more than one place.

6. Make a newspaper for parents from dictated or written stories children have prepared, turning some event that happened to them into "news."

Ann E. Fordham (1989), Assistant Professor of Reading and Early Childhood Education at Shippensburg University, describes classrooms in which teachers tell their own personal narratives (often about their experiences with students in the classroom) to demonstrate form and content and to involve children in telling their own personal narratives. "Telling personal narratives," Fordham (1989, p. 21) explains, "leads naturally into writing narratives. Teachers can write class-experience storybooks." Here is one such story, written by Mrs. Betty Gilchrest, a first-grade teacher in Millboro, Virginia, and edited by her students:

Jakey had packed, so he bought his milk and hustled through the narrow hall to his seat—WITHOUT his milk. Tiffany was s-l-o-w-l-y carrying her tray of beef with gravy, spinach, peaches, and milk into the lunch room when—KA-BOO! Jakey and Tiffany collided with Jakey catching most of Tiffany's beef with gravy, spinach, and peaches in his arms, on his shirt,—everywhere! Jakey's mouth flew wide open, his eyes blinked rapidly and he breathed heavily. Tiffany quietly smiled and got another tray. Mrs. G sent Jakey to get his milk, and as he returned empty-handed, he said, "There's girls everywhere!" Mrs. Hileman gave Jakey a BIG T-shirt to wear the rest of the day.

Summary

- This chapter addressed the many uses of stories in classrooms. There are numerous formal instructional uses of stories in classrooms. Stories are ubiquitous early reading materials and a very common form of early writing requested of children. Less ubiquitous potential instructional uses include use of stories in teaching science and history. Stories circulate in classrooms in informal, social ways as well. Such social uses of narrative are important to remember because it is in this way that cultural differences in storytelling traditions may impede relationships between children of different cultural backgrounds.
- There are many basic functions of stories and personal narrative. First, stories and narratives are the means by which children make sense of experiences. Children are often engaged by content that adults may find disturbing. For example, many children are curious about death. The only content that should be banned from stories in the classroom is cultural stereotyping, and this is a realizable goal. Concern to avoid stereotyping, however, can sometimes lead to avoidance of authentic stories from various cultural backgrounds or to denial of some unpleasant realities faced by many children of color in the United States. Teachers are encouraged to include numerous books about people of any one background, and to make sure that the representations of such people reflect the real diversity within that tradition. Stories are an important means of passing on many life lessons.
- Self-presentation is a second basic function of personal narratives. This self-presentation reflects the roles of protagonists children encounter in the stories they read or hear. Such roles include that of hero, victim, scrapper, perpetrator, jokester, participant, reporter, and mere bystander. Children are increasingly adept at differentiating their own past roles in their oral personal narratives, a skill that could be put to curricular use. Unfortunately, some girls may avoid presenting themselves heroically. These children might be encouraged to be heroic more often in their narratives.
- Narratives and stories make past events present and vivid and abstractions memorable. It is this function that enables stories to engage children in subjects such as science and history. Narratives are certainly not the only kind of reading material teachers should include in classrooms. Some children may prefer expository materials, and all children need to read some expository materials. Nonetheless, stories are harder to forget than a series of facts and may attract some children to subjects that have traditionally been taught in a largely expository fashion.
- The exchange of personal narratives is a means of forging relationships between teachers and students and between students themselves. This largely social function has a surprising academic impact, a topic for further discussion in Chapter 2.

References

AARDEMA, V. (1975). *Why mosquitoes buzz in people's ears*. New York: Scholastic Book Services.

AMES, L.B. (1966). Children's stories. *Genetic Psychology Monographs, 73*, 337–396.

BARTON, B. (1986). *Tell me another: Storytelling and reading aloud at home, at school, and in the community*. Markhum, Ontario: Heinemann.

BEALS, D., & SNOW, C. E. (1994). Thunder is when the angels are bowling upstairs. *Journal of Narrative and Life History, 4*(4), 331–352.

BETTELHEIM, B. (1975). *The uses of enchantment*. New York: Vintage Books.

BRIDGE, C.A., & TIERNEY, R.J. (1981). The inferential operations of children across text with narrative and expository tendencies. *Journal of Reading Behavior, 13*(3), 201–214.

CALKINS, L.M. (1986/1994). *The art of teaching writing* (new edition). Portsmouth, NH: Heinemann.

COLE, J. (1990). *The magic school bus: Lost in the solar system*. New York: Scholastic Inc.

DEMOS, J. (1994). *The unredeemed captive: A family story from Early America*. New York: Alfred A. Knopf.

DENNETT, D.C. (1991). *Consciousness explained*. Boston: Little, Brown.

DICKINSON, D.K. (1991). Teacher agenda and setting: Constraints on conversation in preschools. In A. McCabe & C. Peterson (Eds.), *Developing narrative structure* (pp. 255–302). Hillsdale, NJ: Lawrence Erlbaum.

DICKINSON, D.K., & MCCABE, A. (1993). Beyond two-handed reasoning: Commentary on Egan's work. *Linguistics and Education, 5* (2), 187–194.

DONALDSON, M. (1978). *Children's minds*. N.Y.: W.W. Norton & Co.

EGAN, K. (1993). Narrative and learning: A voyage of implications. *Linguistics and Education, 5*(2), 119–126.

ELLENWOOD, S., & RYAN, K. (1991). Literature and morality: An experimental curriculum. In W.M. Kurtines & J.L. Gewirtz (Eds.), *Handbook of moral behavior and development, Vol. 3*, pp. 55–67.

FINGER, C.J. (1924). *Tales from silver lands*. NY: Scholastic Book Services.

FLOOD, J., LAPP, D., & FLOOD, S. (1984). Types of writing found in the early levels of basal reading programs: Preprimers through second grade readers. *Annals of Dyslexia, 34*, 241–255.

FLOOD, J., LAPP, D., & NAGEL, G. (1991). An analysis of literary works in district core reading lists. *National Reading Conference Yearbook, 40*, 269–275.

FORDHAM, A.E. (1989). The benefits of telling personal narratives. *The Children's Literature Council of Central Pennsylvania, 2*(2), 20–22.

FREEDMAN, A. (1987). Development in story writing. *Applied Psycholinguistics, 8*, 153–170.

GARDNER, H. (1983). *Frames of mind: The theory of multiple intelligences*. New York: Basic Books.

GARDNER, H. (1993). From conflict to clarification: A comment on Egan's "Narrative and learning: A voyage of implications." *Linguistics and Education, 5* (2), 181–186.

GRAVES, D.H. (1983). *Writing: Teachers and children at work*. Exeter, NH: Heinemann.

GREENE, J.D. (1994). *One foot ashore*. New York: Walker.

HARRIS, V.J. (1991). Multicultural curriculum: African American children's literature. *Young Children, 46*(2), 37–44.

LEVI-STRAUSS, C. (1970). *The raw and the cooked*. New York: Harper & Row.

LIPKE, B., & LIPKE, P. (1992). Tales from science. *Science Scope, Nov/Dec*, 28–31.

LURIE, A. (1990). *Don't tell the grown-ups: Subversive children's literature*. Boston: Little, Brown.

MacIntyre, A.C. (1981). *After virtue.* Notre Dame, IN: University of Notre Dame Press.

McCabe, A., & Peterson, C. (1984). What makes a good story? *Journal of Psycholinguistic Research, 13,* 457–480.

McCabe, A., & Peterson, C. (1985). A naturalistic study of the use of causal connectives in personal narratives. *Journal of Child Language, 14,* 145–159.

McCabe, A., & Peterson, C. (1987). Adults versus children's spontaneous use of *because* and *so. Journal of Genetic Psychology, 55,* 257–268.

McCabe, A., & Peterson, C. (1990). What makes a story memorable? *Applied Psycholinguistics, 11*(1), 73–82.

McCabe, A., & Peterson, C. (1991). Getting the story: A longitudinal study of parental styles in eliciting narratives and developing narrative skill. In A. McCabe & C. Peterson (Eds.), *Developing narrative structure,* pp. 217–254. Hillsdale, NJ: Lawrence Erlbaum.

McCabe, A., Capron, E., & Peterson, C. (1991). The voice of experience: The recall of early childhood and adolescent memories by young adults. In A. McCabe & C. Peterson (Eds.), *Developing narrative structure,* pp. 137–174. Hillsdale, NJ: Lawrence Erlbaum.

Menig-Peterson, C., & McCabe, A. (1977–78). Children talk about death. *Omega—Journal of Death and Dying, 8,* 305–317.

Michaels, S. (1991). The dismantling of narrative. In A. McCabe & C. Peterson (Eds.), *Developing narrative structure,* pp. 303–351. Hillsdale, NJ: Lawrence Erlbaum.

Miller, P.J., & Sperry, L.L. (1988). Early talk about the past: The origins of conversational stories of personal experience. *Journal of Child Language, 15,* 293–315.

Murrow, L.K. (1987). *West against the wind.* Mahwah, NJ: Troll.

Newkirk, T. (1987). The non-narrative writing of young children. *Research in the Teaching of English, 21* (2), 121–143.

O'Brien, T. (1990). *The things they carried.* New York: Penguin.

Paley, V.G. (1990). *The boy who would be a helicopter.* Cambridge, MA: Harvard University Press.

Pappas, C.C. (1993). Is narrative "primary"? Some insights from kindergartners' pretend readings of stories and information books. *Journal of Reading Behavior, 25* (1), 97–129.

Peterson, C., & McCabe, A. (1978). Children's orientation of their listeners to the context of their narratives. *Developmental Psychology, 14*(6), 582–592.

Peterson, C., & McCabe, A. (1983). *Developmental psycholinguistics: Three ways of looking at a child's narrative.* New York: Plenum.

Petry, A. (1964). *Tituba of Salem Village.* New York: HarperTrophy.

Piaget, J. (1960/1976). *The psychology of intelligence.* Totowa, NJ: Littlefield, Adams.

Pitcher, E.G., & Prelinger, E. (1963). *Children tell stories.* New York: International Universities Press.

Vitz, P.C. (1990). The use of stories in moral development: New psychological reasons for an old education method. *American Psychologist, 45,* 709–720.

Wigginton, E. (1976). *"I wish I could give my son a wild raccoon."* Garden City, NY: Anchor/Doubleday.

Wigginton, E. (1977). *Foxfire 4.* Garden City, NY: Anchor/Doubleday.

Zabrucky, K., & Ratner, H. (1992). Effects of passage type on comprehension monitoring and recall in good and poor readers. *Journal of Reading Behavior, 24* (3), 373–391.

Zipes, J. (1988). *The Brothers Grimm: From enchanted forests to the modern world.* New York: Routledge.

Zipes, J. (1989). *Beauties, beasts, and enchantment: Classical French fairy tales.* New York: New American Library.

CHAPTER 2

The Structure of Stories and How That Develops

Allyssa McCabe

OVERVIEW

This chapter begins with a consideration of the links between stories told, read, and written and contrasts our viewpoint with some others with which readers may be more familiar. Some authentic stories from cultures not our own puzzle us, and this is no accident or mistake. There are cultural differences in the way stories are structured. Frequently, however, such differences have been erased by translators. For example, we look at number, which is one means of structuring many folktales and other stories in various cultures. Although the magic numbers vary from one culture to the next, even this relatively accessible kind of variation has tended to be altered to conform with European preferences.

Divergent forms of storytelling should not be rewritten to conform to European traditions in the process of translating them into English. Cultural differences in structuring stories are not rare and need to be appreciated instead of effaced. Cultural differences should be distinguished from the kinds of storytelling differences that have been attributed to socioeconomic status.

Narrative structure represents a particular way of understanding stories, and the same story can be depicted as having various kinds of narrative structures. In other words, the problem-solving structure of a story will differ from the structure of its emotional buildup. Both these structures will differ from the poetic structure of the same story, a topic to be pursued in Chapter 3.

This chapter also addresses how narrative structure develops. That is, we discuss cognitive and linguistic prerequisites for producing well-formed narratives. In connection with the former, we debunk the idea that lack of explicitness in a child's story is due to the cognitive constraint of egocentrism. In other words, we argue that children have the cognitive capacity to tell stories as soon as they develop the linguistic capacity to do so. The profound connection between language and culture, as well as the linguistic equality of all varieties of English, are two concepts stressed here. Children's oral narrative structure, as we will see, is most canonical, meaning distinctly representative of the ideal form of storytelling in their culture, during the early elementary school years.

This description of the prerequisites of developing narrative structure is complemented by a consideration of the means by which narrative structure develops. Specifically, monologic narrative originates in dialogic conversation between children and the adults who socialize them, most often parents. We conclude by offering some suggestions for putting research into practice.

CULTURAL DIFFERENCES IN NARRATIVE AND STORY STRUCTURE

Telling, Reading, and Writing Stories

Oral-Literate Distinction Revisited

Much has been made of a contrast between an oral storytelling tradition and a literate one (Bernstein, 1974; see Hemphill, 1989, for review), with the general implication being that literate-style language allows for a smoother transition to literacy than does oral-style language (for example, Michaels & Collins, 1984). Some (Heath, 1982; Snow, 1983) have taken issue with this use of "literate-style" to refer to any form of oral language, arguing that such usage blurs the meaning of the terms. This book will follow Snow (1983, p.166) in defining *oral language* as "all oral forms of communication, speaking and listening," and *literacy* as "the activities and skills associated directly with the use of print—primarily reading and writing." Historically, literacy itself began with writing (Ong, 1982). The thrust of our approach is (1) that any kind of oral language can be made literate by the simple act of writing it down, (2) that the smoothness of transition from oral language in preschool years to literacy in the primary school years depends just as much on the kind of literate language to which the child is exposed as it does on the kind of oral language the child brings to the task, and (3) that understanding the literature of any culture not one's own one is greatly facilitated by understanding the oral discourse style that participants in that culture value; without such background knowledge, a reader is likely to be severely constrained in comprehension.

Story Form Transcends Mode of Presentation

The form of storytelling transcends the medium through which it is told. That is, a number of researchers have found that children's facility with storytelling in one mode predicts their facility with storytelling in another mode. For example, good readers tend to be good writers who achieve more cohesive harmony in their written productions (Cox, Shanahan, & Sulzby, 1990). And while children differ in the degree to which they specify information, they provide equivalent amounts of information whether they tell or dictate a story to an adult who writes it down (Sulzby, 1981). Another study (Clemente, 1990) looked at many aspects of both oral and written stories from thirty-two Spanish children, aged 6 to 7 years. There were virtually no differences in the coherence, use of formal opening and closing sentences, and complexity of narratives told in the two modes, although written narratives were more formal and briefer than oral compositions. Several studies have found few differences in children's oral and written retellings of stories previously read to them (for example, Geva & Olson, 1983; Cameron, Hunt, & Linton, 1988). Instead, significant relationships *are* found between reading comprehension and story rewriting and retelling (Cameron et al., 1988). When children struggle with certain forms, it is the form, or genre, of the material (narrative or expository), rather than the mode of presentation (oral versus written), that accounts for such difficulties (Hidi & Hildyard, 1983). That is, children's written productions were essentially identical to their oral productions in the way that meaning was structured. Those authors concluded that children's difficulties with writing can be traced not to the writing process per se, but to the nature of the discourse that the children were required to produce.

Bartlett's Great Experiment: Familiar Ways of Telling Stories Affect Ways That Other Stories Are Understood, Retold, and Remembered

Consider the following narrative:

The Ghosts

One night two young men from Seattle went down to the river to hunt seals, and while they were there it became foggy and calm. Then they heard war cries, and they thought: "Maybe this is a war party." They escaped to the shore and hid behind a log. Now canoes came up, and they heard the noise of paddles, and saw one canoe coming up to them. There were five men in the canoe, and they said:

"What do you think? We wish to take you along. We are going up the river to make war on the people."

One of the young men said: "I have no arrows."

"Arrows are in the canoe," they said.

"I will not go along. I might be killed. My relatives do not know where I have gone. But you," he said, turning to the other, "may go with them."

So one of the young men went, but the other returned home.

And the warriors went on up the river to a town on the other side of Walla Walla. The people came down to the water, and they began to fight, and many were killed. But presently the young man heard one of the warriors say: "Quick, let us go home: that Indian has been hit." Now he thought: "Oh, they are ghosts." He did not feel sick, but they said he had been shot.

So the canoes went back to Seattle and the young man went ashore to his house, and made a fire. And he told everybody and said: "Behold I accompanied the ghosts, and we went to fight. Many of our fellows were killed, and many of those who attacked us were killed. They said I was hit, and I did not feel sick."

He told it all, and then he became quiet. When the sun rose he fell down. Something black came out of his mouth. His face became contorted. The people jumped up and cried.

He was dead.

All the words are English words, not even particularly unusual ones. All the sentences are grammatically well-formed sentences, not even complicated in structure. However, to most English-speaking English and American adults, the story makes little sense. Among other structural differences from European North American stories, there is no resolution. The story ends disturbingly at a climactic moment that is never explained in the fashion that such adults have come to expect. Every year when I read this example to graduate students, I see their faces change from alert interest to puzzlement to empathic embarrassment for me, a professor who is making no sense whatsoever to her audience.

What I am actually doing when I present this North American Indian folktale is replicating an experiment done by a British psychologist, F.C. Bartlett (1932, p. 65), many years ago. In a book that would eventually revolutionize the way psychologists viewed the act of *Remembering* (also the title of his book), Bartlett presented this tale to British citizens of various ages and had them recall the tale repeatedly. Over these retellings, Bartlett noticed that his subjects omitted much information and began to reshape other information, substituting words more familiar to them, leaving some enigmatic things out and putting other information in—essentially making the tale into something closer to an English tale than the original North American Indian one.

Bartlett's experiment has been corroborated by more recent studies. Adult readers wrote better summaries of stories for which they had an appropriate schema than for stories from a different culture, and repeated retellings of a North American Indian story that deviated from these English-speaking white college students' own schemas resulted in poor performance (Kintsch & Greene, 1978). Foreign scripts were misremembered to be more like North American scripts by North American subjects (Harris, Lee, Hensley & Schoen, 1988). Both Americans and illiterate and schooled villagers in Botswana recalled stories (themes and episodes) from their own culture better than stories from the other one (Dube, 1978). Recently, Palauan and American eleventh grade readers read culturally familiar and unfamiliar passages in their own language. Students used different, less efficient strategies when confronted by texts from the other culture. Students also recalled significantly more ideas and elaborations and produced fewer distortions for the culturally familiar rather than for the unfamiliar passage (Pritchard, 1990).

Of more relevance for the present project is that when preschool children of different ethnic backgrounds heard a story, they retold the same story in distinctive ways. Specifically, while the total amount said by Puerto Rican children in this project did not differ from that said by African American children, the nature of what they recalled was quite different; Puerto Rican children recalled far more description and far less action than did African American children (John & Berney, 1968). A recent study of European North American and Ponam children from Papua, New Guinea, also examined the ways in which these elementary school-aged children recalled two European tales. While the Ponam children recalled significantly more propositions from both stories than did the American sample, they omitted many of the constituents (affect, consequence, resolution, and moral) that would be required in order for their recalls to meet good story grammar standards (Invernizzi & Abouzeid, 1995).

What all these studies mean is that children, as well as adults, comprehend and remember more of stories that conform to the structure of the kind of stories they have heard at home. Narrative is the primary means by which children make sense of their experience (Hymes, 1982). To put together a coherent narrative of some event you've heard about or that has happened to you is to sort through the blooming, buzzing confusion of life's happenings, extract the most salient component events, arrange them in some order, highlight the importance of these events for your listener—in short, to make sense of that experience. We remember stories from different cultures in ways that make those stories conform to the kind we expect *because such stories become more sensible to us in the reshaping of them.*

Why Not Rewrite Stories So They Make Sense To Everyone?

Paula Gunn Allen (Coltelli, 1990) discusses translation in the context of formal published translations of American Indian stories like the one above. Even authors extensively involved in such cultures tend to retell indigenous stories in English with a European North American frame of reference. Allen discusses the case of her uncle, who extensively adapted indigenous stories he translated into English. Spirit people were called fairies, and European concepts like princess and prince were imported. Her uncle would, she says, "translate from the Laguna, which he spoke, not only into English but into Western thought, and that's what causes the thing to turn upside down . . . So the best you can do is translate intuitively and then readers have to read intuitively because there is no other way to do it" (Coltelli, 1990, pp. 23, 24). Discussing other translations of Laguna stories, she says: "They are good. From a Laguna point of view. The reason they're good is because they make no sense [to European North Americans]. She has enough sense not to try to make sense. And as a result, you can read between the lines of her work in such a way that you begin to be able to get what goes on there in ways that you can't when the recorder tries to restructure. When Uncle John puts the stuff into a structure, immediately the reader looks at the structure and says, 'Oh, I recognize this.' And the reader, the Western reader, should not be saying, 'I recognize this.' Believe me, if that's what readers are saying, they're making a terrible mistake. And there's something wrong with the text" (Coltelli, 1990, pp. 24, 25).

In other words, to answer the question posed as the title of this section, you cannot rewrite stories to make equal sense to everybody. The more you approximate the form preferred by one culture, the farther removed you are from the form preferred by another. To match all children's sense of storytelling at least some of the time, then, you must at the same time challenge the sense of storytelling of children from other cultures. This should not be seen as threatening because no one has ever found understanding to be a zero-sum game. That is, so far as we know, children are quite capable of understanding an enormous number of things to which they are exposed.

The Importance of Number in Narrative Structure: How Eight Chinese Gods Got Translated into Seven Chinese Brothers

Belief in the universality of European story forms and concepts has led to unconscious imposition of European forms on discrepant stories from a variety of other cultures. Apparent universals in storytelling form may in fact be artifacts of translation. Egan (1993, p. 121) notes that "ubiquity of abstract binary concepts undergirding classic fairy stories and children's invented narratives suggests that their presence is hardly an incidental or casual matter," implying some universal aspect of mind at work. However, two is not the only engaging integer of importance in children's fairy tales from around the world. Three is the dominant integer in titles, let alone plots, of *Grimm's Complete Fairy Tales*, appearing in 15 of 211 titles. In Calvino's collection of *Italian Folktales*, the number three appears in 13 of 200 titles. Neither of these collections includes such classic stories as "Three Billy Goats Gruff," "The Three Little Pigs," or "Goldilocks and the Three Bears." In a famous Japanese story, "Peach Boy," the peach boy, Momotaro, is assisted by three animals who usually hate each other, a spotted dog, a monkey, and a pheasant. Three is a number of particular importance to Japanese culture (Minami & McCabe, 1991). Three freshly killed killer whales are the epitome of wealth in a Haida story, "The Wasgo and Three Killer Whales."

Three dominates themes and images in fairy tales from a number of countries, but thirteen, twelve, seven, nine, and four also appear frequently in European tales (Heuscher, 1963, pp. 100, 154), as does six (Grimm), and fourteen (Calvino).

While there seems to be widespread incorporation of numbers such as two and three into folklore in many cultures, cultural differences in the symbolism of particular numbers exist and affect stories, including the numerology in such stories. For example, in China three and nine are lucky numbers, and eight symbolizes riches, money, and happiness. But four is a taboo number, at least in the north, as it is in Japan, because the word for four in these regions is also the word for death. While the number eight does not appear dominant in European folktales, it is somewhat more prominent in China. A famous Chinese proverb consists of eight words, "Ba Xian Guo Hai Ge Xian Sheng Tang" (Eight gods cross the sea, each expressing a magic skill). This is said to highlight the fact that everyone has different abilities. Like many Chinese proverbs, it is associated with a very famous story, "Eight Gods.*" In the story, each of eight gods tries using his own particular skill to cross an ocean inhabited by a fierce King Dragon. Each manages to succeed in his own way. Interestingly, when this story was translated into English by an English author (Mahy, 1990), it became a story of *seven* Chinese *brothers*, dropping out the sole female.

In sum, while eight is almost never privileged in Western fairy stories, it is prominent in some Eastern ones. And while four appears often enough in Western tales, it would be very rare indeed in Eastern ones. While reading about

---

*Based on information in *A Chinese-English Dictionary*, 7th edition, compiled by Beijing Foreign Languages Institute, English Department, published in 1986 by Commercial Printing House.

eight brothers would hardly pose any great challenge to a European North American child's mind, even this very accessible facet of cultural difference in structuring was changed.

Some Cognitive Functions of Number in Story Structure

The fact that numerical motifs in folktales are not confined to twos may be related to some aspects of children's thought processes in the preschool and early elementary school years. The motif of three in such tales as "Goldilocks and the Three Bears" might well be related to children's acquisition of the ability to understand serial ordering (size of bears, chairs, bowls, beds). Children do seem quite able to grasp the concept of serial order in this narrative long before they are capable of demonstrating it in the context of Piagetian tasks, such as arranging sticks progressively from shortest to tallest.

Another kind of concept played with in the tale of the Three Bears, and others, is the establishment of a pattern and then the reversal of that pattern (for example, two chairs are not right and then the third one fits Goldilocks perfectly). While storytellers could use more than three incidents to establish a pattern and then reverse it, three is the most efficient way of doing that.

In "Why Mosquitoes Buzz in People's Ears" (Aardema, 1975), a West African Folk Tale, a series of six incidents reveal the complex chains of causal links that can determine a person's motivation for doing something; a mosquito annoyed an iguana, who frightened a python, who scared a rabbit, who startled a crow, who alarmed a monkey, who killed an owlet, and therefore its grieving mother wouldn't wake up the sun so that the day could come.

In "The Magic Ball" (Finger, 1924), a tale of the Chaput Country in Latin America, five birds in some way help to rescue a little girl who has been trapped by a witch. A condor who "sees far and knows much" tells the girl's brother that fire will conquer the witch's spell. Two birds—a turkey and a goose—fail in their attempts to bring blazing sticks to the rock in which the girl is imprisoned because they drop the blazing sticks in water or snow. A flamingo succeeds, but is burned in the process. Finally, an ostrich assists in transporting the brother, so that he is there when the flamingo frees his sister. The story provides mythical explanations for the coloring of the turkey, goose, and flamingo, and portrays the kind of ideal caring brother-sister relationship celebrated also in the Hansel and Gretel story.

Narrative is a means of stimulating children to use what have been conceptualized as potentially separable intelligences (Gardner, 1983). Gardner (1983, p. x) defines intelligence as the ability to solve problems or create a product that is valued in one or more cultural settings. He argues that there are seven distinctly different kinds of intelligence: verbal, visual-spatial, logico-mathematical, musical, physical, and both inter- and intra-personal intelligences. The world's fairy tales appeal to children's verbal intelligence through language. Their visual-spatial intelligence gets engaged by having them picture these stories in their minds. Interpersonal and intrapersonal intelligence are stimulated by giving children lots of information about all sorts of human interactions, and many words for various feeling states. What is surprising is to realize that logico-mathematical intelligence is activated by stories as well. In other words, through words plotted in various ways mindful of a culture's numerology, vivid images are conjured up, and children, as well as those who teach them, may put these images to many different uses.

Are Cultural Differences in Narrative Structure Relatively Rare?

Variation Within Cultures

Before considering the variety of stories found cross-culturally, we must draw attention to how much variation exists within one culture. For example, European and European North American tastes for detailed description in novels has declined dramatically from Victorian to modern times (Logan, 1993). Contemporary European North American parents (and their children) differ in the extent to which they foreground description (setting) versus plot in conversational narratives (Peterson & McCabe, 1992, 1994), as well as in the lengths of narrative they tell on a regular basis. European North American girls tend to foreground conversation when they tell about past personal experiences more than do boys (Ely & McCabe, 1993). Thus, variation within a culture is as remarkable as variation between cultures.

Variation Among Cultures Often Grouped Together

Moreover, cultures that are grouped together with such labels as European North American, African American, Asian American, or Latino actually are comprised of distinctly different cultures themselves, and such differences have an impact on storytelling. For example, Sioux stories tend to emphasize action, while Navajo stories are often quieter and more contemplative, and may include many references to members of the hero's family (John-Steiner & Panofsky, 1992).

Differences in narrative structure also have been found among groups that share some European heritage. For example, Hungarian children, unlike Anglo-American children, often embellish the stories they retell (John-Steiner & Panofsky, 1992). In spontaneous dinner-time narratives, American children tend to talk more about themselves, often with adult assistance, while Israeli children talk less about themselves and more about shared family events such as trips (Blum-Kulka & Snow, 1992).

Cultural Differences

We enter into a discussion of some cultural differences in storytelling having highlighted the diversity among members of various groups. We are mindful of what an explosive issue labels can be in any discussion of diversity, with their unplanned but seemingly inevitable obsolescence. We have sought to use labels that many individuals within a group agree on as the ones preferred at this time, but even these labels meet with objections from some.

Although there are enormous gaps in our knowledge of the structure of stories in many cultures, some information is available about storytelling styles in which children from a few other cultures are steeped (for example, Miller, Potts, & Fung, 1989; Miller, Potts, Fung, Hoogstra, & Mintz, 1990). Hawaiian children occasionally tell a teasing kind of story, with much overlapping contribution from their peers (Watson, 1975). Children of mixed race and language backgrounds in South Africa often tell narratives that increasingly employ repetition, parallelism, and refrains in a hauntingly poetic fashion (Malan, 1992). Children from Athabaskan communities may periodically tell narratives consisting of repetition sequences (Scollon & Scollon, 1981). Cultural differences in adults' narratives have also been established (Chafe, 1980), as have differences in adults' conversations with children about past events (Ochs, 1982; Schieffelin & Eisenberg, 1984). Such cultural differences extend to the expository writing of adults; Kaplan (1966/1972) found that adult students for whom English is a second language import distinctive writing styles from their native languages to their English compositions. In short, both cultural variation and variation within cultures seem relatively common in narrative structure.

Are Cultural Differences in Narrative Structure Really Due To Differences in Socioeconomic Backgrounds?

Twenty-five years of research has established a number of ways in which working-class speakers differ from middle-class speakers, but these differences are distinct from the ones that have been attributed to culture per se. Hemphill (1989) has reviewed research on socioeconomic status. Working-class speakers make greater use of pronouns as compared to nouns, while middle-class speakers rely more on use of specific nouns. Working-class speakers also use fewer subordinate constructions than do middle-class speakers. Compared to middle-class speakers, working-class speakers tend to take shorter turns and more frequently overlap with other speakers (Hemphill 1982, in Hemphill, 1989). Middle-class speakers from various ethnic backgrounds, on the other hand, are more likely to give long individual speeches, rarely overlapping each other, except for interruptions to gain the conversational floor. Hemphill attributes the working-class approach to a greater concern for collaborative meaning construction, while the middle-class approach is more focused on individual contributions to conversation. In short, the kind of discourse differences documented for socioeconomic status are different from the cultural differences that we will focus on in this book. If readers look at the narratives told by Natalie (p. 7) and Larry (p. 15), they will see the use of unspecified pronouns that has been the focus of so much research on socioeconomic differences in discourse.

What Exactly Is Narrative Structure?

Some years ago, Carole Peterson and I argued that narrative structure was a linguistic representation, not a structure of memory as others had argued (Peterson & McCabe, 1983, p. 13). Subsequently, I argued that narrative structure represented our understanding of a particular narrative or set of narratives (McCabe, 1991, p. xiii), a view to which I still subscribe.

When teachers ask their students either to (1) look for the problem that some story solves or (2) the beginning, climactic, and concluding events, along with those that build up to and lead from the climax, they are asking students to perform a specific kind of reading of stories. These two different ways can often be used with the same stories, but will result in differences of focus. There are many other ways that students can read the same stories, and teachers may wish to explore how different students' understanding of a story can be depending on these differences of focus. For example, if you ask a fifth-grader to read *Banner in the Sky* and to focus on the problem to be solved, she would tell you that the problem for the protagonist, Rudy, is to get to the top of the mountain and thus attain the goal his father had set for himself (his father died trying to get to the top of Citadel Mountain). If you ask the fifth-grader to read the same story and focus on the climax, she would tell you that it occurs just before Rudy's expedition gets to the top of the mountain, when one of Rudy's partners falls and the rest wonder what has happened to him. These are two very different readings of the same story.

The kind of narrative structure we document for various traditions of storytelling represents our readings of stories told by children from those traditions. We do not pretend that these are exhaustive readings by any means. In the following chapter, we will suggest several approaches to discerning structure in children's narratives, some of which will probably be considerably less familiar to teachers than others.

How Does Narrative Structure Develop?

Decontextualized Language

Cognitive Prerequisites of Storytelling. Children have the cognitive ability to tell narratives and stories even before they have the linguistic capacity to do so, though there is some confusion about this. Confusion about children's cognitive capabilities derives from the esteemed psychologist, Jean Piaget. Piaget used many methods to establish his point that children behaved egocentrically, meaning that they did not notice whether they were talking to someone with a different perspective from their own or not. He observed children talking out loud to themselves without any attempt to communicate, for example. While Piaget (1926, in Flavell, 1963) called this behavior "egocentric speech" and attributed it to an inability to take the role of their listeners, Vygotsky (1986) took issue with Piaget's interpretation. Children who talked out loud to themselves, said Vygotsky, were not unaware of that fact. They were instead beginning to use language for cognitive purposes, in addition to their original social purposes. Specifically, children were beginning to use language to control their own behavior. For example, one 3-year-old girl watched a play about a mischievous boy rabbit. At one point she became so incensed by his naughty tricks that she said out loud (to no one and apropos of no conversation with anyone), "No, I will *not* take my shoe off and throw it at that bad boy rabbit, no!" Of course, no one had suggested any such thing. The point is that the little girl was using language to control her own impulses.

Piaget used other methods to argue the point that children were egocentric. He even included narrative materials in his efforts. Specifically, Piaget had children retell fables to imaginary children or adults (Flavell, 1963, pp. 272–273). He found ample evidence of childhood egocentrism, he thought, in the unspecified pronouns and otherwise confusing language children used.

However, the materials Piaget selected were rather elaborate fables, involving such adult concepts as jealousy about infertility. Retelling stories, also, is something young children rarely do spontaneously outside of school (Preece, 1987). Using a genre of narrative more practiced by children, then, other researchers have drawn quite different conclusions regarding children's capacities. From the time that they are at least 3 years old, for example, children are more inclined to tell an elaborate story to an adult who did not share an experience with them than to an adult who did and who, consequently, already knew the story (Menig-Peterson, 1975).

In short, children are no more egocentric than adults. Their narrative language makes it clear that they know when someone needs to be filled in about an experience and when they do not. Nevertheless, unfortunately, one of the most well-known facets of childhood is children's supposed egocentrism. And it is true that occasionally young children *appear* to be very egocentric. Here is an example of a 4-year-old boy who leaves a lot of pronouns unspecified:

INTERVIEWER: Did you ever go swimming in a lake?
LONNY: Yeah, one time my dad took me.
INTERVIEWER: Oh, he did?
LONNY: Unhuh, and he said, we want to go swimming in the lake. And I said, "Yeah."
INTERVIEWER: Then what happened?
LONNY: I sunk. My dad went under water and got me then. We had it once still on. We had it once still on me, but it wasn't mine, it was the lakeman's.
INTERVIEWER: Oh, it wasn't yours, it was the lakeman's. The orange thing.
LONNY: Yeah, and it kept me up.
INTERVIEWER: It kept you up?
LONNY: Yeah. The blue thing, but, but my blue badge didn't. I just sunk. The blue vest sunk.

Such confusing narratives may invite many teachers to agree with Piaget that young children are hopelessly egocentric. And if teachers believe the problem is a cognitive incapacity of young children in general or particular children, they would be inclined to simply smile and nod with acceptance. Yet on close scrutiny of confused narratives such as the one above (I have probably read this narrative a thousand times), it seems that this boy's problem is a typical one and boils down to his lack of vocabulary. He forgot the word *vest* and did not recall that or the word *badge* until the very end of his story. The lakeman's orange life vest failed to keep the child afloat. What about the "blue thing"? I infer that he had a beginning swimming course at the end of which, as was common at the time, he received a blue badge. He was probably told that now that he could swim he wouldn't sink. He may have confusedly attributed flotation powers to the badge because of such a comment, and consequently felt doubly betrayed when not only did the lakeman's orange life vest fail, but so too did his blue badge.

In other words, a lack of skill (in vocabulary, for example) may result in a narrative that appears egocentric. But it is a lack of skill that causes that "egocentrism," rather than the egocentrism that causes the lack of skill, as Piaget (for example, 1960) claimed. The following narrative was told by the same child at the same time; with vocabulary in hand this child seems anything but egocentric:

> LONNY: I got a big dog. Don't ever try take a little cat by it. Or don't ever take little stuffed animals. Don't ever take little biddy animals by it 'cause it will eat them up. It ate a annarule, a baby animal. Somebody took a baby puppy by her. A TAN PUPPY! Then he ate him up. That was stupid. I watched him, said, "Don't no eat him." And he just still ate him, ate him up.

The little boy saw the need to warn others—*who had not shared his upsetting experience*—about his ferocious pet. In short, children are no more egocentric than adults or than Piaget himself was.

To say that even very young children have the ability to take the perspective of their listeners by adapting their personal narratives to suit those listeners' needs is not to say that children do not improve in their ability to tell decontextualized narratives. Children do continue to refine their orientative ability with age. From 5 to 6 years, they improve in the way they specify context in telling, dictating, and writing various genres of stories (Tinzmann, Cox, and Sulzby, 1983). Improvement continues past the age of 6 in this regard (Menig-Peterson & McCabe, 1978); by 9 years of age, just like journalists, children give the who, what, where, and when of their oral narratives at the outset, where it is most optimally useful. Most of their orientation describes who was present during an experience, with additional information as needed. Older children present their listeners with a greater variety of contextual information in any given narrative. They are also more complete about the information they do provide than are younger children.

Piaget also took as a sign of childhood egocentrism the fact that children often completed story stems that he gave them with effects rather than causes. For example, Piaget would ask them to complete something like, "The man fell down because . . ." Children prior to the age of 9 or 10 would often respond with "The man fell down because he broke his glasses." However, we examined children's use of *because* in their narratives and found that they seldom reversed causes and effects when they talked about the real experiences they had (McCabe & Peterson, 1985). Furthermore, we (McCabe & Peterson, 1987) found that adults, just as often as children, occasionally make the same sorts of reversals. For example, one child said, "It was cold outside because I was marching," meaning that she knew it was cold outside because she was marching. Adults do the same thing from time to time in spontaneous speech. In other words, even though children on rare occasions may use causal language in an incorrect fashion, it is no more revealing of some childhood condition such as egocentrism than it is of a similar condition of adults.

From the beginning, then, childhood narration is a communicative act. When a child's narrative fails to communicate it is most often due to a lack of skill rather than a lack of cognitive ability. Teachers are in a position to offer the right words to a child struggling to find these, something that will not only improve their stories, but also is likely to expand their vocabularies. Children can tell very *explicit* stories at very young ages and should be assisted in doing so. They are not cognitively incapacitated by their youth.

Linguistic Prerequisites. To tell stories and narratives, children must have sufficient language to be able to do so. Before they tell stories, children pass through a predictable set of earlier linguistic milestones. They cry at birth, coo at the age of 1 or 2 months, babble repetitively at about six months, produce their first word sometime around their first birthday, and talk with their parents about the here-and-now using one word at a time for another six months or so. Vocabulary at first builds slowly. Then, at about 18 to 22 months children begin what some call a "vocabulary explosion," learning an average of two to four new words a day (Smith, 1926, in Gleason, 1993). By the end of their second year, then, children begin to put words together and begin to add grammatical niceties such as prepositions *(in/on)* and plural markings.

Children must be able to mark an event as past in order to narrate unambiguously. The irregular past tense (such as *went*) is the fifth grammatical morpheme to be acquired by English-speaking children (Brown, 1973). Sometime after their second birthday, children begin to talk about past events with their parents, beginning with past events that just occurred and over time extending such discussion to more remote occurrences (Sachs, 1979).

There are many varieties of English spoken in this country, as well as all over the world. Children will acquire the particular dialect or dialects of English to which they are exposed in their culture. From a linguistic point of view, all dialects of English are equally rule-governed and valued (see Labov, 1972 for further discussion of this point).

Monologic Narrative Begins in Dialogic Conversation

Children acquire language in general and storytelling in particular in the context of talking with their parents (Snow, 1972; McCabe & Peterson, 1991, respectively). These are among the many intrapersonal processes that begin in interpersonal conversation, as Vygotsky (1986) argued. Adults scaffold their children's early narratives about past events (Fivush, 1991; McCabe & Peterson, 1991; Sachs, 1979), asking their children information, supplying that information if the children cannot do so, and in other ways consciously or unconsciously giving their children practice in storytelling.

Adults in different cultures talk about past events in distinctive ways (Heath, 1986; Schieffelin & Eisenberg, 1984), and these differences can be quite profound. In discussing each of the traditions represented in this book, we will give at least one example of exemplary parent-child conversation about past events for two reasons. First, we wish to reinforce our point that cultural differences in narrative structure are not superficial habits, easily changed. First-graders, for example, have oral narrative structure that is the result of six years of daily conversation with their parents. Narrative structure is deeply embedded in cultural and familial contexts.

Second, we wish to provide a model for teachers of the kinds of questions and comments that may seem natural to children from various backgrounds. Perhaps teachers could be more effective in drawing stories out of their students if they match the students' expectations about how such conversations should proceed.

Canonical at 6 Years

By the age of 6 years, children have acquired the ability to produce narratives that contain all the basic parts of a story valued by their culture (Peterson & McCabe, 1983). Only three years later, many of their narratives are so long and complicated that most major ways of analyzing narrative have become strained, unable to capture the overall shape of those narratives in a satisfying way (Peterson & McCabe, 1983). Adult narratives are even lengthier, more idiosyncratic, and more difficult to analyze using standard methodology. Thus, children in the early elementary school years display more canonical narrative structure than either younger or older individuals in their cultures. In other words, their narratives conform more to orthodox narrative structure than do those of adults, at least as that structure has traditionally been defined. For this reason, 6- to 9-year-old children are the best group to study if your focus is on cultural differences in storytelling, and that is the group we focus on in this book. Such children are old enough to have internalized the kind of storytelling

---

Box 3: Research into Practice

1. When doing a unit composed of, for example, eight stories from a particular culture, encourage children to use literature response logs to record their honest reactions, even if those reactions are negative. At such times, teachers will probably wish to restrict such logs to a written dialogue between themselves and their students (rather than a springboard for student discussion) to avoid offend-

ing children from that culture. It is only by confronting struggles in appreciating stories from different cultures that we can promote genuine appreciation and understanding. Outlawing negative reactions will likely lead to tacit dismissal of the unit by those students who struggle the most. Xiaofang Xu (1993) used an oral version of the literature response log when she read groups of stories

---

Box 3: Research into Practice—cont'd

from various cultures to preschool-aged children. She found that even such young children initially voiced distaste for stories from cultures not their own. She also found, however, that the more stories she read from those cultures, the more those students came to like them in a genuine way.

Here is a series of reactions to eight stories from a particular culture written in a literature response log by an 11-year-old European North American girl. To avoid offending anyone, and because the culture being presented is not relevant (these could have been stories from any culture unfamiliar to her), we have deleted specific references to either culture or books. Note how her reaction changes over time as she becomes familiar with a new tradition *without any outside requirement to do so*. Though comments from a teacher might have been inserted, they were not and were not necessary in this case. Increased familiarity in and of itself simply increased her appreciation.

Book 1: I thought it was weird how she was a spirit & I thought it had no point.

Book 2: I thought it was kind of stupid because [particular kinds of holiday] are no big deal.

Book 3: I thought it was really good because it was clear. I loved the illustrations.

Book 4: Awesome illustrations & a cool story. It made the book fun & exciting.

Book 5: Exactly like [another story she read], but it was good.

Book 6: Cool book. Great tricks and it was funny.

Book 7: It's neat because it's interesting to find out what [people in culture X] do for [a particular holiday].

Book 8: It is fun to learn how to make a [cultural object].

I can think of no better record of a successful unit in a multicultural literacy program.

2. Have children read several folktales from a particular culture. Work with them to see patterns of preference for particular numbers (for example, the number three in European folktales).

3. After completing a study of the ways in which a particular culture uses particular numbers to structure stories, have children pick a number and use it in their own composition. Have them write a story that involves similar incidents with three sisters or eight kittens, for example.

---

preferred by the adults around them, yet they are not old enough to have become peculiarly individual.

Summary

- Oral narrative or story structure refers to genres of spoken discourse, not subcategories of spoken discourse. Thus, all children may be said to produce oral stories before they produce written ones.

- Familiar ways of telling stories affect the way other stories are understood, retold, and remembered.
- When European or European North American authors translate stories from cultures not their own, they often revise even such minor aspects of structure as the number of participants.
- Stories cannot be translated so that they make equal sense to everyone. Sense-making in the culture of origin is traded off against sense-making in the culture into which these stories are imported.
- Cultural differences in story form are not uncommon. There are numerous bodies of research that document these differences in many aspects of story form and storytelling practices.
- Cultural differences in storytelling form can be distinguished from differences that have been documented as attributable to socioeconomic status.
- Narrative and story structure represents an understanding of such discourse, and there are numerous ways of understanding (representing aspects of structure) any particular story.
- Narrative structure begins to develop after children achieve certain linguistic prerequisites. Children have the cognitive capacity to produce narratives of personal experience before they have the linguistic capacity to do so. Children are no more egocentric than adults, despite Piaget's claims that they are, and children's occasional struggles to produce narratives cannot be attributed to youthful cognitive incapacity.
- Linguistic prerequisites include the acquisition of sufficient vocabulary, acquired in the context of talking about present events with parents or other caring adults, and of the past tense.
- All dialects and languages are held in equal esteem by linguists. All are equally rule-governed and logical, and children acquire the dialect(s) and/or language(s) to which they are exposed.
- Monologic narrative begins in dialogic conversation. That is, children's performances at age 6 result from their internalization of habitual conversations with their parents.
- Adult language is often held up as an ideal to which all children should aspire. However, if one is interested in studying the most canonical forms of a culture, as opposed to the most idealistic, one would be well-advised to consider the oral narratives of 6- to 9-year-old children. Such children have acquired the basic form of narration valued by their culture but are not old enough to have developed idiosyncrasies in this regard.

References

BARTLETT, F.C. (1932). *Remembering.* Cambridge, England: Cambridge University Press.
BERNSTEIN, B. (1974). *Class, codes, and control,* (Vol. 1). *Theoretical studies towards a sociology of language* (2nd ed.). London: Routledge & Kegan Paul.

BLUM-KULKA, S., & SNOW, C. (1992). Developing autonomy for tellers, tales, and telling in family narrative events. *Journal of Narrative and Life History, 2,* 187–218.

BROWN, R. (1973). *A first language.* Cambridge, MA: Harvard University Press.

CALVINO, I. (1980). *Italian folktales.* Trans. G. Martin. New York: Pantheon Books. (Original work published 1956).

CAMERON, C.A., HUNT, A.K., & LINTON, M.J. (1988). Medium effects on children's story rewriting and story retelling. *First Language, 8,* 1–18.

CHAFE, W.L. (1980). The deployment of consciousness in the production of a narrative. In W.L. Chafe (Ed.), *The pear stories: Cognitive, cultural, and linguistic aspects of narrative production* (pp. 9–50). Norwood, NJ: Ablex.

CLEMENTE, E. (1990). Narraciones orales y escritas en ninos: Un estudio sobre sus diferencias. *Estudios de Psicologia, 41,* 7–19.

COLTELLI, L. (1990). *Winged words,* pp. 11–39. Lincoln, NE: University of Nebraska Press.

COX, B.E., SHANAHAN, T., & SULZBY, E. (1990). Good and poor readers' use of cohesion in writing. *Reading Research Quarterly, 25,* 47–65.

DUBE, E.F. (1982). Literacy, cultural familiarity, and "intelligence" as determinants of story recall. In U. Neisser (Ed.), *Memory observed.* San Francisco, CA: Freeman.

EGAN, K. (1993). Narrative and learning: A voyage of implications. *Linguistics and Education, 5*(2), 119–126.

ELY, R., & MCCABE, A. (1993). Remembered voices. *Journal of Child Language, 20* (3), 671–696.

FIVUSH, R. (1991). The social construction of personal narratives. *Merrill-Palmer Quarterly, 37* (1), 59–81.

FLAVELL, J.H. (1963). *The developmental psychology of Jean Piaget.* New York: Van Nostrand.

GEVA, E., & OLSON, D. (1983). Children's story-retelling. *First Language, 4,* 85–110.

GLEASON, J.B. (1993). *The development of language* (3rd ed.). New York: Macmillan.

Grimm's complete fairy tales. Garden City, NY: Doubleday.

HARRIS, R.J., LEE, D.J., HENSLEY, D.L., & SCHOEN, L.M. (1988). The effect of cultural script knowledge on memory for stories over time. *Discourse Processes, 11,* 413–431.

HEATH, S.B. (1982). What no bedtime story means: Narrative skills at home and school. *Language in Society, 11,* 49–76.

HEATH, S.B. (1986). Taking a cross-cultural look at narratives. *Topics in Language Disorders, 7*(1), 84–94.

HEMPHILL, L. (1989). Topic development, syntax, and social class. *Discourse Processes, 12,* 267–286.

HEUSCHER, J.E. (1963). *A psychiatric study of fairy tales.* Springfield, IL: Charles C. Thomas.

HIDI, S.E., & HILDYARD, A. (1983). The comparison of oral and written productions in two discourse types. *Discourse Processes, 1,* 97–117.

HYMES, D. (1982). Narrative form as a "grammar" of experience: Native Americans and a glimpse of English. *Journal of Education, 2,* 121–142.

INVERNIZZI, M.A., & ABOUZEID, M.P. (1995). One story map does not fit all: A cross-cultural analysis of children's written story retellings. *Journal of Narrative and Life History, 5*(1), 1–19.

JOHN, V.P., & BERNEY, J.D. (1968). Analysis of story retelling as a measure of the effects of ethnic content in stories. In J. Helmuth (Ed.), *The disadvantaged child: Head Start and early intervention,* (Vol. 2). New York: Brunner/Mazel.

JOHN-STEINER, V., & PANOFSKY, C. (1992). Narrative competence: Cross-cultural comparisons. *Journal of Narrative and Life History, 2,* 219–234.

KAPLAN, R. (1966/1972). Cultural thought pattern in intercultural education. *Language Learning, 16,* 1–20.

KINTSCH, W., & GREENE, E. (1978). The role of culture-specific schemata in the comprehension and recall of stories. *Discourse Processes, 1,* 1–13.

LABOV, W. (1972). *Language in the Inner City.* Philadelphia: University of Pennsylvania Press.

LOGAN, T. (1993). Victorian treasure houses: The novel and the parlor. *Journal of Narrative and Life History, 3*(2-3), 283–298.

MAHY, M. (1990). *The seven Chinese brothers.* New York: Scholastic.

MALAN, K. (1992, October). "Structure and coherence in South African children's personal narratives." Paper presented at the 17th annual Boston University Conference on Language Development, Boston, MA.

McCABE, A. (1991). Editorial. *Journal of Narrative and Life History, 1* (1), 1–2.

MENIG-PETERSON, C. (1975). The modification of communicative behavior in preschool-aged children as a function of the listener's perspective. *Child Development, 46,* 1015–1018.

MENIG-PETERSON, C., & McCABE, A. (1978). Children's orientation of a listener to the context of their narratives. *Developmental Psychology, 74,* 582–592.

MICHAELS, S., & COLLINS, J. (1984). Oral discourse styles: Classroom interaction and the acquisition of literacy. In D. Tannen (Ed.), *Coherence in spoken and written discourse,* (pp. 219–244). Norwood, NJ: Ablex.

MILLER, P.J., POTTS, R., & FUNG, H. (1989, March). "Minority perspectives on narrative development." Paper presented at the annual meeting of the American Educational Research Association, San Francisco, CA.

MILLER, P.J., POTTS, R., FUNG, H., HOOGSTRA, L., & MINTZ, J. (1990). Narrative practices and the social construction of self. *American Ethnologist, 17*(2), 292–311.

MINAMI, M., & McCABE, A. (1991). Haiku as a discourse regulation device. *Language in Society, 20,* 577–599.

OCHS, E. (1982). Talking to children in Western Samoa. *Language in Society, 11*(1), 77–104.

ONG, U.J. (1982). *Orality and literacy.* New York: Methuen.

PETERSON, C., & McCABE, A. (1983). *Developmental psycholinguistics: Three ways of looking at a child's narrative.* New York: Plenum.

PETERSON, C., & McCABE, A. (1992). Parental styles of narrative elicitation: Effect on children's narrative structure and content. *First Language, 12,* 249–321.

PETERSON, C., & McCABE, A. (1994). A social interactionist account of developing narrative orientation. *Developmental Psychology, 30*(6), 937–948.

PREECE, A. (1987). The range of narrative forms conversationally produced by young children. *Journal of Child Language, 14,* 353–373.

PRITCHARD, R. (1990). The effects of cultural schemata on reading processing strategies. *Reading Research Quarterly, 25*(4), 273–295.

SACHS, J. (1979). Topic selection in parent-child discourse. *Discourse Processes, 2,* 145–153.

SCHIEFFELIN, B.B., & EISENBERG, A.R. (1984). Cultural variation in children's conversations. In R.L. Schiefelbusch & J. Pickar (Eds.), *The acquisition of communicative competence,* (pp. 378–420). Baltimore, MD: University Park Press.

SCOLLON, R., & SCOLLON, S.B.K. (1981). *Narrative, literacy, and face in interethnic communication.* Norwood NJ: Ablex.

SNOW, C.E. (1972). Mother's speech to language-learning children. *Child Development, 43,* 549–565.

SNOW, C.E. (1983). Literacy and language: Relationships during the preschool years. *Harvard Educational Review, 53,* 165–189.

SULZBY, E. (1981). *Kindergartners begin to read their own compositions: Beginning readers' developing knowledges about written language project.* Final report to the Research Committee of the National Council of Teachers of English. Evanston, IL: Northwestern University.

VYGOTSKY, L. (1986). *Thought and language.* Trans. A. Kozulin. Cambridge, MA: The MIT Press.

WATSON, K.A. (1975). Transferable communicative routines: Strategies in group identity in two speech events. *Language in Society, 4,* 53–72.

XU, X. (1993). "Familiar and strange: A comparison of children's literature in four cultures." Unpublished master's thesis, Tufts University, Medford, MA.

CHAPTER 3

How to Translate Narrative Structure and to Appreciate What It Means

Allyssa McCabe

OVERVIEW

In this chapter we present the methods used to collect and analyze oral narratives from children in various cultures. Results of this approach form the basis of this book. Methods useful for research may also be useful in instruction. We note children's frequent use of conjunctions and suggest ways for using, instead of fighting, this oral habit when children begin to write down their stories. Personal narratives may be displayed as poetry, consisting of sentences or phrases grouped together in stanzas. Personal narratives may also be analyzed into information and emotion. Suggestions are made for putting research into practice.

METHODS OF COLLECTING AND ANALYZING ORAL NARRATIVE STRUCTURE

How Oral Narratives Were Gathered and Analyzed for This Book

Collecting Oral Narratives

Over the past few years, I have developed a methodology for coming to understand narratives from different cultures. First, a full participant in a particular culture expresses an interest in articulating the rules for telling good narratives and stories in that culture. Then we interview children from that culture who are between the ages of 6 and 8 years. Such children are old enough to have developed the basic cultural form for storytelling but not so old that their stories have become unduly complicated and idiosyncratic (Peterson & McCabe, 1983). We use a translation of a conversation that has been used successfully for hundreds of children from many different kinds of backgrounds. We operate on the principle that children, like adults, are much more likely to tell a narrative about their experiences if their listener shares one or more stories about his or her own experiences first. Thus, an adult interviewer tells brief narratives about getting hurt, taking a pet to the veterinarian's office, and so forth, and then responds to the child's story with open-ended questions (such as, "Umhum, and then?") or simply repeats the child's statements.

Analyzing Oral Narratives

After these interviews are collected, conversations are transcribed, narratives are identified, and scoring of these narratives begins. As we score narratives, my collaborator and I discuss various aspects of the culture in which the children and the adult live. The operating assumption is that all unified cultures develop a kind of aesthetic taste that pertains to all senses. For example, some cultures (like Japan) prefer small things—small trees, small houses, small portions of food, and small literary forms, for example (Lee, 1983). Perhaps this taste reflects an adaptation to physical circumstances in the country of origin (for example many people sharing a small amount of space), as one prominent anthropologist has argued (Harris, 1974). However, even if members of that cultural group come to America where physical circumstances are vastly different, an aesthetic sensibility may remain the same over generations. Thus, my group tries to ascertain the ways in which cultural differences in narrative structure are embedded in larger cultural concerns. Our method uses both a member of the culture of interest to provide information and a member of a foreign culture to ask questions and comment on what may strike outsiders as the most distinctive features of that culture. Those distinctive features are often taken so much for granted that little, if any, attention is paid to them by insiders.

The approaches we will mention serve two purposes. First, they are the ones my collaborators and I have found most useful for the majority of the thousands of children's narratives, written and oral, that we have encountered over the years. Thus, the findings we present in later chapters will be based on the analyses detailed here. Second, we believe these analyses hold considerable potential for educational application although they are far less well known than other approaches. These approaches are only a few among many possible approaches. The more kinds of analysis children are asked to apply to their own and others' stories, the broader their understanding of those stories will be.

Practical Periods: Oral Habits That Can Be Used to Analyze Structure

There are many aspects of children's personal narratives that reward close scrutiny. Consider the lowly and ubiquitous *and*. This conjunction, and its close relative *and then*, are the subject of many admonitions and even tirades by educators attempting to teach children to write in a literate manner. Careful analysis of hundreds of *ands* in children's narratives (see Peterson & McCabe, 1991) has led us to realize that these conjunctions are not slung about meaninglessly by children. Instead, these conjunctions usually introduce actions rather than orientation or evaluation (Peterson & McCabe, 1991 a, b). For example, in the following section of a narrative (the full account is given on page 11), a fast-paced sequence of actions is linked with *ands* (emphasis mine):

> Walter: ... *and* I just had put it [a snake] in a cage. *And* I was looking through this snake book *and* I read that water snakes are poisonous, *and* I said, thought, "Ohh, I lifted a poison snake up." *And* my Mom came out there *and* she said, "What happened?" *And* I said, "I lifted a poison snake up."

In general, "and" functions as a signal that a narrative event is coming up.

Note that African American and European American children do this kind of prosodic punctuation, and so do children of other cultures, using, of course, conjunctions of their own. Japanese children tend to use (or overuse, from an educator's point of view) "ne," as do South African children. Latino children use "y" or "pero," among other possible conjunctions to mark the ends of sentences or the beginnings of stories, as well as more traditional links.

This habit of introducing events in a narrative with "and" is not confined to children. In an interview a few years ago, a well-known actress, who has been speaking in public ever since she was a small child and thus presumably has received ample instruction about the importance of *not* using *and* so much, nonetheless lapsed into introducing all the events in an emotional narrative about her father's last public performance with *and*.

These "practical punctuation devices" can be used by teachers to help children come to understand the use of punctuation in written narratives, as well as to display their work poetically, as we will see. Teachers can ask children to substitute punctuation devices for many *ands* in revising written work, which can shift public opinion of *ands* from an annoying habit to be gotten rid of to a clue that some kind of punctuation is in order.

Displaying Narratives As Poetry

Many children's stories benefit from being rewritten or retyped as if they were poems. This exercise is based on a form of analysis developed by researchers to study narratives from cultures not their own (Gee, 1985, 1991a, b; Hymes, 1981, 1982). For example, Hymes (1982) analyzed a short story from the Zuni, an American Indian tribe in New Mexico, and found a culture-specific pattern of narrative structure.

There is variation in the method by which researchers break transcriptions of oral language into sentences or phrases. Some (Hymes, 1981, 1982) subdivide grammatical sentences into smaller components called "lines." Others (Gee, 1991b) use speaker pauses to break oral language into component parts. In my own adaptation of these approaches, I have found that children often introduce what I would call a sentence by means of a conjunction *(and, so, then, because, but)*. *Sentences* in oral language include grammatically complete independent clauses but also could be phrases where the grammatical subject of the sentence is appropriately implied.

The next step is to group these lines or sentences into larger units, called "stanzas" here. Frequently, children will have several sentences with themselves as grammatical subject, sentences that can be grouped together. Then there will be a slight change of focus—still within the same narrative—to another grammatical subject or location, which calls for a new stanza. In other words, *stanzas* are rough oral equivalents of paragraphs.

This kind of approach to narratives, depicting them as poems, surprises people with its usefulness. First of all, it reveals regularities even in children's productions that were not readily apparent before the rewriting. Second, it helps teachers and researchers see structure in and make sense of narratives that were hard for them to follow before the rewriting. Third, child narrators can come to recognize what eventually becomes paragraph structure in their early productions. Note that this approach will work for oral or dictated narratives even in preschool years, but will only be useful for narratives written by children toward the end of second grade and thereafter. Before that time, children's written narratives are not likely to be long enough to include more than one stanza.

We have found that this technique works better for the productions of children from some cultures than for others. Specifically, narratives of Japanese children (Chapter 5), African American children (Chapter 6), and many American Indian and Canadian Aboriginal children (Chapter 8) show remarkable regularity in terms of the number of lines per stanza, while those of European American culture (Chapter 4) and Latino backgrounds (Chapter 7) do not. Japanese children have a tendency to say about three lines on any subtopic, while African American children show an equally consistent tendency to use four lines per topic.

Another aspect of children's narratives that is revealed by this technique is their tendency to bring a subtopic to a close with what I call a "punch line." That is, stanzas may end in a refrain of some sort (for example, "And we had a lot of fun"), repeated at regular intervals throughout a narrative. Two narratives collected (and one translated) by Karen Malan (1992) illustrate the way in which children develop subtopics to a kind of punch line (italicized below) that ends that topic and precedes a slight shift of topic within the overall narrative. Note also the frequent use of conjunctions to begin sentences, as well as "ne" to end many sentences, another one of those prosodic punctuation devices we have described.

Jamie (4-year-old South African boy):

We got a gate, ne.
But yesterday, ne, we left to school again, ne.
So we say, "bye-bye" to my mommy, ne.

Chippy was running around
and we just took Chippy,
and we tied him up again.

And so one day, it was late, ne.
So he jumped over the gate again.

And then, the next time, I went home, ne,
So my daddy say hello for Chippy
but so he was running around in the big road.

So he was running over the road, ne.
Then the car bumped him,
and so now he's again tied up.

So the next morning, I went with the train, ne.
So that man said that that is another train, ne.
He goes to town center only, ne, to a lot of stations, ne.
So they said that goes to a lot of stations.
Now we go again that way, that way.
Then our train must go, ne.

And then the next morning Chippy and we came home again, ne.
So when we came home, ne.
And so we saw Chippy running around.

Now there's more dogs, ne, a lot of dogs, ne.
He was running around, ne.
So he run there, ne.
so a dog came and bite him right here.

At times these punch lines are repetitions of the same or similar phrases, which gives them a poetic quality much like refrains in musical compositions, as in the following narrative (refrains are italicized):
Analicia (4-year-old South African girl who speaks Afrikaans here):

En toe my uncle het verdrink in die water in 'n klein boatjie verdrink, hy. Die water was diep. En toe verdrink hy. En toe waaj die winde. En toe verdrink, hy. Dan begrawe hulle hom.

translation:
And then my uncle drowned in the water.
In a small boat he drowned.

The water was deep,
and then he drowned.

And then the winds blew,
and then he drowned.

Then they buried him.

In short, as this extremely poignant example illustrates, children's oral narratives can truly be very poetic indeed, and this type of analysis reveals such poetry the way no other approach can.

Displaying Narratives As Emotional and Informative Events

A number of years ago, Labov and his colleagues (Labov, 1972) devised linguistic techniques to evaluate narration of experiences within Black English vernacular. Carole Peterson and I (1983) adapted Labov's analysis to formulate what we called High Point Analysis (Peterson & McCabe, 1983) because of the central importance of ascertaining the emotional climax—the high point—of a child's narrative. The results of this analysis are presented in Chapter 4, and the gist of this analysis has become part of many elementary school teachers' curricula. Specifically, in some process writing workshops, children are asked to write a story outline, with (1) a beginning, (2) events building to (3) a climax, (4) events after that climax, and (5) an end, or conclusion. In reading exercises, children are asked to determine the comparable parts of some story.

However, this approach to narrative may be used in another, less familiar way, as is described in Box 4. Furthermore, the approach may be deepened by pointing out all the different kinds of components to be found in narratives and stories. Such components include (1) boundary markers, (2) information (including description and action), (3) dialogue, and (4) evaluation.

Box 4: Research Into Practice

1. Children can be encouraged to take either one of their own stories or a story they have read and use different kinds of highlighters to pick out different kinds of information. Children may be asked to break the story down into the four components of the highpoint approach.

   In the following narrative, **boundary markers** are bold-faced. Description is neutral print. Actions are italicized. As is conventional, reported speech will be included in quotation marks. Evaluative information is written in capital letters.

   Jasmine (a fifth-grade girl) wrote a story and analyzed the components as follows:

   It was a dark & Stormy night and INSIDE THE BOORE HOUSE A STARTLING THING WAS ABOUT TO HAPPEN. *It all started when Mrs. Boore asked her daughter to get the* FOOLISH *cat from out of the washing machine. When the daughter made several attempts,* the FOOLISH *animal would just claw at her and hiss.*

   When the Mother started loading the laundry, THE CAT MADE NO ATTEMPT TO GET OUT OF THE WASHER, SO MRS. BOORE DID NOT KNOW PEPPER, THE CAT, WAS IN THE WASHER. *She dumped* the thick, gooey, light blue detergent into the large white washer, *closed the lid,* and *started the machine.* Just 1 minute after, *the daughter noticed* some muffled sounds coming from near the washer.

   "MOM! THE CAT IS IN THE WASHER!" *She screamed.* Then her long slender legs *turned* TO JELLO *as her Dad came rushing in and stopped the washing machine. He took out Pepper.* WHAT A SAD SIGHT HE WAS.

   He was alive, but he was soaked and shivering. His BEAUTIFUL short silky black fur was sopping wet and matted. His eyes were WIDE AS

box continues

Box 4: Research Into Practice—cont'd

MEATBALLS WITH FRIGHT. *The daughter held him close to her chest, and Pepper started a* RUMBLING PURR.

Now whenever the Boore family does the laundry, they do a "Pepper check" to make sure he isn't in the washer! THE END

After she had finished her own analysis of her work (done in highlighters), Jasmine commented that she was good on actions but could use some more description, an apt self-criticism.

2. Teachers, especially of very young children, may wish to encourage parents to emphasize various components of narrative in talking about past events with their children. Very few parents see such conversation as having any educational significance. They would probably do more of it and do a better job if they knew that it did have such an impact. Encourage all parents to habitually question their children about when and where something happened for several months. Then ask them to focus on asking their children about why they think people do the things they do.

Boundary Markers. Things like "Once upon a time" or "This is a story about when I broke my arm" are typical ways of beginning a fictional story or a factual narrative, respectively. These are ways of letting your audience know that a story is coming up. Other phrases like, "And they lived happily ever after" or "And I never broke my arm again" or just "That's all" or "The End" mark the formal closing of a fictional or factual story. Older children may include what Labov (1972) called "codas," which are statements that bring the impact of an experience up to the present (for example, "And he's [a pet] dead right now too"). Teachers could ask children for other kinds of boundary markers they could use at either end of their writing and be on the alert for interesting ones they encounter in their reading.

Information. Information in a narrative is of two sorts, description and action.

Description. Sentences that describe who, what, when, and where things happened, what objects, if any, were involved, and what ongoing activities there were. (for example, " . . . those great big ones, those fisher bags, was taped shut.")

Action. Events given in the simple past tense that may occur in a sequence of some sort. ("And I turned around . . . ")

Reported Speech, or Dialogue. Stories can be developed through exchanges of words as well as actions. For example, one 9-year-old girl concluded her narrative about seeing a snake while fishing with: "Dad said, 'If you would have saw that snake and scared 'em, something would have happened to that.'" When children remember or compose speech, they should be encouraged to make it really sound like someone is talking. Dialogue is a good place to take a time-out from enforcing correct grammatical form. If children are writing personal narratives, teachers may wish to promote the use of dialogue, even if students do not remember exactly what was said. Truth about a specific experience is less important than drama, as far as writing a good narrative goes.

Evaluation. Emotional meaning is embedded throughout children's narratives. What follows is a list of all the types of evaluation found in the narratives of 4- to 9-year-old white English-speaking children, along with real examples (taken from Peterson & McCabe, 1983, and McCabe & Rollins, 1994):

Onomatopoeia ("It went bam.")

Stress ("I screamed and I *screamed*"—heightened tone of voice)

Elongation ("We had to stay a looong time.")

Exclamation ("Oh boy!")

Repetition ("I screamed and I screamed and . . . I screamed and I screamed")

Compulsion words ("We had to come in then.")

Similes and metaphors ("His eyes got as big as tomatoes.")

Gratuitous terms ("very," "really," "just")

Attention-getters ("I got to tell you the important part.")

Words per se (*finally, accidentally, squished, scared*)

Exaggeration and fantasy ("I picked them [trees] up with my pinky.")

Negatives ("He didn't shot me or nothin'.") Negative events, which are infinite in number and therefore reflect expectations a narrator had, are among the least obvious ways of evaluating the meaning of some experience.

Intentions, purposes, desires, or hopes ("I hoped Santa would bring me a new one.")

Hypotheses, guesses, inferences, and predictions ("We didn't think it would rain.")

Results of high point action (. . ."I cut myself with the knife. *Blood came running out.*")

Causal explanations ("He hit me in the head with a rock, *so* I threw one at him.")

Objective judgments ("My brother liked my snowman much better than he liked my sister's.")

Subjective judgments ("That was my favorite.")

Facts per se ("I caught the biggest fish.")

Internal emotional states ("She didn't care about me.")

Tangential information ("She gave me ten dollars for going in there. *Ten dollars is a lot of money when you're little.*)

Children typically evaluate their experiences rather heavily. Children as young as 2 years begin to use evaluation (Miller & Sperry, 1988) and it becomes increasingly more frequent with age. In fact, Peterson & McCabe (1983, pp. 52, 57) found that half of all comments from normal children aged 4 to 9 years were evaluated in some way. While evaluation permeates the narratives of young children, not all evaluation constitutes an evaluated high point. What distinguishes an evaluated high point from other types of evaluation is that the evaluation at the narrative's high point is concentrated in some way. For example, the evaluated high point or emotional heart of the following narrative is italicized:

> Kate (8-year-old European North American girl): I really fight pete. Well whenever we get home from school, he starts an argument. He says, "You got to do that. You got to do that." Which is, when it's really his turn. I get so mad I punch him in the STOMACH about that hard and he goes screaming, "Mommy, Kim hit me." I mean it. But when he gets in trouble . . . and I have arguments with Pete, especially one. Well, it was the day he went into my room. I was at school still, this was when I was in kindergarten and he went in my room and *tore all my pictures down that I painted and he tore them up. And he broke one of my best, my very best doll, my Raggedy Ann, she was my favorite.* I got another one. I love Raggedy Ann dolls. Then I told my mother and she came and he got it. Then we started arguing all over again. Boy once Pete talks, he can't stop talking.

Here, the narrator clearly articulates the heart of this experience for her, although there is some evaluation earlier in the narrative (for example, *stomach* is stressed, "I mean it").

Individual Differences in Relative Attention to Components

Children bring oral narrative expertise to school with them. That is, there are considerable differences in the extent to which individual children tend to include the various components of narration in their oral narratives, tendencies that they will subsequently display as they begin to write their stories down. In past research with many colleagues, we have traced the origins of these individual preferences to early conversations children have with their parents. These results are based on a longitudinal study of some children living in Newfoundland.

Description versus Action

English-speaking parents differ from each other in the extent to which they emphasize asking children questions about plot versus description, and these differing emphases are echoed later in their children's narrations to other adults (Peterson & McCabe, 1992). The extent to which parents pay attention to description, or setting, information in their conversations about past events with their children predicts the extent to which children subsequently include information about *where* and *when* something happened in their conversations with other adults (Peterson & McCabe, 1994). Thus, the element of narration most responsible for making narratives stand on their own in a manner some have called decontextualized can be traced to early parent-child conversation about the past. It is this orientative, descriptive component more than any other narrative component that has been linked to school success because description of setting decontextualizes a narrative from its social context (for example, Feagans, 1982).

Causality, an Important Kind of Evaluation

The psychological motivation of characters ("Why did the family leave Russia?") is a common component of assessments of reading comprehension. Some children receive quite a bit more practice than others talking to their parents about such issues, which gives them a decided advantage. That is, the extent to which parents discuss psychological motivation ("Why did he hit you?") with their children predicts the extent to which children include such information in subsequent conversational narratives to other adults (McCabe & Peterson, in press).

Dialogue

The ability to mark past speech explicitly is a mark of advanced emergent literacy (Sulzby & Zecker, 1991). Children's narratives contain numerous references to past speech (Ely & McCabe, 1994). Richard Ely, Jean Berko Gleason, and I (Ely, Gleason, & McCabe, in press) examined the extent to which differences among parents in attention to past speech would predict later child attention to this component of narration. Again, children whose parents frequently asked questions about past conversations or used reported speech were generally the same children who later were likely to talk spontaneously about past speech events in their experimenter-elicited narratives.

Cultural Differences in Relative Attention to Components

In addition to individual differences in the use of these narrative components, my colleagues and I have also found cultural differences. As is shown in Table 1, the groups we examined tend to focus on different components of narratives, a fact that will be discussed at much greater length and in appropriate cultural contexts in chapters to follow.

In view of these demonstrated cultural and individual predilections for emphasizing certain aspects of narration over other aspects, teachers may want to consider several options. First, teachers should ask themselves what their own preferences are. Usually, these preferences remain more or less intuitive,

TABLE 1. Some Major Formal Dimensions of Cultural Variation in Oral Personal Experiences of 7-Year-Olds

	African American	Japanese American	Latino: English Dominant	Spanish Dominant	European N. American
Typical number of experiences/ narrative	multiple	multiple	multiple	multiple	multiple
Number of lines/ stanza	4	3	varies	varies	varies
Percent of comments that are:					
Evaluation	28%	24%	29%	34%	15%
Actions	48%	49%	36%	30%	57%
Description	15%	27%	28%	28%	23%
Boundary markers	8%	n.a.	7%	9%	4%
Sequencing of actions	yes (74%) +themes	yes	not in 37% of narrs.	not in 49% of narrs.	yes in 100%

Data from Algonquin children this age are not available.

revealed primarily by means of the comments we make in the margins of students' papers: "Good descriptive language," "You need to make something happen here," and so forth. Knowing what you value and that others value rather different kinds of stories gives perspective to such expectations.

Second, teachers may want to make some adjustments. Keep in mind that even at the tender age of 6, a particular child has had at least four years of practicing a certain kind of storytelling in his or her family. How reasonable is it to expect them to change these well-established preferences in the writing of one or two stories at school? Is it a good idea to push Spanish-speaking children who do not focus on actions in their oral narratives to do so in their written ones? In the next few chapters, we will address such cultural issues in much more detail, keeping in mind as always the enormous individual variation to be found within any one culture.

Summary

- Research on oral narratives forms the basis for this book, and various research efforts are potentially useful in class instruction.
- Children's ubiquitous use of conjunctions like *and* is not haphazard and may be used in teaching them about punctuation.

- Oral and written narratives may be displayed as poetry, broken down into lines that are then grouped together in stanzas. This strategy reveals form in narratives that otherwise surprise teachers.
- Another approach to studying stories and narratives (in the classroom or for research purposes) is to break them down into their component parts: boundary markers, information (description and action), dialogue, and evaluation.
- There are notable individual differences in the extent to which children within any one culture tend to use these component parts. Some children prefer description, others action, still others evaluation.
- These individual differences originate in the kinds of conversations children have had with their parents from the age of 2 years on.
- There are also cultural differences in the extent to which children within any one culture tend to use these component parts.

References

ELY, R., GLEASON, J.B., & MCCABE, A. (in press). "Why didn't you talk to your Mommy, Honey?" Gender Differences in talk about past talk. *Research on Language and Social Interaction.*

ELY, R., & MCCABE, A. (1993). Remembered Voices. *Journal of Child Language, 20* (3), 671–696.

ELY, R., & MCCABE, A. (1994). The language play of kindergarten children. *First Language, 14,* 19–35.

FEAGANS, L. (1982). The development and importance of narratives for school adaptation. In L. Feagans & D.C. Farran (Eds.), *The language of children reared in poverty* (pp. 95–116). New York: Academic Press.

GEE, J.P. (1985). The narrativization of experience in the oral style. *Journal of Education, 167,* 9–35.

GEE, J.P. (1991a). Memory and myth. In A. McCabe & C. Peterson (Eds.), *Developing narrative structure* (pp. 1–26). Hillsdale, NJ: Lawrence Erlbaum.

GEE, J.P. (1991b). A linguistic approach to narrative. *Journal of Narrative and Life History, 1* (1), 15–40.

HARRIS, M. (1974). *Cows, pigs, wars, and witches: The riddles of culture.* New York: Random House.

HYMES, D. (1981). *"In vain I tried to tell you": Studies in Native American ethnopoetics.* Philadelphia: University of Pennsylvania Press.

HYMES, D. (1982). Narrative form as a "grammar" of experience: Native Americans and a glimpse of English. *Journal of Education, 2,* 121–142.

LABOV, W. (1972). *Language in the Inner City.* Philadelphia: University of Pennsylvania Press.

LEE, O.Y. (1983). *Haiku de nihon o yomu: Naze "furuike no kawazu" nanoka—nihon-jin no bi-ishiki, kodo-yoshiki o saguru* [Reading Japan in haiku: Why "a frog in an old pond"—examination of sense of beauty and behaviors of the Japanese]. Kyoto: The PHP Institute.

MALAN, K. (1992, October). *"Structure and coherence in South African children's personal narratives."* Paper presented at the 17th annual Boston University Conference on Language Development, Boston, MA.

McCabe, A., & Peterson, C. (in press). Meaningful "mistakes": The systematicity of children's connectives in narrative discourse and the social origins of this usage about the past. In J. Costermans & M. Fayol (Eds.), *Processing interclausal relationships in the production and comprehension of text*. Hillsdale, NJ: Lawrence Erlbaum.

McCabe, A., & Rollins, P.R. (1994). Assessment of preschool narrative skills: Prerequisite for literacy. *American Journal of Speech-Language Pathology: A Journal of Clinical Practice*, 45–56.

Peterson, C., & McCabe, A. (1983). *Developmental psycholinguistics: Three ways of looking at a child's narrative*. New York: Plenum.

Peterson, C., & McCabe, A. (1991). Linking children's connective use and narrative macrostructure. In A. McCabe & C. Peterson (Eds.), *Developing Narrative Structure* (pp. 29–54). Hillsdale, N.J.: Lawrence Erlbaum. (a.)

Peterson, C., & McCabe, A. (1991). On the threshold of the storyrealm; Semantic versus pragmatic use of connectives in narratives. *Merrill-Palmer Quarterly, 37* (3), 445–464. (b.)

Peterson, C., & McCabe, A. (1992). Style differences in eliciting personal experience narratives: Are they related to differences in how children structure narratives? *First Language, 12*, 299–321.

Peterson, C., & McCabe, A. (1994). A social interactionist account of developing decontextualized narrative skill. *Developmental Psychology, 30* (6), 937–948.

Sulzby, E., & Zecker, L.B. (1991). The oral monologue as a form of emergent reading. In A. McCabe & C. Peterson (Eds.), *Developing narrative structure* (pp. 175–214). Hillsdale, N.J.: Lawrence Erlbaum.

CHAPTER 4

Telling Plots: Some European North American Traditions

Allyssa McCabe

OVERVIEW

The historical background of European storytelling reveals fluctuations in an emphasis on action plots, as well as a kind of cultural unconsciousness about various storytelling traditions often assumed to be universal. Narratives of real personal experiences are exchanged at the dinner table in many European North American families. Fictional stories are usually not told, but read. An exemplary mother is presented, whose lengthy habitual conversations with her daughter predate outstanding monologic narratives from that child years later. In the past, scholars who have dealt with this storytelling tradition have done so without focusing on its cultural origins. Instead, some have emphasized psychoanalytic content, while others have focused on cognitive problem-solving in the fantasy stories produced by children. Common features of narration and storytelling in this tradition are presented, as well as the relationship between these features and the structure of European music and visual art. Information about how European North American children develop is abundant and is summarized.

STORYTELLING IN THE EUROPEAN AND EUROPEAN NORTH AMERICAN TRADITION

Historical Background

From the mid-eighteenth century until the mid-twentieth century, Europeans and European Americans valued temporally sequenced plots, a practice that has fallen into disrepute in the somewhat esoteric professional literary and critical circles in the latter half of the twentieth century (Brooks, 1984). But while literary critics debate about whether "'reading for the plot' ... is a low form of activity" (Brooks, 1984, p. 4) or not, the educational system for elementary school children does not question the importance of such an activity. Most ordinary European Americans have been taught throughout elementary school that narratives are by definition temporal sequences of events with clear beginnings, middles, and ends, just as Aristotle told us years ago. Americans of all ethnicities are surrounded by stories that display this format in books, films, television, and comics, as well as in evolutionary science, religion, and so forth. Many European North Americans are highly rejecting of novelists or playwrights from their own Western cultural background who attempt to tamper with this basic kind of sense-making device. Samuel Beckett's play, *Waiting for Godot,* may have been critically acclaimed, but it has never attracted the audience that murder mysteries or Sylvester Stallone's "Rocky" films have.

Because European North Americans dominated public storytelling forums in America for years, exceptions to sequentially plotted stories could be missed or avoided. European North Americans have often been the medium through which stories of other cultures were filtered, so that American Indian or Haitian folktales that could not be retold in a sequential form could simply be ignored. Thus it may be easy for European North Americans to believe that there really is a universal kind of storytelling that involves sequential action plots. In this respect they are, for the most part, unconscious that the European North American tradition is a cultural tradition deriving from a specific group of cultures rather than a generic expression of mind.

Storytelling Practices in Community

In this tradition, perhaps the single most common forum for the exchange of narratives about daily experiences is the dinner table (Blum-Kulka & Snow, 1992). Many European North American families regularly engage in ritual narration about what happened during the day over their mealtime meat and potatoes. Each family member takes a turn, and is expected to offer at least one experience. Generally, interruptions are considered rude, and overlapping conversation is avoided. Speakers are expected to talk about one experience at a time, and to give enough details to make the account vivid, but not so many as to seem to be going off on a tangent. During these times, adherence to truth is more important than telling dramatic stories in many families. Siblings, if not parents, may directly challenge any departures from the facts. "He's doing the dream machine again," one little girl said disgustedly when her brother attempted to embellish his experience.

If families are able to eat breakfast together, there may be a morning version of the dinner table reports. That is, families may engage in a ritualistic recounting of what they dreamed during the night. Narratives of personal experiences are told over the phone, in occasional letters, and at bedtime. In fact, some children seem particularly adept, like Scheherazade, in postponing bedtime goodbyes with lengthy recapitulations of the day's events (for example, Nelson, 1989).

Perhaps in the past, there were traditional settings in which narratives were told for the sheer sake of entertainment and truth could take a back seat. But almost no one from this tradition sits on porches or gathers around particularly skilled individuals just to hear their stories these days. Parents might take their children to the library to hear an oral storyteller in the 1990s, but not to Grandpa's house, nor to some other private setting.

Telling fictional stories of one's own devising or even recalling stories from memory is not common. Most European North American parents would find these activities very difficult. Fictional stories, then, are encountered primarily in printed storybooks, which are read frequently to children in some families, less frequently or seldom in others (Heath, 1982).

Exemplary Mother Talking with Young Child

Carole Peterson and I have followed ten European North American families since the children were 2 years old. At 6, we could measure which children were the strongest narrators. Consider the following exchange between a 27-month-old girl (who would be one of our best $3^1/_2$-year-old narrators) and her mother:

> MOTHER: And did you get sick at school, Helen?
> HELEN: Yeah.
> MOTHER: What made you sick?
> HELEN: I got (unintelligible) my pants fall, fall down.
> MOTHER: You got wee-wees in your pants and you fell down. Is that what you said? And who looked after you when you got sick?
> HELEN: Suzanne.
> MOTHER: Suzanne did. Did Suzanne look after you when you were sick?
> HELEN: Yeah.
> MOTHER: Did you lie on the mat? Suzanne put a blanket over you?
> HELEN: Yeah.
> MOTHER: Did you fall asleep?

This is a brief excerpt from a conversation that stayed on the same topic for fifty-nine more turns. This mother really wanted to find out what had happened to her child at the day care center, and she had to make guesses about what might have happened in order to do so. By repeatedly collaborating with young children to talk about what has happened, parents facilitate their child's ability to know what a good story is, including the kind of information others expect you to give about who was there and what happened. Helen, like every other child, was no born storyteller at age $3^1/_2$. But after four years of interested and informative interviewing, she became a very good one.

In every measure we employed, one girl emerged as the best storyteller. We have numerous examples of what kind of interviewing her mother had engaged in, how much interviewing she did, and how such interviewing compared to other parents' styles. Consider, for example, the following dialogue between a girl we call Eva, $4^1/_2$ years old at the time, and her mother. It is a lengthy dialogue, but we present it here for precisely that reason—as a model of how long you can spend getting a child to spin out a good story, of how you can encourage them to give elaborate descriptive details, of how you are well advised to encourage storytelling at the expense of truth sometimes:

> EVA: And you know what? We even saw a bear track.
> MOTHER: Bear tracks?
> EVA: Yeah.
> MOTHER: Out behind the children's center?

EVA: Yes.
MOTHER: What did they look like?
EVA: Big hairy footprints.
MOTHER: Who found those?
EVA: I me Joey Nicholas.
MOTHER: Ohhh.
EVA: And Frazer.
MOTHER: Did you follow the tracks?
EVA: Yes.
MOTHER: And what did you find?
EVA: A bear!
MOTHER: Where?
EVA: In the field.
MOTHER: And what was the bear doing in the field?
EVA: It was eating our soup, our snack—honey and peanut butter.
MOTHER: And what did you say to that bear when you found that bear in the field?
EVA: Said "go get your own honey."
MOTHER: You wouldn't even share with the bear?
EVA: I did.
MOTHER: Was it a girl bear or a boy bear?
EVA: A girl.
MOTHER: Did you find out what her name was?
EVA: Yes xx [= unintelligible comment].
MOTHER: Pardon?
EVA: xx.
MOTHER: Oh that's a nice name for a bear. Was she friendly?
EVA: No.

The two regularly talked at length about a wide variety of topics. At age 5, Eva told lengthy, well-formed narratives like the following, which more resembles narratives typical of 6- or 7-year-olds than those of 5-year-old children. Again, this narrative is lengthy, but its length is a most important point:

EVA: We had a game with a face and everybody had a piece of
ADULT: Everybody had a what?
EVA: Piece of face, and we stuck it on and know what?
ADULT: What?
EVA: I almost put the eye where I was supposed to. Know what Molly said?
ADULT: What?
EVA: And somebody put the mouth by the eye and Molly said, "That's a good place for a feed—right by your eye like [makes eating sounds]. Right on your forehead. And then, then we turned it upside down.
ADULT: You turned it upside down, yeah.
EVA: And then the mouth was like at the bottom and the head and the eyes were . . . the mouth was on the bottom and the eyes were on the top. But, but one eye was down there and one eye was up there.
ADULT: Were you blindfolded when you put those things on?
EVA: Yeah.
ADULT: I see, so you had a very funny face then?

EVA: If we weren't, it wouldn't be so much fun.
ADULT: That's right because you'd know where everything went.
EVA: And I got things from my loot bag, and you know what they were?
ADULT: What?
EVA: But Ivan (brother) broke his up before the party right when we were get-
ting them ready. He broke his up.
ADULT: Did he?
EVA: His own and he almost wanted to break mine up.
ADULT: He almost wanted to break yours up?
EVA: And almost wanted to break one of my friend's one up and that was
purple.
ADULT: Oh, and so what happened?
EVA: We took it away from him, because we didn't want him, for him to spoil
my other friends' fun at the party. But Alex, my friend, wanted the loot bag
before he was going.
ADULT: Alex your friend.
EVA: [xxx] want the loot bag when he was going. He just had to see his
mother's toe and then he said, "Loot bag."
ADULT: He just had to do what?
EVA: See his mother's toe.
ADULT: His mother's toe.
EVA: And then Alex said, "Loot bag," and then we give it to him without; he
goes so fast he doesn't want, he forgets his balloons. [HIGH POINT]
ADULT: He goes so fast he forgets his balloon.
EVA: Yeah. Because he wants to see what's inside it.
ADULT: Oh, he wants to see what's inside it.
EVA: Yeah, and then we gave somebody else his balloon.
ADULT: Gave somebody else his balloon, ah ha.

This story takes a topic—birthday parties—that could (and often does) produce dull laundry lists of activities and structures it into a narrative that builds
to the emotional highpoint, nicely evaluated by means of her friend's action—
as soon as he sees his mother's toe he takes off so fast he even forgets his balloons just because he can't wait to see what is in the loot bag. The rest of the
narrative is a nice example of resolution—clearing the stage by means of explaining what was done with the forgotten balloon. As was mentioned earlier,
monologic narrative begins in conversation, and this child's ability to tell a
lengthy, well-developed narrative was preceded by many lengthy conversations with her parents.

Other Scholarly Treatments

Past treatments of European North American children have usually not
been identified as such. There were two traditions of research on children from
this tradition: a psychoanalytic tradition and a more recent cognitive one. The
psychoanalytic approach (for example, Ames, 1966; Pitcher & Prelinger, 1963)
emphasized the content of preschool-aged children's stories. Children's stories
were depicted as often involving violence, including harm to animals and objects, aggression, and accidents. Gender differences were noted in this tradition,

with boys paying even more attention to violence than girls. Such tendencies were linked with Freud's idea of aggressive instincts.

The relatively more recent cognitive approach to European North American children's storytelling (Botvin & Sutton-Smith, 1977; Mandler & Johnson, 1977; Stein & Glenn, 1979) likened the form of fictional stories told by children to the form of Russian fairy tales as delineated by Vladimir Propp (1968). Such an approach focused on the extent to which children, as they grow older, increasingly organize fantasy tales around the precipitation and resolution of some conflict or problem.

Features of Narration in This Community

The features of the European North American tradition are so familiar to teachers that they may not seem to have a cultural origin: (1) children following this tradition go into great detail about single experiences of particular poignancy to them; (2) from the age of 5 years, they sequence events in oral and, later, written stories; (3) in their narratives about real past experiences, they often recognize some problem confronted by themselves or others. They articulate the goals that were precipitated by facing that problem and whether or not such problems were resolved; and (4) narratives and stories in this tradition have clear beginnings, middles, and ends. In factual narratives, children often begin with an attention-getter ("You know what?") and/or a summary (such as "I broke my arm!") and end with a coda ("That's all."). In fictional stories, children typically begin with "Once upon a time," and end either with "The end," or "And they lived happily ever after."

Thus, European North American children come well equipped for the kind of stories they hear in school, which tend to be exactly of this form, and there is research to the effect that teachers know exactly how to listen to such stories and that they both appreciate and extend them in written form (Michaels, 1991).

Relationship of Narrative Features to Structure of Other Art Forms in the European North American Tradition

There is an old tradition, prior to the twentieth century, of painting scenes of the peak moments of religious or secular history. Room after room in castle after castle in Europe is covered in frescoes and paintings and decorated with statues of momentous battles or famous myths or biblical events. There are many explicit "epiphany" scenes. Numerous paintings attempt to summarize and suggest critical stories. Thus the emphasis on highlighting some key event in an experience is common in visual traditions of European and European North American children. In fact, in the history of Western art, the stories told by a culture and the means visual artists have devised to portray these narratives have constantly interacted (E.H. Gombrich, *Art and Illusion*. Princeton University Press, 1960, p. 131).

Such aesthetics relate to larger aspects of culture as well. Central perspective is commonly interpreted as a manifestation of Renaissance individualism (Arnheim, 1974, p. 294). Paintings that give the illusion of depth by funneling from a center are attempts to present the world as seen from the viewpoint of an individual observer. Such a centered world would hardly fit the Taoist or Zen philosophies of the East, which express themselves in the centerless continuum of the Chinese and Japanese landscapes shaped by isometric perspective (Arnheim, 1974, p. 295).

In the field of mathematics, there is a famous phenomenon known as the Golden Rectangle or the Golden Section. The mathematical fine points of this phenomenon are more complex than the scope of this discussion warrants, but the critical element of the Golden Section here is that it plays an important role in painting, sculpture, and architecture (*Columbia Encyclopedia*, p. 1103). While there is some evidence that Egyptians and Babylonians knew the principles embodied in the Golden Section, the Greek philosopher Pythagoras (500 B.C.) is the individual who made it famous (*Prentice-Hall Encyclopedia of Mathematics*, pp. 227–228). The relevance of this phenomenon to our present discussion is that the Golden Section occurs approximately 61.8 percent of the way through a line. The ratio of the smaller section to the larger one is identical to the ratio of the larger section to the whole, combined segment. The Greek sculptor Polyclitus articulated the idea that beauty is no simple quality of an object being depicted, but instead has more to do with this kind of interrelation of parts of the sculpted representation of that object (Gardner, 1959; Sewall, 1961). The influence of this famous philosopher and sculptor on subsequent Greek and Roman artists cannot be underestimated.

Such aesthetics apply to music, as well. In many classical musical compositions from the European tradition, themes build to a climax, often performed with a peak crescendo. More specifically, during the classical era in the late-eighteenth and early-nineteenth centuries, the sonata form reigned supreme. In sonata form, a composition begins in a certain key, called the tonic key. After this section, called the exposition section, the composition moves to a different key in what is termed the development section. Different keys are explored and themes are inverted and otherwise elaborated. Then about 62 percent of the way through the piece, the climactic moment is reached when the composition returns to the original key (Pascoe, 1973). After this, the beginning section is recapitulated. What is of greatest interest here is that this happens at the point in the composition that is analogous to the spatial position of the focal point in many paintings: about two thirds of the way through a piece.

Thus a Western tradition of clearly defined climaxes, often to be found about 61.8 percent of the way into a work of art or music is the aesthetic backdrop for a consideration of children's narrative form. A similar structure centered around a clearly defined climax—amazingly also often about 60 percent of the way through a story—is to be found in accomplished narratives of ordinary European American children beginning at a surprisingly young age.

Developmental Information

European North American children begin narrating by referring to one past event at about 27 months. For example, a little girl told her mother, "I hied the big boy," informing her that she had just said hello to a waiter. By 31 months, they begin to chain two past events together. For example, a mother asked her 31-month-old son, "Did you like the puppy?" He said, "He taste my knee." She echoed this, "He tasted your knee?" Her son replied, "Yeth. An' puppy *chase* me."

At 3 and 4 years of age, children typically put together more than two events, but they often do so erratically, by violating chronology, contradicting themselves, or leaving out important events. Consider the following narrative a little boy told to a friend of his parents when he was 3 years and 5 months old:

> FRIEND: What did you do on your picnic?
> NICKY: We just played hide and seek. We were just lost in the woods. We just found mushrooms. We wasn't lost anymore.

Now the little boy had never really been lost in the woods, though he had played hide-and-seek. Perhaps part of the thrill of that game for him was flirting with the terror of being lost from his parents. The stories of 3- and 4-year-olds often require careful exegesis to be interpreted correctly.

Sometimes the events deleted by a 3- or 4-year-old seem convenient. For example, when she was 4, one little girl deliberately pushed her brother down and slapped him when he prematurely knocked over a stack of blocks she was making for him. Her father sent her to bed and forbade her bedtime story. She began to sob. Her mother came in to say good night and asked her what happened. She said that she was stacking blocks and her brother knocked them over and then her daddy sent her to her room. Asked several times to repeat what happened and questioned about whether she had left something out, she repeatedly, consistently deleted her own naughty act, the one that precipitated her punishment.

This is not the only example of such self-serving editorial work. In the following example from the corpus of over a thousand narratives collected by Carole Peterson and myself (Peterson & McCabe, 1983), the $3^1/_2$-year-old narrator conveniently omits what she did that broke her sister's arm and led to being spanked:

> BETH: My sister had, she's had, she broke a arm when she fell in those minibike. She had, she went to the doctor, so I, my dad gave me spanking, and I
> INTERVIEWER: Your dad gave you what?
> BETH: A spanking to me. And she had to go to the doctor's to get a cast on. She had to go get it, get it off, and, and it didn't break again. She still got it off. She can't play anymore. She *can* play rest of us now.

When transgressions are remembered spontaneously, it is often with the point of revealing the more mature perspective of the "much older" child. For example, a little boy spontaneously reminisced one day: "This was really naughty of me. I scribbled on the wall when I was a baby." This was done with no reminders at all, neither visual ones such as the scribbles nor verbal ones such as admonitions not to do such a thing. The whole point of the story was to show how mature he was at the advanced age of $3^1/_2$ years.

At 5 years, children almost always tell a well-ordered story, but they often end it prematurely, at the high point. The high point is the emotional climax of a narrative, which happens to be getting a shot in the following two narratives from our study:

LARRY: And, um, and, uh, uh, you want to hear another one? I went to the hospital?

INTERVIEWER: Sure.

LARRY: Well, I don't like to go to the hospital, and, and I had to have a operation about TONSILS. About my tonsils weren't getting very good. See, part of my food couldn't get down 'cause I had to take milk and this is

INTERVIEWER: The food couldn't get down?

LARRY: Yeah, 'cause I had to take milk. Right here, two little bumps that were causing all the trouble. And I kept getting sore throats and colds so many TIMES, and so we went and got those out. Man we went SO EARLY. Nobody was up yet. Nobody, nobody was up 'cept us when we had the operation in the morning when nobody was up. 'Cept me and my dad and my grandma were up. Nobody, and my brother. Yeah, and, those were who were up, and nobody was else up 'cept the hospital was already up, yeah. I had to wait a few hours but, but while I was there they had brought stor- library stories along. And, and then the doctor came in—one of the girl doctors—and gave me a shot like a mosquito bite. Anyway you don't feel a mosquito bite, but she gave me one.

The emotional climax, as in the previous narrative, is often not a positive event. Sometimes it does not even seem to be a resolvable one. In the following narrative the little girl hauntingly tells us the meaning of her trip to the doctor, the climax of which also was getting a shot. What more could she add?

Marilyn: Know something? The other day I had to go to the doctor's. And I had to get a shot. In the arm. And my MOMMY, she didn't CARE about me getting a SHOT. And my babysitter took me to get a SHOT. With my brother. And my MOTHER didn't CARE. And so my mother didn't CARE. I cared, but my MOTHER didn't. My MOTHER cares now, but not much. SHE don't care a LOT. She only cares a little bit. My mom don't care much about me. She DON'T care much about me. Just a little . . . NOT much.

At 6 years in this culture, however, children typically do go on to provide a resolution (italicized) after the climax of a narrative, as in the following narrative:

INTERVIEWER: Have you ever been in a hospital?

DONALD: Uh-huh.

INTERVIEWER: You have? Tell me about it.

DONALD: When I got, when I drank glue. But, that's when I was about one or two. Had to go to the hospital. They gave me some kind of pills to make me get all of it out. *Then I just went back home.* They don't take too long. They just take about one minute. I, I, I, gue-, I guess it's, if the pills won't help you, gotta, gotta, They got to operate on you. They didn't operate on me.

In contrast to the two preceding narratives, here we find out what happens after the treatment received at the doctor's office. The mention of going back home and of how rapidly the treatment worked, the alternatives had it not worked—all of this material is narrative resolution that is usually missing from the narratives of 5-year-olds.

By 6, then, children tell stories that meet expectations of what a good story is: they begin, often, by using some *boundary marker* such as an abstract. Then they orient their listener to who and what was involved and where and when things took place (*description*, to use the terminology of Chapter 3). They present a series of *actions* and *dialogue* that builds up to a heavily *evaluated* high point, and then go on to resolve the events with further actions or more dialogue. They often conclude with another boundary marker such as "That's all."

Resolutions. The provision of resolution is the most remarkable narrative accomplishment between the ages of 5 and 6, and children continue to devote even more of their narratives to this end as they grow older. Initial resolution of a narrative is often as cursory as in the preceding one. How much resolution is eventually provided, like much else in narrative, depends on many factors.

European North American preschool-aged children's resolutions tend to be one of three sorts: (1) some version of "and then I/we/they went home," as in the narrative about the glue-drinking calamity above; (2) the solution of some problem (for example, a man brought a tow truck and fixed the family car); or (3) the aftermath of some problem that could not be or was not solved (such as extensive gore after a splinter removal—see Mark's narrative below). About a third of the early resolutions of 4-year-olds fall into each of these categories.

In the following narrative from our study, the 6-year-old narrator provides a much more elaborate and extensive narration than, "And then we went home." He actually tells quite a bit about what happened after the climactic event of getting poked. The high point of a narrative is technically defined as that event often alluded to in summary form by the initial abstract and then explicitly evaluated in a clause that stops the action, as in the following example. Note that the terminology describing the parts of narrative below is adapted from Labov (1972) and summarized in Chapter 3:

MARK: There's um where I got poked. [ABSTRACT] You know them pencil things that Eversharp thing that you sharpen that you open and you sort of go like that? [DESCRIPTION]

INTERVIEWER: That you open so they go like that?

MARK: Yeah, and one side's the sharp side and the other side's just a handle like? You know they have these little holes and the pencil goes right down there? [DESCRIPTION CONTINUED]

INTERVIEWER: Uh huh?

MARK: And also they have a poker and stuff. But the poker went right through there and came right through here, and hit that (points to arm). And it got over there and came out. [COMPLICATING ACTIONS] And it was all dirty cause there was pencil lead down there. [HIGH POINT EVALUATION] and we had to get it out and we had to squeeze and squeeze and all the blood just ROLLED on the floor. Just like this (gestures). It just falled. Goed like this, and it hit the floor. [RESOLUTION ACTION]

The resolution of a personal narrative is sometimes the solution of some human problem, but not always so. That is, another dimension of narratives is the extent to which problem-solving is the focus of what might be called plot development. In the preceding narrative the problem of "getting poked" precipitates action on the part of the boy and his family: "And we had to get it out and we had to squeeze and squeeze." Here this resolution of the narrative coincides with the solution of a problem, which is common in the narratives of children aged 6 or older.*

Nevertheless, there are narrative resolutions that have nothing to do with solving problems. Going home from the hospital resolved the story but certainly not the problem in the glue-drinking episode above, for example.

Similarly, there are solutions of problems that do not function as resolutions of narratives. For example, in the following unusual narrative from our study, the 8-year-old girl provided none of the evaluation of her experience that would have transformed this problem-solving episode into a satisfyingly resolved narrative:

INTERVIEWER: Have you ever gotten jabbed with anything?
BOBBIE: By a bee.
INTERVIEWER: By a bee. Oh, tell me about it.
BOBBIE: It got kind of cool one day and my grandma came. She called me and she wanted to know where Daryl was.
INTERVIEWER: Where Daryl was?
BOBBIE: Yeah, and I ran outside to tell her and I was running and I stepped on a bee.
INTERVIEWER: You went outside to tell her and you were running and you stepped on a bee. Ah. Then what?
BOBBIE: Nothing. I just went in the house and had to have something on it.

This girl's experience seems to mean little to her, and her listeners are left with the feeling of, "So what? Why are you telling me about this?" The fact that a bee sting was dealt with did not in and of itself constitute the kind of narrative that seems worth listening to. In short, resolving a story and solving some problem in life are two very different tasks, which only occasionally overlap.

Telling versus Writing. Even though 6-year-olds *can* tell an elaborate story, they at times turn their attention to other aspects of narration. They are much more adept at telling a story than they are at dictating one, because the need to wait for the inevitable slowness of their scribe distracts their attention from their stories. In turn, they are more adept at dictation than they are at writing, as we will see.

---

*Peterson and McCabe, 1983, p. 167, discuss a similar point. However, there the focus is on the way in which the high point of a narrative is often the solution of a problem. In the narrative discussed here, the high point as abstracted by the narrator is getting poked, although the consequence of the curative squeezing—the solution of the narrator's problem—is also heavily evaluated.

In other words, although 6-year-olds *tell* elaborate stories such as those above, they *write* stories that consist of only one event: "I brace my foot its my friends folt," which translates from invented spelling into "I breaked my foot. It was my friend's fault." The mechanics of handwriting and spelling absorb too much attention for them to say anything more than the one main event, and perhaps, as above, one explanatory comment about that event.

Fact versus Fiction. When children begin to write narratives, they often opt for fiction instead of fact, probably in part because they have confronted virtually nothing but fiction in printed form. In other words, the idea that printed stories are made up ones is part of the emergent literacy they bring to early literacy endeavors, and they may adamantly resist efforts to have them write about real personal experiences. After all, they have almost never read a printed story that was a true one.

This cultivated preference for fiction poses a threat to elaboration above and beyond that posed by the need to attend to making letters, spelling, and so forth. As a rule, children tell much more elaborate factual narratives than fictional ones (Peterson & McCabe, 1983, pp. 101–103; Hudson & Shapiro, 1991), and so this choice of genre in writing is not necessarily one designed to showcase their most elaborate narrative accomplishments.

Moreover, the content of the fictional stories children compose has an unfortunate tendency to consist of recycled plots drawn from television, video games, and storybooks they have heard or read. In contrast, their factual narratives are more compelling because life forces them to be original, at least to some extent. This is analogous to the realm of art: drawing from imagination is likely to be schematic in kindergarten and early elementary school years, whereas drawing from observation requires original lines.

Perhaps, then, we need to let children read more narratives about real experiences if we expect them to write factual narratives. Picture book biographies for preschool and kindergarten-aged children are not as plentiful as they might be.

Issues for Instruction

Perhaps the most important general issue concerning instruction about European North American storytelling is that teachers need to make clear that it is just one tradition in storytelling. At present, children receive ample instruction about the importance of sequencing, problem-solving, talking about one important thing at a time, having a clear beginning, middle, and end. Many, many teachers' manuals give numerous very specific exercises for teachers and students in all these facets of narrative, and I would not presume to reiterate them here. The new issue for teachers is to present this material with reference to its cultural basis and not as if such traditions are simply the "right" way to do things.

Box 5: Research Into Practice

1. Sergei Prokofiev's *Peter and the Wolf* is an ideal composition with which to explore the connections between classical music form and the classic European folktale. Prokofiev composed this piece for the Moscow Children's Theatre Centre. He wrote his own text and produced a piece "that is more classical than the classic" musical works of Haydn or Mozart (Griffiths, 1990). Teachers may wish to play the piece with narration (a performance by the Chamber Orchestra of Europe, narrated by Sting, is readily available) and without narration (such as Leonard Bernstein's performance with the New York Philharmonic Orchestra). In this composition, there are several dramatic moments (when Peter warns the bird about the cat, when the wolf eats the duck, when the hunters almost shoot the wolf), but the climax of both music and folktale is Peter's capture of the wolf. The musical highpoint occurs approximately 63 percent of the way through the Chamber Orchestra's performance (fifteen minutes into the piece), just as the Golden Section would describe. Note that while narration accompanying the music clarifies the link between the two for novice listeners, the musical climax is more evident in performances without narration.

2. After a *Peter and the Wolf* exercise, teachers may wish to select a different musical composition and have children compose their own stories to accompany it, working with the children to build up to a clear high point and then resolve it.

3. Many European North Americans feel a strong attachment toward stories from the countries of their ancestors. Greek Americans have told me how much they truly prefer Greek stories. French Americans may enjoy Zipes' *Beauties, Beasts, and Enchantment: Classic French Fairy Tales*. Italian Americans often enjoy Italo Calvino's *Italian Folktales*. Of course, these stories also amuse many individuals whose ancestry includes no Greek, French, or Italian lines. In keeping with the themes of this book, then, teachers may find themselves connecting to students and students' parents by selecting folktales of the cultures represented by students and/or by highlighting the specific cultural origins of those tales. Coming to recognize and emphasize the specifically European origin of folktales once presented as generically universal has considerable appeal.

Summary

- Action plots have not always been in vogue in the European storytelling tradition, but they are quite popular.
- European North American families often exchange personal narratives at the dinner table. Telling fictional stories is a much rarer event.
- Parents of outstanding narrators have conversed at length about past experiences with their children from the time they were 2 years old.

- Past scholarly treatments have not focused on the cultural context of this storytelling tradition. Instead, they have focused on psychoanalytic content or cognitive problem-solving.
- Features of storytelling valued in this community include: (1) talking about one important thing at a time, (2) sequencing events, (3) representation of problem-solving, and (4) having a clear beginning, middle, and end.
- The structure of many classic European stories is quite similar to forms of classical music and visual art. Specifically, numerous works have a climactic centerpiece.
- Oral narration of personal experiences develops between the ages of 2 and 6 years.

References

AMES, L.B. (1966). *Children's stories. Genetic Psychology Monographs, 73,* 337–396.

ARNHEIM, R. (1974). *Art and visual perception: The new version.* Berkeley: University of California Press.

BLUM-KULKA, S., & SNOW, C. (1992). Developing autonomy for tellers, tales, and telling in family narrative events. *Journal of Narrative and Life History, 2,* 187–218.

BOTVIN, G.J., & SUTTON-SMITH, B. (1977). The development of structural complexity in children's fantasy narratives. *Developmental Psychology, 13,* 377–388.

BROOKS, P. (1992). *Reading for the plot.* Cambridge, MA: Harvard University Press.

CALVINO, I. (1980). *Italian folktales selected and retold by Italo Calvino.* Trans. George Martin. New York: Pantheon.

GARDNER, H. (1926/1959). *Art through the ages* (4th ed.). New York: Harcourt, Brace.

GOMBRICH, E.H. (1960). *Art and illusion.* Princeton, NJ: Princeton University Press.

GRIFFITHS, P. (1990). Prokofiev: Peter and the Wolf Classical Symphony. Hamburg: Deutsche Grammophon GmbH.

HARRIS, W.H., & LEVEY, J.S. (1975). *The New Columbia Encyclopedia.* New York: Columbia University Press.

HEATH, S.B. (1982). What no bedtime story means: Narrative skills at home and school. *Language in Society, 11,* 49–76.

HUDSON, J.A., & SHAPIRO, L.R. (1991). From knowing to telling: The development of children's scripts, stories, and personal narratives. In A. McCabe & C. Peterson (Eds.), *Developing Narrative Structure* (pp. 89–136). Hillsdale, N.J.: Lawrence Erlbaum.

MANDLER, J.M., & JOHNSON, N. (1977). Remembrance of things parsed: Story structure and recall. *Cognitive Psychology, 9,* 111–151.

MICHAELS, S. (1991). The dismantling of narrative. In A. McCabe & C. Peterson (Eds.), *Developing narrative structure* (pp. 303–351). Hillsdale, NJ: Lawrence Erlbaum.

NELSON, K. (Ed.). (1989). *Narratives from the crib.* Cambridge, MA: Harvard University Press.

PASCOE, C. (1973). "Golden Proportion in Musical Design." Unpublished doctoral dissertation, University of Cincinatti, Cincinatti, OH.

PETERSON, C., & MCCABE, A. (1983). *Developmental psycholinguistics: Three ways of looking at a child's narrative.* New York: Plenum.

PITCHER, E.G., & PRELINGER, E. (1963). *Children tell stories.* N.Y.: International Universities Press.

Prentice-Hall Encyclopedia of Mathematics. (1982). Englewood Cliffs, NJ: Prentice Hall.

PROPP, V. (1928/1968). *The morphology of the folktale.* Austin: University of Texas Press.

SEWALL, J.I. (1961). *A history of western art* (revised ed.). New York: Holt, Rinehart, & Winston.

STEIN, N.L., & GLENN, C.G. (1979). An analysis of story comprehension in elementary school children. In R.O. Freedle (Ed.), *New directions in discourse processing* (Vol. 2, pp. 53–120). *Advances in discourse processes.* Norwood, N.J.: Ablex.

ZIPES, J. (1989). *Beauties, beasts, and enchantment: Classical French fairy tales.* New York: New American Library.

CHAPTER 5

Compressed Collections of Experiences: Some Asian American Traditions

Masahiko Minami
and
Allyssa McCabe

OVERVIEW

This chapter addresses the historical background of Asian and European North American relations, a background based on exclusion and avoidance of Asians and Asian culture. Many Asian traditions place a premium on brevity. Speakers are expected to take short turns and rely on their listeners to empathize and fill in the details of what is discussed. The focus of the chapter is on Japanese narration, but some Chinese and Korean traditions are briefly discussed. Narrative form relates to various cultural and literary traditions in these countries.

SOME ASIAN STORYTELLING TRADITIONS

Historical Background

More than half a million immigrants from nearly 100 different countries and cultures come to the United States each year. Most speak languages other than English (Crawford, 1989, 1992; Hakuta, 1986). The last one and a half decades in particular have witnessed a rapid influx of immigrants from Asian and Latin American countries. The *New York Times* (April 28, 1993) summarized preliminary census data concerning demographic changes from 1980 to 1990 and reported that the number of U.S. residents for whom English is a second language jumped by nearly 40 percent to 32 million. The inevitable consequence of this spike in immigration has been that a large number of children whose first language is not English are entering U.S. schools. According to the

U.S. Department of Education (1992), in 1990–1991, approximately 2.3 million elementary and secondary school students lived in language-minority households, made substantial use of minority languages, and were identified as limited-English-proficient (LEP) children. The Stanford Working Group (1993) estimated the number of LEP children to be much higher—3.3 million between the ages of 5 and 17.

As the *Times* (April 28, 1993) also reported, there was a sharp increase in the number of Asian-language speakers, including Koreans (127 percent), Chinese (98 percent), and Japanese (25 percent). This rapid expansion in the Asian population in the United States is a rather recent trend. The Chinese Exclusion Act of 1882 and the Oriental Exclusion Act of 1924 prohibited immigration of Chinese, then Japanese people to the United States. Only in 1965, when immigration laws were revised, were Asian immigrants permitted to enter this country (Crawford, 1992; Marger, 1994). Because of this regrettable exclusion of certain people on the basis of race, European North Americans are generally relatively unfamiliar with Eastern culture and stories.

This chapter focuses on storytelling practices and forms observed in narratives told by Asians, Japanese in particular, in the United States. Regardless of the language spoken—their native language or English—we would like to examine the narrative structure they produce and value. Of course, if different languages are spoken by a narrator and a listener, critical communication problems will occur. However, even if both speak English, if the manner of presentation and the habitual interaction style of the narrator is different from what the listener is accustomed to, communication may be difficult.

As was mentioned in the preface to this book, it is much more difficult to recognize cultural differences in narrative structure than it is to hear a foreign accent or understand differences in word choice or grammar. For example, imagine a 7-year-old Japanese boy who sounds like a native speaker of English but was, in reality, raised in a Japanese-speaking family in a Japanese neighborhood in the United States. Asked by an American teacher whether he has hurt himself, the boy might answer, "Yes, I have." The teacher takes pains to ask him to continue his injury story. The boy finally says, "I was playing on the monkey bars. And I got a splinter. And I had it pulled out." Because empathic consideration for others is highly valued in Japanese culture, even though the 7-year-old does not give any evaluative comments about his injury story, Japanese listeners in his family or neighborhood have always empathized with the boy's hidden feelings (Doi, 1973). The boy told his story without making explicit his emotions because he had been trained to count on his listener to fill them in. Perhaps, however, an American teacher might not understand that the boy's background culture has such a long-standing preference for communicative conciseness. Perhaps, believing that children at age 7 should show imagination and creativity by telling lengthy stories (as shown in the previous chapter), the teacher might judge the boy to have difficulty in expressing his feelings.

Storytelling Practices in Community

General Practices. Although in certain respects Asian cultures resemble each other more than they do Western culture, they should not be lumped together in one category. For example, while Japan and China are both Asian societies in which group-oriented, rather than individualistic, norms prevail, these two nations differ considerably in their standards of early childhood education (Tobin, Wu, & Davidson, 1989). More specifically, Stigler and Perry (1988) conclude that whereas Western elementary school math educators tend to emphasize children's inherently unique limitations or excellence, Asian educators are more comfortable with the idea that all children have potential and that with proper effort can attain almost anything. In spite of such similarities between Japan and China, however, these researchers warn about the danger of overemphasizing similarities between these two groups. "Chinese classrooms are more performance oriented and Japanese classrooms more reflective" (Stigler & Perry, 1988, p. 40).

Obviously, because Asians who live in the United States are from different groups, cultures, and ancestries, carelessly extrapolating from one Asian culture and its underlying values to another culture is inappropriate at best, and perpetuates sweeping generalizations about Asian cultures at worst. The goals of this chapter are, therefore, to present characteristic features of Japanese children's narratives, and then to carefully consider whether some of those findings can be applied to narratives told by children from other Asian cultures such as China and Korea. We believe that Japanese narrative can serve as a good basis for understanding narratives told by Asian children, because Confucian paradigms (for example, the malleability of human behavior) that have supported East-Asian cultures for centuries still underlie contemporary Japanese culture.

Exemplary Mother-Child Interaction

The origins of Japanese children's narrative patterning can be traced back to conversations between parents and children. That is, through dialogues during dinner-table conversations or before falling asleep, Japanese mothers' style of interviewing children about past events forms a template for Japanese children's narrative form. A conversation between a 5½-year-old girl, Yumiko, and her mother illustrates this; their conversation (originally in Japanese) exemplifies the way that many Japanese mothers converse with their young children, frequently acknowledging their children's efforts in a verbal way. When Yumiko's American peers drank Japanese wheat tea, which she brought from home to school, the taste of the tea must have been strange to them:

YUMIKO: um you know, all (kids) said that they wanted (to drink wheat tea), you know
MOTHER: uh huh.
YUMIKO: and you know, when (they) drank (it), you know, (they) said "yucky."
MOTHER: When (they) were looking at (the wheat tea), (they) said that (they) wanted (to drink it), and then once (they) had drunk (it), (they) were saying "yucky," right?

The mother acknowledges her child after a brief initial turn and then confirms what the child narrated. This frequent exchange of brief turns between Japanese mothers and their children is typical (Minami & McCabe, in press) and functions to demonstrate maternal interest at the same time that it ensures children do not become verbose. In Japanese society, proverbs such as "silence is golden," "still waters run deep," and "a talkative man is embarrassing" are common and reflect a preference for "implicit, nonverbal, intuitive communication" over lengthy, explicit, verbal exchanges of information (Lebra, 1986).

Other Scholarly Treatments

Different Types of Minorities. Asians are often considered "model minorities" in the United States. John Ogbu (1992) classifies minorities into two groups, castelike or involuntary minorities, and immigrant or voluntary minorities. Whereas African Americans belong to involuntary minorities, Asians, such as Chinese, Koreans, and Japanese, are representative of voluntary or immigrant minorities. According to Ogbu, involuntary minorities try to preserve linguistic and cultural differences as symbolic of their ethnic identity and their separation from a more dominant culture. In contrast, Ogbu argues that voluntary minorities generally believe that their lives in the United States are better than their lives in their native countries. They are therefore more likely to assimilate to the dominant culture and hence succeed than are involuntary minorities, particularly in academic arenas.

Unfortunately, voluntary minorities are at times stigmatized and treated in the same way that involuntary minorities are. Voluntary minority students are sometimes not allowed to speak their first language in school settings (Crawford, 1989, 1992): "until 1973 it was a crime in Texas to use a language other than English as the medium of public instruction" (Crawford, 1989, p. 26). In such situations voluntary minorities may feel that they are treated as if they were castelike involuntary minorities. Therefore, regardless of their status, minority students (either voluntary or involuntary) may feel that they belong to subordinate groups and that they are looked down on, or even rejected, by peers or teachers from the dominant culture.

Furthermore, Asian students often adopt a generally observant but passive participation style in classrooms. European North Americans may tend to interpret this behavior as a sign of passivity and thus may consider Asians as not so bright or even dull (Miyanaga, 1991). As Japanese researcher Kuniko Miyanaga (1991) noted, however—and, moreover, as one high school student who had recently immigrated from China to the United States proudly protested at an interview—Asians consider that being quiet and listening intently in the classroom is active, not passive, participation (Shaw, Michahelles, Chen, Minami, & Sing, 1994).

Features of Narration in This Community: Japanese Narratives

Background Information. For this study we gathered data—Japanese data in particular—in a suburban town in the Northeast United States. About

10 percent of the town population of approximately 55,000 is Asian, 3 percent is African American, and small numbers of other groups are present. However, residents of the town are predominantly European North American.

Consider the following narrative originally produced in Japanese by an 8-year-old boy, Shun (translated into English and analyzed, using a version of the stanza analysis described in Chapter 3, by the first author).

STANZA A: [First shot]
(a) As for the first (shot), you know,
(b) (I) got (it) at Ehime, you know,
(c) (It) hurt a lot.

STANZA B: [Second shot]
(d) As for the second (shot), you know,
(e) (I) knew, you know,
      (it would) hurt, you know,
(f) Well, you know,
      (it) didn't hurt so much, you know.

STANZA C: [The other shots]
(g) The next (one) didn't hurt so much, either.
(h) As for the last (one), you know,
(i) (it) didn't hurt at all.

To American ears, these stanzas might seem to comprise three short, separate narratives, none of which is fully developed. This type of narrative may strike American classroom teachers as "lacking imagination" (Minami, 1990). Notice, however, the nice progression from the first shot (Stanza A) that must have surprised the boy and was painful, to the second one (Stanza B) that did not seem so bad, and to the third and the last one (Stanza C) that "did not hurt at all." This narrative is a cohesive, unified collection of several experiences that the boy had and, as such, is typical of many of the narratives we collected.

Furthermore, each injury is described in an elegantly succinct three-line form. Almost 60 percent of the narrative stanzas produced by Japanese children in our sample consisted of three lines (Minami & McCabe, 1991).

Finally, because of the nature of the Japanese language, the narrator omits pronouns, copulas, and other linguistic devices (shown in parentheses) that the listener can easily identify by empathizing with the narrator.

Another example of all these features of narrative form follows. It was told by a 7-year-old girl, Sayaka, and juxtaposes three different types of injuries (originally in Japanese): (1) an injury in kindergarten, (2) a fall off an iron bar, and (3) two hernia operations.

PART I: [Injury in kindergarten]

STANZA A: [Got hurt in kindergarten]
(a) When (I was) in kindergarten,
(b) (I) got (my) leg caught in a bicycle,
(c) (I) got a cut here.

STANZA B: [Aftermath of injury]
(d) (I) wore a cast for about a month.
(e) (I) took a rest for about a week.
(f) And (I) went back again.

PART II: [An iron bar]

STANZA C: [Fell off an iron bar]
(a) (I) had a cut here.
(b) (I) fell off an iron bar.
(c) Yeah, (I) had two mouths.

PART III: [Hernia operations]

STANZA D: [The first operation]
(a) Um, well, (I) was born with (a) hernia, I heard.
(b) As for the one hernia,
(c) As a little baby, (I) got an operation.

STANZA E: [The second operation]
(d) But as (I) didn't have an operation for the other one
(e) As an early first grader, (I) was hospitalized.
(f) And (I) got an operation.

Without exception, here, her stanzas consist of three lines. In line (c) in Stanza C, Sayaka, pointing at her chin, meant that the wound was cut open as if it were also a mouth. Japanese listeners may feel that her use of this metaphor is somewhat humorous, but at the same time can easily imagine how severe and painful her injury was, and thus deeply empathize with her.

Finally, Sayaka supported her stories with a kind of reported speech, "I heard" (Part III, Stanza D, line (a), line 11). In Japanese classrooms, such factual representation has traditionally been strongly recommended (Okubo, 1959).

Unfortunately, when some European North American teachers were shown the translated version of Japanese children's narratives such as the ones above, they seemed to misunderstand the communicative compression these Japanese children have learned to practice and value. One teacher said: "These children need help. They need more encouragement. They should be in a different type of program, not only because they themselves need to learn communicative skills, but also because if children who are more advanced are put in the same program, they would get bored. It is important to assess each child's skills, and to really help them improve upon what they have. That is education (Minami, 1990)."

Yet "what has often been viewed as a deficiency in imagination within schoolrooms turns out on close examination to arise because of cultural differences in its deployment; . . . What we tend to think of as imaginative is a highly culturally relative picture" (Sutton-Smith, 1988, p. 19). For example, in many respects, the form of Japanese children's narratives relates to widespread aesthetic values in that culture, as we will show.

Literacy Practices in U.S. School Environments: Two Cases

Cross-cultural Conferencing: The Disownership of Literacy?

Literacy programs for minority children—Japanese children in particular—are integrated into a number of American public school settings. Such children are thus confronted with a pattern of socialization that is an abrupt departure from the earlier one they received not only in their homes, but also in their local communities.

In addition to collecting oral narratives, we gathered samples of written narratives. In spite of certain restrictions due to the demands of writing, the written narratives reflect some of the features of the oral ones (Heath, 1983; Michaels & Collins, 1984). For example, in an historical writing assignment, Katsuo, a fifth-grade Japanese boy in a bilingual literacy program, wrote a fictional piece based on an earthquake that devastated the Tokyo area in 1923. In his first version, Katsuo wrote the following (originally in Japanese):

> Koichi's mother and father died. As many as 167,000 people died because of the earthquake. Koichi's mother died under a pillar. Koichi's father was burned to death. A man who was a friend of Koichi's father carried Koichi on his back, and ran away from the fire. In her last moments, Koichi's mother said, "*I am too old to have a hope. But, Koichi, there are hopes and future for you . . .*

Katsuo's narrative is very succinct, a characteristic we noted was also prevalent in Japanese children's oral narratives. Katsuo briefly described Koichi's father's death. As we previously mentioned, this insertion of other incidents into the narration of a focal incident (the mother's death) is one of the characteristic features of Japanese children's oral narratives.

Additionally, what Koichi's mother said to him in the above story (shown in italics) illustrates traditional, albeit somewhat stereotypical, Japanese cultural beliefs—what Japanese should be like and how strong the mother-child bond is (Lebra, 1986). Because the italicized lines are a cliché from Japanese movies and theatrical plays, we suspect that Katsuo, the author of this story, inserted this so that it would sound humorous or even funny, a point entirely lost on Western readers.

With one of the two American instructors in the school's process writing program, Katsuo developed his original draft through an extensive process of conferencing, drafting, and editing. His finished English version read like this:

> Koichi was standing in his house, too scared to do anything, calling "Mother! Mother!" A man who was a friend of Koichi's father's carried Koichi on his back, and ran away from the fire. The fire ceased, and the earthquake stopped.
>
> Koichi saw a place where many people had jumped in the river. *The sorrow this sight caused him remained in his heart always.* As many as 167,000 people died because of the earthquake.
>
> His house was nearby. He went into his house to look for his mother, but his mother had died under the pillar. Next Koichi looked for his father, but he wasn't there. What am I stepping on, he thought, and he looked down and began to search for bones. Almost at once he saw his father's burned body . . .

When comparing this edited version and the original, we realize what an amazing transformation has been accomplished through the writing and editing process. The original story, which shows a strong resemblance to Japanese children's oral narratives, has been transformed into a more smoothly flowing style. More specifically, the original compactness—one of the characteristic features of Japanese children's narratives—has been replaced with a more lengthy narrative style. The insertion of a brief description of another incident was postponed to the end in the finished version, and the sad (but subversively humorous), melodramatic mother's remarks disappeared altogether. Furthermore, the finished version reflects an imposition of the Western psychodynamic approach—the potential long-term effects of an individual's early childhood experiences on his or her personality—on Katsuo's original fiction (shown in italics). We do not necessarily imply that the finished product represents a case in which this Japanese child was misunderstood in writing conferences. Yet it illustrates possible overediting in the interaction between individuals from two different cultures.

Author's Chair: Ownership of Literacy

A first-grade Japanese boy Makoto "published" a book titled "I was a Fireman," which he wrote with the aid of a Japanese instructor of a Japanese bilingual literacy program. One day, Makoto held the Author's Chair, a ritual in which a first-grade author reads pages from his or her published books in the classroom (Au, 1993; Graves & Hansen 1983). Makoto dedicated his book to his classmate Hiromi, a Japanese girl, because, according to him, she was sweet and gentle and shared her Nintendo game with him (they lived in the same local community). Note that a space indicates a page break (lines added). Each page also originally had a picture drawn by Makoto, which corresponded to the narrative line(s):

I was a Fireman

1   In the night the building caught on fire.
2   The fireman came.

3   They got out their water hoses, Shhhh!!

4   A fire truck came to kill the fire.

5   The fire became big and wild.

6   This house did not catch on fire.
7   There was a slide in the back yard.

8   The church caught on fire.

9   Another building caught on fire a little.

10   Everybody worked hard.
11   The fire died down.
12   We all went home to sleep.

The classroom teacher helped Makoto read his book to the class. He read in halting English, which might have made the story somewhat unclear to the audience. As soon as Makoto finished reading, however, a couple of European North American children raised their hands. One asked, "Is it true?" Makoto responded by shaking his head. The classroom teacher asked him again whether his story was true. Makoto shook his head again, indicating "no," and the teacher seemed to understand him this time. Another child commented that the pictures Makoto drew in the book were beautiful. Since Makoto did not say anything, the teacher told him, "Say thank you." Makoto said in a small voice, "Thank you." Another child asked Makoto whether the slide stopped the fire (see lines 6 and 7). This child probably drew this inference from the sequence of Makoto's story: all houses caught fire except the one with the slide in the yard. Makoto was at first silent. Asked again by the teacher to respond to the boy's question, he said, "Just lucky." Then, another child commented, "Good book."

In this way, children continued to comment on Makoto's book and said something nice to him. Makoto's Author's Chair was over, and he was very proud of it. Even one week after his Author's Chair, he was still proud of his success.

This book also went through the process of conference, editing, and revision, only this time with a Japanese bilingual literacy program instructor, who "scaffolded" Makoto in writing a story in both Japanese and English. As Elfrieda Hiebert (1991, p. 1) puts it, in the old behaviorist view "meaning was assumed to reside primarily within text"; in the social-interactionist view "meaning is created through an interaction of reader and text." The kind of social interaction Makoto received was congruent with the social interactions he had had with his parents and other members of his Japanese community; this cultural compatibility enabled him to make progress in his writing while retaining a sense that this was his kind of writing.

Culturally responsive instruction can happen readily when teachers and students share a cultural background. However, a shared background is neither necessary nor possible in the case of many students in American classrooms. The critical issue here (salient in, but not limited to, cultural diversity) involves the amount and direction of revisions teachers require of their students. Too much revision, especially if it is in a direction quite different from what the child wants to say, amounts to usurping the ownership of the text.

Moreover, the goal of stressing non-European North American students' ownership of literacy (Au, Scheu, & Kawakami, 1990) enables those students to achieve reading and writing competence. Makoto's positive experience will surely help him develop his English competency with a positive attitude. Obviously, one of the long-term goals of multicultural or bilingual literacy programs is to help children function successfully in U.S. society. However, it is also important that teachers understand the cultural rules with which these children grew up.

Cultural Influences Need Not Amount to Subjugation of Minority Cultures nor Plagiarism of Them

We wish to end this section of our chapter on a hopeful note by considering two stories that demonstrate how children can come to be influenced by storytelling forms from cultures not their own, while still retaining a strong sense of authorship. That is, at least in the context of relationships between Japanese American and European North American individuals, one can see the former emulating the latter not as subjugation of the former by the latter, but as choice on the part of Japanese Americans. One can also see European North American imitation of Japanese storytelling style not as some kind of cultural plagiarism, but genuine appreciation instead.

HOP AND BUNNY

1   One little bunny came. It was so little bunny.
2   Little bunny have one sister and one brother.
3   The sister was very good a Artist and brother was so good boy.
4   But little bunny was no good.
5   He doesn't help mother.
6   His little brother was all day help mother.
7   One day he goto shop with sister and brother and mother
8   But he don't wont goto shop.
9   And he goto another way. He walk and walk.
10 He saw the owl. The owl asked him "You'er Easter Bunny?" said the owl.
11 But the little bunny doesn't know [what] Easter mean.
12 And little bunny say "I don't know."
13 "How bout You'er name." Said the owl
14 "My name?" Said the little bunny.
15 "Yes You'er name." Said the owl
16 "My name is Mark." Said the little bunny.
17 "Oh that good name Mark My name is Jon." Said Jon
18 "But I think I am Easter Bunny." Said Mark. And he tell the all Hapns.
19 "Easter bunny was good bunny Oh so you to.
20 Now You'er not so good bunny You'er very good bunny
21 You teik this buskat and eggs and give to You'er brother and sister O.K.?" Said Jon
22 "Yes." Mark Said and he hop and hop and go buk To Home.
THE END

The story above was written at school by an 8-year-old Japanese girl, Tomoko (daughter of the first author) eight months after she came to the United States from her native Japan. She wrote this story without any "scaffolding." Her invented spellings (Chomsky, 1975; Read, 1971) in the story—segmentation errors (such as "bout" on line 13 and "goto" on lines 7, 8, and 9) and phonetic features (such as "teik" "buskat" on line 21 and "buk" on line 22)—represent many aspects of her emerging comprehension of English. (Note that each line indicates a page break and that each page includes a picture drawn by Tomoko.)

Of most relevance to our chapter is the way in which Tomoko draws on Japanese narrative tradition at the same time that she expresses ideas in English words and grammar. More specifically, Tomoko's story was shorter than that of her classmates (though a long one for her) and included relatively less description. This succinctness and focus on action reflects her years of experience telling various kinds of narratives in Japanese. At the same time, Easter is a theme she adopted from her experience in America. Moreover, Tomoko had never written such a story in school in Japan, where language arts are not emphasized so much as mathematics instruction and where emulation of teachers' productions is valued over individual fictional compositions (Stevenson, Stigler, & Lee, 1986; Stevenson et al., 1990). In short, Tomoko's narrative displays subtle differences from those of her North American classmates, differences that might well be overlooked or misread unless one were mindful of general Japanese values.

After reading all of the *Japanese Children's Favorite Stories* (Rutland, Vermont: Tuttle Co., 1958), an 8-year-old European North American boy (son of the second author) spontaneously wrote the following story using invented spellings:

1. Once there lived a man who lived in Japan with his wife.
2. He went one day to sell "komanas."
3. Would you like a "komona?"
4. The person always answered, "Eya domo," wish ment, "no thanks."
5. So he could never sell a komona.
6. He finnly came to a poor woodcuter and asked, "would you like a komona?"
7. "Oi," wish ment, "yes."
8. So the woodcuter gave his "komona" to his wife.
9. The woodcuter din't have eny money, wich ment he couldn't pay with money.
10. So he gave a peach to the guy and said "if you eat this peach then have a wish then your dream will come true."
11. So the man ran home.
12. He showed it to his wife wich said, "Very nice Avery!"
13. Then he gobeld up the peach and said, "I wish that I was the richest man on earth"!!!
14. His wife herd this and scrambled out the door and said, "I devors you."
15. He was very sad of wat he did.
16. So he ran to the woodcuter's house and explaind at what hed done.
17. "Very well, do you take that wish back?"
18. "Yes."
19. So there's your wife.
20. "I soldnt have been that greedy"
21. He said, Thank you.
22. And they lived happaly ever after.

This story blends the boy's own storytelling style with some of the themes (punishment for being greedy), language (obtained from a person who was learning Japanese as a second language), and imagery (a magical peach) he picked up from the Japanese stories, and is the mirror image of Tomoko's story.

While the story is not as lengthy as others Nick has written (perhaps an un-conscious reflection of the relative conciseness of the Japanese stories, perhaps not), it is relatively more expansive than the stories of some of his Asian peers at school. Interestingly enough, Nick and Tomoko have written stories of al-most identical length, despite coming from contrastive value systems in this re-gard. Both have learned a great deal about the other's culture and valued story forms, yet both felt quite proud of their efforts. Such voluntary, active, playful appreciation of diverse storytelling forms should be a goal of any multicultural literacy program. The fact that the young authors retain elements of their orig-inal storytelling practices at the same time that they emulate those of a differ-ent culture needs to be understood and expected. We suspect some ingenious teachers could even find a use for these "imports."

Relationship of Narrative Features to Structure of Other Art Forms in the Community

Haiku as Representative of Japanese Narrative Discourse. In many ways, Japanese children's narratives are reminiscent of *haiku,* a form of Japanese po-etry with a distinctive three-line format. Recall that Japanese children tend to devote approximately three lines to a topic (stanza) in their oral narratives.

Since depicting an actual scene in detail is impossible in a *haiku*'s seventeen syllables, a prerequisite of *haiku* is communicative compression. To write good *haiku,* one must use allusion, suggesting moods by selecting symbolic aspects of some situation, telling a whole story poetically. Japanese children's narra-tives (even with all the stanzas taken together) are strikingly succinct, a prac-tice that prepares them for fitting a whole story into three lines. As readers can see from the parenthetical insertions in the narratives above, Japanese children do not specify pronouns, nor do they need to. European North American chil-dren may need explicit instruction about the value of deleting pronouns, arti-cles *(a, an, the),* copulas *(is, was),* and other filler words that are neither neces-sary nor desirable in *haiku.* When you have only seventeen syllables, each one should count for something.

Japanese children's narratives are usually about a collection of isolated, similar events, a tendency that may relate to the practice of publishing collec-tions of *haiku* by different authors in Japan. For example, there is a record of an ancient collection of one thousand chained poems, poems composed by each person adding to the verses of another person (Shimazo, Yunoue, & Uryu, 1978). There are also many modern *haiku* genres, such as kitchen-*haiku,* com-posed by housewives (Shibata, 1984), or convalescence-*haiku,* composed by in-valids (Murayama, 1984).

In addition, since *haiku* historically developed as an oral comic dialogue between two different people (Minami, 1990; Minami & McCabe, 1991a; Yamamoto, 1969), *haiku* has a close relationship to Japanese narrative discourse style, where conversational partners exchange frequent, short turns. *Haiku* is thus representative of underlying cultural values, such as empathy and collab-oration.

Japanese children have been abundantly exposed to this *haiku*-like, succinct storytelling style from early childhood on. One distinctive practice in Japanese society is a *kamishibai* picture-story show, a series of large cards each consisting of a picture on the front and the narrative lines to be read by the storyteller on the back. *Kamishibai* storytelling is often used in Japanese preschools—nursery schools as well as day-care centers—as a support for children's emergent literacy (Tobin, Wu, & Davidson, 1989), and *kamishibai* storytelling has traditionally been very influential for children in Japan (Norton, 1991; Pellowski, 1977).

Momotaro (The Peach Boy) and *Hanasaka Ji-San (The Old Man Who Made Trees Blossom)* are the best-known traditional folktales that are read to preschoolers using *kamishibai*. In both folktales the protagonists are a nameless, good-natured, childless old couple; both start with the same opening, "Long, long ago, in a certain place," which flavors storytelling in classrooms with some authenticity (Norton, 1991). Likewise, both stories end with Heaven's reward for the good (Mino, 1986). *Momotaro*, scripted by Saneto (1986), and *Hanasaka Ji-San*, scripted by Yoda (1986), begin as follows (both originally in Japanese):

The Peach Boy

1   Long, long ago, in a certain place there were an old man and an old woman.
2   The old man (went) to the mountain every day to cut brushwood.
3   And the old woman went to the river to wash some clothes.

The Old Man Who Made Trees Blossom

1   Long, long ago, in a certain place there were an old man and an old woman.
2   They had a little dog named Shiro.
3   They loved Shiro very much.

Because they are written narratives, both stories later include a series of complicating actions (Labov, 1972; Peterson & McCabe, 1983). As can be seen, however, the beginning parts of these Japanese folktales illustrate a culturally nurtured traditional storytelling style that includes three-line structures similar to those seen in *haiku* and in the oral narratives of Japanese children.

In U.S. schools, unfortunately, *haiku*'s literary dimension is slightly exaggerated and, inversely, its narrative aspect is made light of or ignored altogether. Some textbooks correctly explain that *haiku* consists of three lines (Norton, 1991); others, against the original norm, transform it into four lines. For example, the famous Japanese *haiku* poet Buson Yosa's (Aso, 1959) rather unusual (in terms of syllables) *haiku*, "Willow leaves have fallen/Spring water has dried up/Stranded stones here and there" (note: a slash indicates a line break), is changed into "Ah leafless willow . . . /Bending over/The dry pool/Of stranded boulders (Houghton Mifflin, 1988).

Further, the use of personification—attribution of personal qualities to trees in this case—is explained as evidence that *haiku* is a form of poetry (Houghton Mifflin, 1988). However, personification is sometimes used even in daily conversations among Japanese people. For example, mothers are expected to provide children with explicit training in empathy and a frequent way they do this is to appeal to the feeling of inanimate objects (Clancy, 1985, 1986). In other words, personification is a typical language game played between Japanese mothers and children, not an especially poetic practice. Nor, we might add, is personification some repercussion of the kind of primitive animistic child thinking Piaget emphasized but which has been questioned in recent years (McCabe & Peterson, 1985).

Thus, although the form of *haiku* is often taught in U.S. classrooms and we assume that American children can appreciate *haiku*, it is introduced in a way quite different from the authentic, Japanese way.

The following are two pieces of *haiku* (both originally in Japanese). One was written by another famous Japanese *haiku* poet, Basho Matsuo (Lee, 1983), and the other one was written by a fourth-grade Japanese boy living in New York (Gakken, 1989). Note that both pieces of *haiku* are composed of three lines, one each addressing the three dimensions of location, object/event, and time:

On a withered bough,	(Location)
A crow perched;	(Object or event)
Autumn evening.	(Time)
Although it is cold,	(Time)
The Statue of Liberty	(Object and location)
Stretches herself.	(Event)

Readers are likely to feel that Matsuo's *haiku* is very poetic and sophisticated, whereas the child's is just cute, charming, or humorous. Yet the child's composition still displays major features characteristic of *haiku:* (1) *haiku* as narrative poetry, and (2) *haiku* as everyday speech.

Other Asian Children's Narratives: Chinese and Korean Narratives

Some Chinese Traditions. Chien-Ju Chang (1994), a native speaker of Mandarin Chinese, interviewed 7-year-old Chinese children living in the United States, some originally from China and some from Taiwan. The most common type of personal narrative produced by these children was the type of narrative also common from European North American children this age, as follows (collected, transcribed, translated, and analyzed by Chien-Ju Chang):

Jenny: Then (I) fell down again. I wanted to jump up to a place. Then (I) did not jump well. (I) fell down. Then (it) BLED. Then one of my friends, she helped me stand up. Then she, then she went to play. Then my papa applied that something . . . (I) don't remember. Then there was a SCAR. Then (it's) gone now. Then I came to America. Then (I) have never fallen down. (I) have never fallen down after that.

Although it is relatively short and does not contain the kind of description characteristic of European North American children's narratives, the overall form is similar to the classic European North American narrative. That is, her story begins with an abstract telling us this will be a story about falling down. It builds to a high point, the bleeding, and the situation is resolved through the intervention of the child's friend and then her father. The story concludes, as do many European North American stories, with a coda about her scar and her experiences of not falling down so far in America.

Along with the similarities between personal narratives told by Chinese and American children, however, there were also some subtle differences. First of all, Chinese children, like Japanese children, often talk about multiple experiences in one narrative, whereas European North American children almost never do so. For example, the following narrative follows the classic pattern of building up to a high point and then resolving it, but it weaves together several injuries, more similar to Japanese than to European North American narrative practices. Also, note that it ends with a moral.

> Shiuan-Shiuan: Many times (I have been hurt). Sometimes my hamster gave me a small "jiou!" (He) bit (me). Sometimes, but not this one . . . another hamster bit (me). I had to go to the sink to "ruo pa pa ba" (sound of running water) for ten minutes. (I) put a bandage on it. Sometimes I climb on the kitchen counter, stayed there and forgot how to get down . . . Like this (goes to kitchen counter). Sometimes I had to "biau" (sound of something jumping down) down from here. Many times, I got my knee hurt. BRUISE. Be careful!

[Note that in all these translations, use of the past tense, which is required in English, is a matter of guesswork, as Mandarin Chinese does not mark tense morphologically. Also note that the interviewer is frequently echoing the child's comments and/or saying "Uh Huh" throughout these conversations, although her comments are deleted here to save space and promote readability.]

Another distinctive feature is that these Chinese children ended a third of their narratives at the climactic moment, without resolving them, as in the following examples:

> Lu-Lu: (I) did (get a shot). I often get a shot. Once there was really no place for the shots. (I) got shots everywhere in my hands and arms. (They) could not really find the vein for shots. So the only way (they could do the procedure) was to give (me) a shot IN MY LEG. My leg felt PARALYZED after the shot!

> Tommy: That is . . . I was originally very afraid. Then, check up. The dentist filled up my tooth. After filling up, I did not feel painful. But I came the second time. I felt painful here. Then the dentist said that (it) must be pulled out. So he pulled it out. I was afraid. Then he used drugs . . . Then I was very pained. Pain was gone, he asked me. Then he asked me to rinse the mouth. After rinsing, he pulled it out again. Finally, once more. This time (he) put the tooth in my mouth. Gold tooth. This one (shows interviewer).

In this latter narrative, the narrator combines several experiences into one story as well as ending at the climactic moment: the insertion of the gold tooth.

Ostensibly Chinese stories for children that are widely available in America strike some Chinese adults as strange (Xu, 1993). For example, Chinese names are never as long as *Tikki Tikki Tembo*. As was mentioned in Chapter 2,

Five (or Seven) Chinese Brothers is an Americanized version of a well-known story about *Eight Gods,* one of whom is a woman who was dropped out of the American version.

In China, Chinese children's literature is abundant and often emphasizes the importance of prosocial behavior and altruism, as well as the shame of selfishness. For example, in one story, "Companions on Ice," a little yellow duck gives up trying to win a race in order to save a rabbit and a squirrel who have fallen through ice into the water below. The little grey duck who wins the race gives his medal to the little yellow duck at the end. Another story, "Two Little Kittens" contrasts a bad kitten who is rude and very selfish and who eats up all the fish she catches with a good little kitten who is polite, who is very willing to go out to get fish for the family, and who "wanted to share (the fish she caught) with her mother and the younger kittens" in her family even though she was hungry. The story ends by asking the children "what have you learned from this story?"

Though many, if not all, cultures use narrative to pass on moral lessons to children, not to mention adults, the Chinese culture is particularly clear that this is a goal of telling narratives and stories to children. Chinese mothers may make very explicit reference to selfish acts their children have committed in the past and emphasize their displeasure with those past acts (Miller et al., 1990). Congruent with such familial practices, the Chinese government identifies moral education as the number one requirement for school-aged children (Guidebook for Preschool Education, 1989, cited in Xu, 1992), and numerous stories—traditional and commissioned, printed or in movie form—are deployed to the end of moral instruction (Xu, 1992).

Another interesting and extremely popular Chinese storytelling tradition is the "Little Man's Book" (Breedlove & Zhang, 1990). More than half of the 246 million books that have been published today in China are so-called Little Man's Books. These books recount a story or an event with an artistic series of narrative pictures. The stories are often adapted from novels, short stories, dramas, films, or other literary works, and include historical events, biographies, great literary works of China and the world, and folk tales. These are inexpensive and are available in most of China's city or town railway stations, bus stops, parks, and streets. What is most distinctive is that although these books are written to educate and entertain children, they continue to be popular with adults. The educational value of these small picture books is widely recognized in China, as well as outside that country (Japan, West Germany, and a few other countries have expressed their wish to cooperate with Chinese artists to publish these picture books in their own countries), and evidently does nothing to diminish their tremendous popularity (Breedlove & Zhang, 1990).

Some Korean Traditions. Korean children also were interviewed in their native language, Korean, by a native adult speaker of Korean, for this book. Sang Ki has lived in the United States for five years; the girl Young Hee was born in the United States. Although they have lived for a long time in the

United States, their narratives still show a great degree of reticence, similar to that observed among Japanese and Chinese children. In the following narratives, both talked (originally in Korean) about what happened after they got a shot.

Sang Ki (7-year-old boy):

STANZA A: [A nurse came]
(a)   A nurse came.
(b)   With a cotton ball, she rubbed.
(c)   Then, I came home.

STANZA B: [The nurse gave a present]
(d)   After she rubbed it with a cotton ball,
(e)   she gave me a present.
(f)   I got a bandage.
(h)   And I got presents.

Young Hee (6-year-old girl):

STANZA A: [A nurse gave a sticker]
(a)   It (the shot) hurt.
(b)   The nurse gave me a sticker.
(c)   She gave me a bandage, too.

As can be seen, these Korean children, like Japanese children, always stayed on the subject and did not talk much about the details surrounding an event. Both focused on actions rather than description or evaluation, in contrast to European North American children.

The value of avoiding verbosity is incorporated into some popular Korean folktales for children. For example, "The Golden Amber" tells a story of a foolish, talkative dog and a clever cat. The story eventually depicts the cat and dog retrieving a magic golden amber stone for their master. During this process, the cat, who doesn't know how to swim, crosses a river on the back of the dog, who does. The cat carries the amber stone in his mouth. The dog begins to get worried because the cat is so silent (naturally—the stone is in his mouth). The dog pesters the cat with questions about whether the cat still has the stone or not until the cat finally answers him, dropping the stone into the river in the process. Suffice it to say that the stone is eventually retrieved by the cat, who lives happily inside the house forever. In contrast, the bad, overly talkative dog is banished to the outdoors. Useless talk is the source of misfortune.

Children's stories from the Korean tradition emphasize additional themes similar to those from other Asian traditions, themes deriving from Confucianism, Buddhism, and shamanism (Adams, 1981). For example, "Two Brothers and their Magic Gourds" contrasts a greedy versus a charitable brother. "The Blindman's Daughter" is a beloved tale about a daughter who is willing to sell herself for 300 bags of rice so that her blind father might see again. Although the sailors who buy her are reluctant to go through with sacrificing her to the monstrous sea dragon when it strikes, she knows what she must do and jumps in. Happily, her filial piety is rewarded when the Sea Dragon King (a shamanistic spirit) takes pity on her and returns her to land in a lotus blossom (a Buddhist symbol). Sailors take the blossom to the king of the land, whose son falls in love with the princess sleeping in the lotus blossom and marries her. In the end, she is even reunited with her father, who sees for the first time.

Issues for Instruction

Perhaps the most important issue for instruction of some Asian and Asian American students pertains to the issue of how much they should be forced to participate in class discussion or to write lengthy compositions or be penalized for not doing so. In our opinion, some accommodation to their deeply ingrained socialization to avoid verbosity needs to take place. Furthermore, when Asian or Asian American children *are* talking, teachers may want to give frequent brief verbal acknowledgments (such as "Uh huh").

Teachers also may want to explain to their classrooms that while some cultures value individuals talking at length, others, including many Asian countries, value taking relatively short turns. Some cultures value spelling everything out, while others, like Japan, value leaving some things to listeners' or readers' imaginations. Teachers may even want to ask their students to do some empathic listening: "What do you think Character X really felt like at this point?"

EXEMPLARY INSTRUCTION

In one bilingual education program, at the end of every Friday there is a period called "Good News," when first and second graders from all classrooms gather to see movies and to sing songs. One early spring afternoon, at the break between two movies, classroom teachers asked children—European North American children, as well as children from other backgrounds—to sing together a Japanese song *Haru ga Kita* (Spring has come) in the Japanese language. Note (1) that this song, reminiscent of *haiku,* consists of a series of three line stanzas and (2) that, moreover, there is an oral dialogue between two groups, A and B.

IA	*Haru ga kita,*	Spring has come,
	Haru ga kita,	Spring has come,
	Doko ni kita?	Where has (it) come?
IB	*Yama ni kita,*	(It) has come to the mountains,
	Sato ni kita,	(It) has come to the village,
	No ni mo kita.	(It) has come to the fields, too.
IIA	*Hana ga saku,*	Flowers are blooming,
	Hana ga saku,	Flowers are blooming,
	Doko ni saku?	Where are (they) blooming?
IIB	*Yama ni saku,*	(They) are blooming in the mountains,
	Sato ni saku,	(They) are blooming in the village,
	No ni mo saku.	(They) are blooming in the fields, too.

IIIA	*Tori ga naku,*	Birds are singing,
	Tori ga naku,	Birds are singing,
	Doko de naku?	Where are (they) singing?
IIIB	*Yama de naku,*	(They) are singing in the mountains,
	Sato de naku,	(They) are singing in the village,
	No de mo naku.	(They) are singing in the fields, too.

Inclusion of this song was exemplary multicultural education because it incorporated a form of authentic discourse that would match the discourse values of the Japanese children in that classroom while at the same time exposing other children to a new discourse form in a memorable, pleasurable way.

Box 6: Research Into Practice

LISTENING AND TELLING.

Below, we list steps that teachers can take to encourage multicultural learning and sensitivity in the classroom. In "listening and telling," however, we are describing an integrated classroom, not a separate bilingual classroom.

1. Encourage minority children's parents to become involved in their children's education; for example, ask them to talk about some aspects of their cultural heritage in classrooms. Facilitating participation by various cultural communities is important.

2. Invite a Japanese *kamishibai* storyteller into classrooms. Not only can Japanese children feel pride in their own cultural identity and heritage, but also teachers and children from other backgrounds can appreciate traditional Japanese stories presented by means of pictures on miniature frames that function like theatrical stages.

3. Listen to and sing Asian songs— Japanese, Chinese, or Korean— whose lyrics contain authentic narrative flavor and structures.

READING AND WRITING.

Teachers can get a sense of Asian cultural heritage and of how they can implement an additive approach by reading traditional Asian children's stories.

4. Japanese *kamishibai* picture-stories are also published as children's books. *Momotaro (The Peach Boy),* one of the best-known Japanese folktales, depicts a nameless, good-natured, childless old couple's receiving a reward from Heaven in the form of a baby, who later punishes wicked - inhabitants on Ogres' island and returns to his foster parents with treasures (Mino, 1986). An English version is available (Sakade, 1958), through which children from English-speaking backgrounds can appreciate its succinct storytelling style.

5. Another best-known Japanese folktale published in the form of a book is *Hanasaka Ji-San (The Old Man Who Made Trees Blossom),* which, like *Momotaro,* describes a nameless, honest, childless old couple and their dog Shiro, the agent of Heaven's reward (Mino, 1986). This story is also available in English (Sakade, 1958).

Box 6: Research Into Practice — cont'd

(1983), a Nisei (second-generation Japanese American) writer, assigns a variety of roles and characters to Japanese Americans that break European North American students' stereotyped images about Japanese Americans. Such students can also broaden their perspectives about Japanese culture, such as what kinds of daily foods Japanese Americans eat, including *onigiri* (oval-shaped rice balls). Asian American students can take pride in public recognition of their own cultural identity and heritage, while non-Asian American students can gain a better understanding of their Asian American peers.

7. Uchida's autobiographical novel *Journey to Topaz* (1971) describes how difficult Asian minorities' lives in the United States were, and provides an important view of American history. Uchida vividly describes the way that Japanese Americans were forced to evacuate from California during World War II and the severe circumstances and challenges they faced in an internment camp in Utah.

8. "Aekyung's Dream" (Paek, 1988) describes the difficult adjustment a Korean girl faces as she tries to adjust to school in America, where she has trouble with the language and is teased about being "Chinese."

9. "Michi's New Year" (Tanaka, 1980) describes the initial disappointment of New Year's Day for a Japanese girl who has emigrated to Canada, where some things are better, some things not as good, and everything seems different from Japan.

10. Laurence Yep's series of novels (for example, *Child of the Owl*, 1977) describe how strongly Chinese Americans retained their values and self-respect in the United States and, moreover, contributed to the progress of U.S. society.

11. *Japanese Children's Favorite Stories* and *Collection of Korean Stories* (Yale University Press) are two good collections of appealing stories from those cultures.

Summary

- Historical legal exclusion of Asians from the United States has been accompanied by a general unfamiliarity with Asian customs in general and storytelling practices in particular.
- Storytelling in Japan, among other Asian cultures, is influenced by cultural proscriptions of verbosity. From an early age, Japanese children are trained to listen empathically to others and to expect others to reciprocate when they are talking. Japanese children are trained to view talkativeness as insulting to listeners and an embarrassment to the speaker.
- Japanese children tend to tell oral personal narratives that are succinct collections of similar experiences unified into one coherent discourse. Often, these children have been observed to narrate three lines per subtopic or stanza.

- Japanese children are accustomed to conversations consisting of frequent brief turns exchanged with their partners.
- In assisting children with storytelling at school, teachers might want to refrain from overediting compositions, imposing so much of a Western approach to storytelling that the children relinquish a real sense of authorship in the process.
- Cultural influences on storytelling can be reciprocal, however, and can avoid both subjugation or cultural plagiarism so long as children's simultaneous imports from their original culture are accepted.
- In many ways, Japanese children's oral narratives resemble *haiku*, a form of poetic storytelling often practiced, but just as often misunderstood, in American classrooms.
- Both Chinese and Korean children's oral narratives are similar to Japanese narratives in their succinctness and de-emphasis of description. Chinese oral personal narratives and certain published stories often foreground moral lessons for the explicit purpose of instructing children in these values.

References

ADAMS, E.B. (1981). *Blindman's daughter.* Seoul, Korea: Seoul International Tourist Publishing Co.

ASO, I. (1959). Chukoki [The restoration period]. In M. Fumiiri (Ed.), *Haiku koza 4* [Haiku lectures 4]. Tokyo: Meiji Shoin.

AU, K.H. (1993). *Literacy instruction in multicultural settings.* Fort Worth, TX: Harcourt Brace Jovanovich.

AU, K.H., & JORDAN, C. (1981). Teaching reading to Hawaiian children: Finding a culturally appropriate solution. In H. Trueba, G.P. Guthrie, & K.H. Au (Eds.), *Culture in the bilingual classroom: Studies in classroom ethnography* (pp. 139–152). Rowley, MA: Newbury House.

AU, K.H., SCHEU, J.A., and KAWAKAMI, A.J. (1990). Assessment of students' ownership of literacy. *The Reading Teacher, 44* (2), 154–156.

BARTLETT, F.C. (1932). *Remembering.* Cambridge, England: Cambridge University Press.

BREEDLOVE, W.G., & ZHANG, M. (1990). A peculiar form of Chinese books for youth and adults—Little Man's Books. *Journal of Reading, 330–333.*

BRUNER, J. (1977). Early social interaction and language development. In H.R. Schaffer (Ed.), *Studies in mother-child interaction* (pp. 271–289). London: Academic Press.

CAZDEN, C.B. (1988). *Classroom discourse: The language of teaching and learning.* Portsmouth, NH: Heinemann.

CHAFE, W.L. (1980). The deployment of consciousness in the production of narrative. In W.L. Chafe (Ed.), *The pear stories: Cognitive, cultural, and linguistic aspects of narrative production* (pp. 9–50). Norwood, NJ: Ablex.

CHANG, CHIEN-JU. (April 8, 1994). "Chinese children's narrative structure." Paper presented at Harvard University, Cambridge, MA.

CHOMSKY, C. (1975). Invented spelling in the open classroom. *Word, 27,* 499–518.

CLANCY, P.M. (1985). The acquisition of Japanese. In D.I. Slobin (Ed.), *The crosslinguistic study of language acquisition,* (Vol. 1, pp. 373–524). *The data.* Hillsdale, NJ: Lawrence Erlbaum.

CLANCY, P.M. (1986). The acquisition of communicative style in Japanese. In B.B. Schieffelin & E. Ochs (Eds.), *Language socialization across cultures* (pp. 213–250). New York: Cambridge University Press.

COOK-GUMPERZ, J., & GUMPERZ, J.J. (1982). Communicative competence in educational perspective. In L.C. Wilkinson (Ed.), *Communicating in the classroom* (pp. 13–24). New York: Academic Press.

CRAWFORD, J. (1989). *Bilingual education: History, politics, theory, and practice.* Trenton, NJ: Crane.

CRAWFORD, J. (1992). *Hold your tongue: Bilingualism and the politics of "English only."* Reading, MA: Addison-Wesley.

CUMMINS, J. (1986). Empowering minority students: A framework for intervention. *Harvard Educational Review, 56* (1), 18–36.

CUMMINS, J. (1991a). Interdependence of first- and second-language proficiency in bilingual children. In E. Bialystok (Ed.), *Language processing in bilingual children* (pp. 70–89). New York: Cambridge University Press.

CUMMINS, J. (1991b). Language development and academic learning. In L.M. Malav & G. Duquette (Eds.), *Language, culture and cognition* (pp. 161–175). Clevedon, England: Multilingual Matters.

CUMMINS, J., SWAIN, M., NAKAJIMA, K., HANDSCOMBE, J., GREEN, D., & TRAN, C. (1984). Linguistic interdependence among Japanese and Vietnamese immigrant students. In C. Rivera (Ed.), *Language proficiency and academic achievement* (pp. 60–81). Clevedon, England: Multilingual Matters.

DELPIT, L.D. (1988). The silenced dialogue: Power and pedagogy in educating other people's children. *Harvard Educational Review, 58* (3), 280–298.

DOI, T. (1973). *The anatomy of dependence.* Trans. J. Bester. Tokyo: Kodansha International. (Original title: *Amae no kozo,* published by Kobundo, 1971.)

DUBE, E.F. (1977). "*A cross-cultural study of the relationship between 'intelligence' level and story recall.*" Unpublished doctoral dissertation, Cornell University, Ithaca, NY.

GAKKEN (1989). *Yonen no gakushu* [Fourth-graders' study], *11.* Tokyo: Gakushu Kenkyusha.

GARDNER, H. (1989). *To open minds: Chinese clues to the dilemma of contemporary education.* New York: Basic Books.

GEE, J.P. (1985). The narrativization of experience in the oral style. *Journal of Education, 167,* 9–35.

GEE, J.P. (1989). Two styles of narrative construction and their linguistic and educational implications. *Discourse Processes, 12,* 287–307.

GRAVES, D., & HANSEN, J. (1983). The Author's Chair. *Language Arts, 60* (2), 176–183.

HAKUTA, K. (1986). *Mirror of language: The debate on bilingualism.* New York: Basic Books.

HARRIS, R.J., LEE, D.J., HENSLEY, D.L., & SCHOEN, L.M. (1988). The effect of cultural script knowledge on memory for stories over time. *Discourse Processes, 11,* 413–431.

HEATH, S.B. (1983). *Ways with words: Language, life and work in communities and classrooms.* New York: Cambridge University Press.

HIEBERT, E.H. (1991). Introduction. In E.H. Hiebert (Ed.), *Literacy for a diverse society: Perspectives, practices, and politics* (pp. 1–6). New York: Teachers College Press.

Houghton Mifflin (1988). *English: Teacher's edition, level 5.* Boston, MA: Houghton Mifflin.

HYMES, D. (1981). "*In vain I tried to tell you": Studies in Native American ethnopoetics.* Philadelphia: University of Pennsylvania Press.

HYMES, D. (1982). Narrative form as a "grammar" of experience: Native Americans and a glimpse of English. *Journal of Education, 2,* 121–142.

JORDAN, C. (1984). Cultural compatibility and the education of Hawaiian children: Implications for mainland educators. *Education Research Quarterly, 8* (4), 59–71.

KINTSCH, W., & GREENE, E. (1978). The role of culture-specific schemata in the comprehension and recall of stories. *Discourse Processes, 1,* 1–13.

LABOV, W. (1972). *Language in the inner city.* Philadelphia: University of Philadelphia Press.

LABOV, W., & WALETZKY, J. (1967). Narrative analysis: oral versions of personal experience. In J. Helm (Ed.), *Essays on the verbal and visual arts* (pp. 12–44). Seattle: University of Washington Press.

LABOV, W., COHEN, P., ROBINS, C., & LEWIS, J. (1968). *A study of the non-standard English of Negro and Puerto Rican speakers in New York City* (Vol. 2) (Cooperative Research Project No. 3288), Washington, DC: Office of Education.

LAMBERT, W.E. (1975). Culture and language as factors in learning and education. In A. Wolfgang (Ed.), *Education of immigrant students: Issues and answers,* (pp. 55–83). Toronto: The Ontario Institute for Studies in Education.

LAMBERT, W.E. (1977). The effects of bilingualism on the individual: Cognitive and sociocultural consequences. In P.A. Hornby (Ed.), *Bilingualism: Psychological, social, and educational implications* (pp. 15–27). New York: Academic Press.

LAMBERT, W.E. (1981). Bilingualism and language acquisition. In H. Winitz (Ed.), *Native language and foreign language acquisition* (pp. 9–22). New York: New York Academy of Science.

LEBRA, T.S. (1986). *Japanese patterns of behavior* (5th ed.). Honolulu, HI: University of Hawaii Press.

LEE, O.Y. (1983). *Haiku de nihon o yomu: Naze "furuike no kawazu" nanoka—nihon-jin no bi-ishiki, kodo-yoshiki o saguru* [Reading Japan in haiku: Why "a frog in an old pond"—examination of sense of beauty and behaviors of the Japanese]. Kyoto: The PHP Institute.

LITCHER, J.H., & JOHNSON, D.W. (1969). Changes in attitudes toward Negroes of white elementary school students after use of multiethnic readers. *Journal of Educational Psychology, 60* (2), 148–152.

MAYNARD, S.K. (1989). *Japanese conversation: Self-contextualization through structure and interactional management.* Norwood, NJ: Ablex.

MCCABE, A., & PETERSON, C. (1985). A naturalistic study of the production of causal connectives by children. *Journal of Child Language, 12,* 145–159.

MCCABE, A., & PETERSON, C. (1991). Getting the story: Parental styles of narrative elicitation and developing narrative skills. In A. McCabe & C. Peterson (Eds.), *Developing narrative structure* (pp. 217–253). Hillsdale, NJ: Lawrence Erlbaum.

MCLAUGHLIN, D. (1990, Winter). The sociolinguistics of Navajo literacy. *Journal of Navajo Education, VII* (2), 28–36.

MCLAUGHLIN, D. (1992). *When literacy empowers: Navajo language in print.* Albuquerque, NM: University of New Mexico Press.

MEHAN, H. (1991). *Sociological foundations supporting the study of cultural diversity, research report, 1.* Santa Cruz, CA: National Center for Research on Cultural Diversity and Second Language Learning.

MICHAELS, S. (1981). "Sharing time": Children's narrative styles and differential access to literacy. *Language in Society, 10,* 423–442.

MICHAELS, S. (1991). The dismantling of narrative. In A. McCabe & C. Peterson (Eds.), *Developing narrative structure* (pp. 303–351). Hillsdale, NJ: Lawrence Erlbaum Associates.

MICHAELS, S., & COLLINS, J. (1984). Oral discourse style: Classroom interaction and the acquisition of literacy. In D. Tannen (Ed.), *Coherence in spoken and written discourse* (pp. 219–244). Norwood, NJ: Ablex.

MILLER, P. (1982). *Amy, Wendy, and Beth: Language acquisition in South Baltimore.* Austin: University of Texas Press.

MILLER, P.J., POTTS, R., FUNG, H., & HOOGSTRA, L. (1990). Narrative practices and the social construction of self in childhood. *American Ethnologist, 17* (2), 292–311.

MINAMI, M. (1990). "Children's narrative structure: How do Japanese children talk about their own stories?" Special qualifying paper. Harvard Graduate School of Education, Cambridge, MA.

MINAMI, M., & MCCABE, A. (1991a). Haiku as a discourse regulation device: A stanza analysis of Japanese children's personal narratives. *Language in Society, 20,* 577–600.

MINAMI, M., & MCCABE, A. (1991b, October). "Rice balls versus bear hunts: Japanese and European North American family narrative patterns." Presented at the 16th Annual Boston University Conference on Language Development, Boston, MA.

MINAMI, M., & MCCABE, A. (1993, July). "Social interaction and discourse style: Culture-specific parental styles of interviewing and children's narrative structure." Presented at the 4th International Pragmatic Conference, Kobe, Japan.

MINAMI, M., & MCCABE, A. (in press). Rice balls versus bear hunts: Japanese and European North American family narrative patterns. *Journal of Child Language.*

MINAMI, M., & OVANDO, C.J. (in press). Language Issues in Multicultural Contexts. In J. Banks & C. McGee Banks (Eds.), *Handbook of research on multicultural education.* New York: Macmillan.

MINO, I. (1986). "Fairy tales and the beginning of moral stage development in children between three and four years of age: An exploratory study." Unpublished doctoral dissertation, Harvard University, Cambridge, MA.

MIYANAGA, K. (1991). *The creative edge: Emerging individualism in Japan.* New Brunswick, NJ: Transaction Publishers.

MURAYAMA, K. (1984). Ryoyo haiku [convalescence haiku]. In K. Murayama & K. Yamashita (eds.), *Haiku-yogo no kisochishiki* [Basic knowledge of haiku terms]. Tokyo: Kadokawa, 286–291.

NORTON, D.E. (1991). *Through the eyes of a child: An introduction to children's literature* (3rd ed.). New York: Macmillan.

OCHS, E., & SCHIEFFELIN, B.B. (1984). Language acquisition and socialization: Three developmental stories. In R. Schweder & R. LeVine (Eds.), *Culture theory: Essays on mind, self and emotion* (pp. 276–320). New York: Cambridge University Press.

OGBU, J.U. (1992). Understanding cultural diversity and learning. *Educational Researcher 21, November* (8), 5–14.

OKUBO, T. (1959). *Shikoryoku o sodateru hanashi-kotoba kyoiku* [Oral-language education to raise thinking power]. Tokyo: Shunjusha.

PAEK, M. (1988). *Aekyung's dream.* San Francisco, CA: Children's Book Press.

PELLOWSKI, A. (1977). *The world of storytelling.* New York: Bowker.

PETERSON, C., & MCCABE, A. (1983). *Developmental psycholinguistics: Three ways of looking at a child's narrative.* New York: Plenum.

PHILIPS, S.U. (1982). *The invisible culture: Communication in classroom and community on the Warm Springs Indian Reservation.* New York: Longman.

READ, C. (1971). Pre-school children's knowledge of English phonology. *Harvard Educational Review, 41* (1), 1–34.

REDMOND, M.V., & Bunyi, J.M. (1993). The relationship of intercultural communication competence with stress and the handling of stress as reported by international students. *International Journal of Intercultural Relations, 17,* 235–254.

REYES, M.L. (1992). Challenging venerable assumptions: Literacy instruction for linguistically different students. *Harvard Educational Review, 62* (4), 427–446.

SAKADE, F. (Ed.). (1958). *Japanese children's favorite stories.* Rutland, VT: Charles E. Tuttle.

SANETO, A. (1986). *Momotaro* [The peach boy]. Tokyo: Doshinsha.

SCHIEFFELIN, B.B., & OCHS, E. (Eds.) (1986). *Language socialization across cultures.* New York: Cambridge University Press.

SCOLLON, R., & SCOLLON, S. (1981). *Narrative, literacy and face in interethnic communications.* Norwood, NJ: Ablex.

SHAW, T., MICHAHELLES, R., CHEN, X., MINAMI, M., & SING, R. (1994). "Adapting to the U.S. classroom: Problems and strategies of Asian high school students in Boston area schools." Unpublished manuscript, Harvard University, Cambridge, MA.

SHIBATA, H. (1984). Daidokoro haiku [Kitchen haiku]. In K. Murayama & K. Yamashita (Eds.), *Haiku-yogo no kiso-chishiki* [Basic knowledge of haiku terms] (pp. 185–189). Tokyo: Kadokawa.

SHIMAZU, T., YUNOUE, S., & URYU, Y. (1978). *Senku-rengashu* [Collection of one thousand chained poems]. Tokyo: Kotenbunko.

SKINNER, B.F. (1957). *Verbal behavior.* Englewood Cliffs, NJ: Prentice-Hall.

SPENER, D. (1988). Transitional bilingual education and the socialization of immigrants. *Harvard Educational Review, 58* (2), 133–153.

Stanford Working Group (1993). *Federal education programs for limited-English-proficient students: A blueprint for the second generation.* Palo Alto, CA: Stanford University.

STEVENSON, H.W., STIGLER, J.W., & LEE, S. (1986). Achievement in mathematics. In H. Stevenson, H. Axuma, & K. Hakuta (Eds.), *Child development and education in Japan* (pp. 201–216). NY: Freeman.

STEVENSON, H.W., LEE, S., CHEN, C., STIGLER, J.W., HSU, C., & KITAHARA, S. (1990). *Contexts of achievement: A study of American, Chinese, and Japanese children.* Chicago: University of Chicago Press.

STIGLER, J., & PERRY, M. (1988). Mathematics learning in Japanese, Chinese, and American classrooms. In G. Saxe & M. Gearhart (Eds.), *Children's mathematics* (pp. 27–54). New directions for child development, 41. San Francisco: Jossey-Bass.

SUTTON-SMITH, B. (1988). In search of the imagination. In K. Egan & D. Nadaner (Eds.), *Imagination and education* (pp. 3–29). New York: Teachers College Press.

TANAKA, S. (1988). *Michi's New Year.* Toronto, Canada: Northern Lights, Peter Martin Associates Limited.

THARP, R.G., & GALLIMORE, R. (1991a). *Rousing minds to life: Teaching, learning, and schooling in social context.* Cambridge, England: Cambridge University Press.

THARP, R.G., & GALLIMORE, R. (1991b). *The instructional conversation: Teaching and learning in social activity, Research Report: 2.* Santa Cruz, CA: National Center for Research on Cultural diversity and Second Language Learning.

TOBIN, J.J., WU, D.Y.H., & DAVIDSON, D.H. (1989). *Preschool in three cultures: Japan, China, and the United States.* New Haven, CT: Yale University Press.

UCHIDA, Y. (1971). *Journey to Topaz: A story of the Japanese-American evacuation.* New York: Scribner's.

UCHIDA, Y. (1983). *The best bad thing.* New York: Atheneum.

U.S. Department of Education. (1992). *The condition of bilingual education: A report to the Congress and the President.* Washington, DC: U.S. Government Printing Office.

VYGOTSKY, L.S. (1978). *Mind in society: The development of higher psychological processes.* Cambridge, MA: Harvard University Press.

YAMADA, H. (1992). *American and Japanese business discourse: A comparison of interactional styles.* Norwood, NJ: Ablex.

YAMAMOTO, K. (1969). *Haiku no sekai* [The world of haiku]. Tokyo: Kodansha.

YEP, L. (1977). *Child of the owl.* New York: Harper & Row.

YODA, J. (1986). *Hanasaka ji-san* [Old man flower blower]. Tokyo: Doshinsha.

XU, X. (1992). "The role of children's literature in Chinese children's moral education." Unpublished paper, Tufts University, Medford, MA.

XU, X. (1993). "Familiar and strange—A comparison of children's literature in four cultures." Unpublished Master's Project, Tufts University, Medford, MA.

CHAPTER 6

Improvising on a Theme: Some African American Traditions

Karen Craddock-Willis
and
Allyssa McCabe

OVERVIEW

This chapter addresses historical background, in which differences between African Americans and European North Americans were exaggerated and dealt with as deficiencies on the part of the former. Storytelling practices in the African American community are described, with particular emphasis on the importance of telling lengthy, dramatic narratives. African American children tell even more narratives that display what has been described as classic European North American highpoint structure than do European North American children of the same age. Some African American children also occasionally tell performative narratives that explicitly or implicitly weave together a number of thematically related episodes. Narrative form resembles distinctive musical form and is drawn upon by numerous successful African American writers.

SOME AFRICAN AMERICAN STORYTELLING TRADITIONS

Historical Background

Historically, examining differences between African Americans and European North Americans has often amounted to stereotyping. Even today, there continues to be commercial exaggeration of both physical and, more subtly, social features of African American life. In the media, the most prevalent depictions of African Americans are hyperbolic, even cartoon-like portrayals of expressive characteristics. Given this history, the movement during the sixties and early seventies to de-emphasize difference was a necessary corrective swing away from such racist ideas. Perhaps some readers will remember song lyrics like "A child is black. A child is white. Together we learn to read and write."

However, the intrinsic value of African American culture must be understood in a way that neither erases its distinctive features nor exaggerates them in a stereotypical fashion. What we have to say about storytelling within this community neither pertains to all individuals of African heritage nor to any individual on all occasions. Nonetheless, there is a distinct African American tradition of storytelling.

Storytelling Practices in the Community

Storytelling in African American communities has long been a key conduit for information in many aspects of daily life. Oral history was and is a way of transmitting vital family lineage. For example, it was traditional in many households to ritualistically recount the family genealogy, something that happens more informally now. With roots in African tradition, the practice of repeating stories about one's ancestors—who they were, what they did, what happened to them—was critical to maintaining a sense of self and community, especially during slavery.

Today, with economic and psychological difficulties still very much present, sharing stories about family is as important as it ever was for preserving identity and family continuity, as well as a means of celebrating family unity. Storytelling is likely to happen on front steps, in kitchens, and at cookouts, as well as on more formal occasions in churches and classrooms. Stories about family members extend far beyond biological relations to include godparents and a host of fictitious relatives such as "play cousins" and the like.

Exemplary Mother-Child Interaction

During conversations with adults or peers, African American children are encouraged to develop themes and to talk at length on a variety of topics. What follows are segments of a conversation between an African American boy, aged $4^1/2$ years, and his family:

MOTHER: Are you going to Barbara's, Ben, for Easter vacation?

SISTER: And Billy and Harriet gonna be there. We goin' to be ridin' our bikes down here!

BEN: I'll be climbing up the tree.

FATHER: You don't plan to take the bus?

BEN: I'll be climbin' up the tree like Superman. And I'll jump onto the roof. (Makes Superman noises.)

FATHER: No you won't either.

BEN: Yes I will. I said, "Ma come open the door," and I said "good morning!"

MOTHER: Oh, sh sh, the last time, Barbara and I were having coffee in the kitchen. All of a sudden, we hear a little knock at the window, and we looked out, and here was Ben. And now this is like another story. And he had climbed up a tree, and got off the tree and climbed on the roof and came to the kitchen window, and was bangin' on the window, and we're having coffee. When I saw him, my heart just dropped. Thought how is he gonna get down this tree?

SISTER: And I was scared to go up there.

FATHER: He has no fear . . .
BEN: You know what? I was in a surfing board?
ADULT VISITOR: Right.
BEN: It was a blue surfing board, and I turned over in deep water? I can swim, and Daddy didn't see, and he saw the board, and you know what? And I got in, when I got in, I turned it out. So I had to hold my nose. I can't I can't, I was tryin' to go like that, when I was 'trying to go over to the rock. When Dad comes in here, he says, "Why are you sittin' down? How'd you get in there? Thought you'd swim under the waterfall? I mean, I thought you went through the cave way and jumped over the table under the sea. Like Superman!"
FATHER: You got a good one [story] tonight!

This conversation included a remarkably lengthy narrative for a 4-year-old child. It also includes parental endorsement of the heroic role the child carved out for himself.*

Other Scholarly Treatments

Within such vital and often vibrant family networks, the exchange of story conveys messages relating love, sorrow, anger, joy, and so forth. Stories are also a forum for showcasing the manner in which you communicate human emotions to your audience. Others (Michaels & Foster, 1985) have described the way that African American children tell stories, calling it a "Performed Narrative," and contrasting this to a "Lecture Demonstration" style typical of European North American children. Traditionally, in American culture broadly conceived, a performance is often understood as a potentially superficial, unilateral reenactment of a previously scripted scene for the purpose of entertainment. This sense of the term "performance" is not the one we wish to highlight here. In our sense, a performed style of presentation is dramatic, animated, openly expressive, improvised, and interactive. Not only is performance in this deeper sense seen in narration, it is a pervasive aspect of effective communication within the overall culture. To perform is not simply to entertain, it is to express the humorous but also the somber, to engage and connect with individuals but also with the larger community. Perhaps no particular feature or features uniquely distinguish the performance aspects of African American narration from aspects of other cultural presentations. But overall, the way that African American children mediate what they say through a variety of verbal and gestural devices needs to be recognized. The performative aspect of their style promotes fluency, and this skill, if tapped, could prove invaluable in writing instruction.

African American children sometimes tell the kind of story typically told by European North American children, for example, the following, told by Mona, a 7-year-old girl:

When I was at the beach, I got stung by a bee. It was, it was when . . . Once I was walkin', and there was this bee behind me, and it was on my street. I was

*We are indebted to Kendra Winner for pointing this out.

still walking', and it stung me on the back of my hand. We had to put this kind of mud on it. It's not like mud, but kinda like mud—a goop. You had to put, they had to put like this—to make it so it won't [hurt]. It stings a little. It doesn't really hurt.

African American children do not always confine themselves to giving just one sequence of events about one past happening at a time; instead, some children often thematically link happenings that occurred in different times and places. However, even when narratives interweave two or three experiences, such as in the examples from Rene and Vivian (pp. 102-107), African American children plot numerous sequences of events within the context of the individual experiences combined (Rodino, Gimbert, Perez, Craddock-Willis, & McCabe, 1991).

Sunny Hyon and Elizabeth Sulzby (1992) studied the narratives and stories of forty-eight African American urban kindergartners told to an adult. Almost 60 percent of the children in this context told stories like Mona's that were centered on a single topic, including some that were retellings of familiar storybooks.

Similarly, Tempii Champion (1995) interviewed fifteen children who spoke African American English about a variety of personal experiences. She found that in these circumstances, children produced narratives like the classic ones described in Chapter 4 66 percent of the time—more often than European North American children do (51 percent of 6- to ten-year-old European North American children's narratives were classically structured in Peterson and Mc-Cabe, 1983). It is impossible to say without research beyond the scope of this work whether such an accomplishment represents adoption of European North American customs so prevalent in American culture or whether indigenous African storytelling developed similar traditions independently.

The point to take from these studies is that distinctions between European North American and African American storytelling traditions should not be exaggerated. Neither should they be ignored. Hyon and Sulzby (1992) found that a third of the children in their study told narratives that contained several episodes whose connections were never overtly stated. Champion (1995) found that 8 out of 71 personal narratives told by the children in her study were performative stories.

Features of Narration

In the African American community, it is often as important to tell a good story as it is to merely recount facts, as can be seen in the conversation between Ben and his family. What happened can be embellished by means of metaphors, jokes, slang, and exaggeration of accomplishments, attributes, and feelings. In lengthier performances, especially for peers, African American children may begin with a real event but proceed to improvise upon that event, just as jazz musicians improvise upon a musical theme, playing variations on the theme a little differently depending on audience reactions. In line with such departures from the facts, it is critical to realize that "lies" is a traditional African American word for figurative discourse, tales, or stories (Hurston, 1935/1990,

p. 8; Gates, 1988, p. 56). The upshot of this aspect of African American story-telling style performed for uninformed white teachers and children is often a profound misunderstanding, with the African American children being accused of, instead of appreciated for, "lying." For example, during observations of mixed classrooms, Rebecca Keebler noted the frustrations many African American children feel when European North American children continually criticize them for not telling the truth in their stories. As one African American boy put it, "Some of the boring parts are true."*

The imagination of African American children has on some occasions, then, been mistakenly seen as a sign of moral turpitude. In fact, however, such differing emphases on the importance of strict adherence to facts derives from parental taste and tolerance for fictionalized versions of experience (Miller, Potts, Fung, Hoogstra, & Mintz, 1990).

By no means do we wish to suggest that African American children never tell the facts nor want to. What we are talking about is not a lack of ability to "stick to the facts." We are simply pointing to a longstanding tradition of exercising poetic license. Conversely, we are not suggesting that non-African American children cannot or do not tell stories without animated or imaginative devices upon occasion. We merely wish to highlight what may be a culturally significant style or form of storytelling.

Consider the following example from a first-grader collected by Michele Foster and Sarah Michaels (1985). As those authors point out, Rene skillfully blends facts and fantasy. This example is remarkably lengthy, especially coming from such a young child, and that is exactly the point we wish to make. We ask readers to appreciate its length and elaboration instead of wishing to curtail it. Rene has a remarkable resource that could be tapped in teaching him to read and write, but only if teachers seek to promote it rather than to whittle it down to some more familiar size.

> Rene: At Thanksgiving when I went to my grandma and grandpa,
> We were, we had, we had all all this FOOD
> and I was at the table, right?
> and . . . it was the day before Thanksgiving.
>
> and I said to my, I was REALLY, REALLY stuffed because we
>   just had finished eating,
> and I said, I'm SO SO full, I could eat a Thanksgiving turkey.
> and she said, "Well you could eat the stuffing too."
> and I said, I said, "why don't you and Daddy put the
>   stuffing in bed?"
>
> and, and, and Daddy, my father looked at me
> and he said, "HUH? HUH?"
> That's what he always does when, um I say something like he
>   should be CHICKEN or something.
> He goes, "HUH, HUH" (laughs)
> He goes like that.

*These classroom excerpts are taken from dissertation work completed by Rebecca Keebler.

And my grandfather always makes um jokes about him being so
    dumb when he was little.
Like he said one time, he said . . . he's at the kitchen table,
He said, "When your father was about ten he didn't know his
    feet from his head,
And he would put his shoes on his head and his feet on top."

And um then he goes, "Well you're BALD Dad." (laughs)
And um then he goes, "Well guess what?"
"You didn't have any hair when you were five."
And he said, and he said, "Now I bet that was a JOKE."

And he said, "No, I don't."
I only have eight plus seven.
And everyone laughed.

And um we heard, um when we were sleeping, I heard a
    scratching noise.
And I snuck out to the um door.
And there was a, there was a mama raccoon scratching at the
    thing with um five babies.
And I um called Nana, my grandmother, and my grandfather and
    my daddy to come

And we let em in for a minute because we were kind of
    allergic to them.
They only let them in for a minute.
And they gave 'em some milk and stuff.
And we gave em some milk and a little bit of, of left-over
    turkey.
And um we let 'em out.

Then uh, and in midnight, actually it was like two o'clock
    in the morning.
I heard a scratch again.
And I went to the same room
And it was just a little, little baby rabbit with his mo—
    with one mother.

And he was SO cute
And I fed THEM some milk and some left-over turkey
And then um then I let THEM out.

A minute LATER I heard another knocking [listening child
    goes, "OOOh" here] at the door.
I opened it up,
And it was my GRANDFATHER (laughs) saying, "What's all that
    noise out there?" (chuckles)
And um after that day, I never let anything, a living thing
    in except um, except uh, I forget.
[Other child: Animals?]

Rene: I almost got, I almost got really scared because of
      it.
There's three HAWKS near their house that live there,
and they try to swoop around and get all the birds 'cause
      they put out bird feeders and stuff.
They, um, my grandma and grandpa, they look down on the bird
      feeders,
and they try to catch all their birds.

And the hawk was flying around.
I could see it.
I walked out,
and I saw this big flying shadow outside.

Now it couldn't be Superman.
It just couldn't be.

I looked up
and I went, "AH" for real.
I was terrified 'cause I thought he was gonna like come down
      and tear me apart or something.
And I was screaming.

I screamed
and I ran back up,
Yeah, I was really scared.
I even spilled the water that, I was supposed to um be
      watering the garden of my grandfather.

I was SCREAMING
and um I went in.
My father said, "Rene, what's the matter?"
I said, "Look up there, Sure ain't Superman." (audience
      laughs)

And he said, "Yes it is,'"
and I go, "It is not, it's a vulture, I mean a hawk."
And um he said, "Oh my God, we'd better, we better close the
      windows,"
'Cause we had all the windows open 'cause it was pretty
      cold.

And the next day I went out
and I rode my bike.
Right before um I opened the door and stuck my head out to
      make sure there was no hawk.
and there weren't.

And then um I was ridin' my bike up and down, up and down,
and all of a sudden I hear this, "AH AH AH AHA BL-BL-BL"

"I wonder if Rene's home?"
And it was Sean.

I wen' I wen', "Ah, I hope it's not him again,"
and instead, then over came Sean by me, a five-year-old and
        a sev-, six-year-old,
and um they were both going (sound effects).
They had drums and whistles

and they were going, "bl-bl toot ch ch ch ch toot
and they were going toot chch ch ch toot and wah wah
        (laughs)
and they were making all these weird noises
and I started saying, "PHEW I'm glad it's you,"

And they said we wanted to warn you about the the HAWK going
        by,
and I said, "OH MY GOD,"
and I took my bike into the garage
and I said "G'BYE." (laughs)

and I went inside again.

And that night I was SCARED half to death.
I couldn't SLEEP.
and I kept remembering my, in my mind I kept um thinking I
        heard ark ark.
and I kept on listening, going (hand to ear, turning head
        from side to side).

I even stopped breathing for a moment. (holds breath for
        effect)
and I thought I hear a, I thought I heard something.
I thought I heard someone going ARK ARK
but I didn't.
I was just hearing things 'cause I was so scared.
[Other child: I have a question.]
And we had some pumpkin pie for dessert.

In displaying Rene's tour deforce using four-line stanza or verse form, we are indebted to the methodology developed by Hymes (1984) and extended by Gee (1991 a, b), a version of which was described in more detail in Chapter 3. It seems that there is a regular poetic form displayed in the narratives of many African American children, and that this form often involves approximately four oral "sentences" per subtopic. Recall that oral sentences are estimated on the basis of beginning with a conjunction or another regular pattern. In Rene's production, fully 62 percent of his sentences begin with *and*. [The rest begin with *I* (17 percent), another pronoun, or a conjunction other than *and*.]

Another feature of African American narratives is the teasing that is frequently either the point of the story or part of what is recapitulated, as in Rene's story above. He and his father tease each other, just as his father and grandfather also tease each other. Teasing (or "Playing the Dozens") has long been noted to be a valued language game in African American communities both in general discourse (Labov 1972) and in the context of storytelling in particular (Coleman, Cosby, & Poussaint, 1989).

Perhaps the most well-documented distinctive feature of African American narrative style, the feature most responsible for the misinterpretation of such narration as "rambling" (Michaels, 1991), is the thematic linkage of events that occurred at different places and times, often involving different participants. Consider the way that a 9-year-old girl pulls together a variety of teeth-pulling stories to establish herself as a "Pullin'-Teeth Expert" in the following narrative. She builds up to a powerful unifying aphorism that encourages self-reliance yet expresses support. Note that children do not always make their themes as explicit as this girl does, though they might be encouraged to do so in written reflections or revisions of an oral performance accepted on its own terms.

> Vivian: We went to the dentist before
> and I was gettin' my tooth pulled
> and the doc, the dentist said, "Oh, it's not gonna hurt."
> and he was lying to me.
>
> It hurt.
> It hurted so bad I coulda gone on screamin' even though I
>   think some . . .
> [I don't know what it was like.]
> I was, in my mouth like, I was like, "Oh that hurt!"
> He SAID no, it wouldn't hurt.
>
> Cause last time I went to the doctor, I had got this spray.
> This doctor, he sprayed some spray in my mouth
> and my tooth appeared in his hand.
>
> He put me to sleep,
> and then, and then I woke up.
> He used some pliers to take it out,
> and I didn't know.
>
> So I had told my, I asked my sister how did, how did the man
>   take [it out].
> and so she said, "He used some pliers."
> I said, "Nah, he used that spray."
> She said, "Nope he used that spray to put you to sleep,
> and he used the pliers to take it out."
>
> I was, like, "Huh, that's amazin'."
> I swear to God I was so amazed that, hum . . .
> It was so amazing, right? that I had to look for myself,
>
> and then I asked him too.

and he said, "Yes, we, I used some pliers to take out your
    tooth,
and I put you to sleep, an, so you wouldn't know,
and that's how I did it."

and I was like, "Ooouuu."
and then I seen my sister get her tooth pulled.
I was like, "Ooouuu"
Cause he had to put her to sleep to, hmm, to take out her
    tooth.
It was the same day she got her tooth pulled,

and I was scared.
I was like, "EEEhhhmmm."
I had a whole bunch cotton in my mouth, chompin' on it
Cause I had to hold it to, hmm, stop my bleeding.

I, one day I was in school.
I took out my own tooth.
I put some hot water in it the night, the, the night before
    I went to school.
and I was taking a test.

And then it came out right when I was takin', when I
finished the test.
And my teacher asked me, was it bleeding.
I said, "No It's not bleeding,
Cause I put some hot water on it."

And so my cousin, he wanted to take out his tooth,
and he didn't know what to do,
so I told him.
"I'm a Pullin' Teeth Expert."

"Pull out your own tooth,
but if you need somebody to do it,
Call me,
and I'll be over."

African American children's narratives in general are far more likely to include metaphors than are European North American children's (Pollio, & Barlow, Fine, & Pollio, 1989). As can be seen in Ben's, Rene's, and Vivian's narratives, dialogue is also prominent and often serves as a device to evaluate a
narrator's experiences (Labov, 1972). African American adolescents' written
narratives contain numerous stylistic devices such as irony, alliteration, rhyme,
and metaphors (Daubney-Davis, 1992). In all these ways, African American
children's and adolescents' narratives mirror the kind of African American
novels that have been appearing on best-seller lists, novels such as Toni Morrison's *Jazz, Song of Solomon,* or *Beloved.*

Relationship of Narrative Features to Structure of Other Art Forms in the Community

In performing stories for their peers, African American children often begin and end with a theme, improvising upon events in between these two points in a fashion reminiscent of jazz compositions (Craddock-Willis, 1990). For example, Rene starts with Thanksgiving dinner, goes far afield from that with his various recapitulations of animal visits, benign and threatening, and comes around again to the same theme: "And we had some pumpkin pie for dessert." In another narrative analyzed by Gee (1991a), a little girl begins and ends a lengthy discussion of how her family baked her grandmother an extraordinary number of cakes with the phrase, "Today it's Friday the 13th, and it's Bad Luck Day." Unless listeners come to appreciate the structure of these compositions with their own version of beginning (theme), middle (improvisation on the theme), and end (return to the theme), they may dismiss them—and in fact have done so—as "rambling" or "not talking about one important thing" (Michaels, 1991).

Improvisation on a theme—Rene's Thanksgiving food for the animals vignettes, for example, or Vivian's tooth-pulling escapades—is stylistically similar to a motif found in some classical European musical compositions (Rondo form) that involves variations on a theme, as well as in some traditional African oral expressions that also exhibit this cyclical pattern. Wynton Marsalis (1994) put it this way: "In jazz the band is like a train. The drums are the engine, the basses the wheels, the piano the body. Or classical music, rondo form, in which a theme keeps coming back, is like going away from home and returning." Marsalis' metaphoric description of jazz could be applied to performative narratives as well.

Another musical feature that African American children may display in their narratives is the use of refrains, or recurring lines that reiterate some main point. One first grader, for example, wrote of going to an amusement park. First she mentioned a ride on a merry-go-round, concluding that stanza with, "And it was so much fun." Then she told of riding a roller-coaster, concluding this stanza, too, with, "And it was so much fun." Finally, she told of eating cotton candy and getting it all over her, concluding with, "And it was so much fun." Some European North American adults and children saw this as "repeating herself," when in reality she was using a most effective rhetorical device, and one with a long tradition in her cultural heritage. Karen Malan (1992) found that South African children increasingly employ refrains in their narratives between the ages of 4 and 6. In other words, this should be seen as a positive, poetic development.

In fact, allusions or cross-referencing to art forms in various modalities is quite salient among African American artists. Toni Morrison (1992) and Bebe Moore Campbell (1992) explicitly link their verbal style to jazz or blues roots, respectively.

Conversely, jazz musicians describe improvisation as speaking, and of "playing a solo as telling a story" (Berliner, 1990). This cross-referencing is also exhibited in dance arenas (for example, the Alvin Ailey American Dance Theater produced "District Storyville," which took its title from the cradle of jazz in New Orleans and was transparently connected with telling stories). Visual artists such as Romare Bearden, whose well-known painting "Three Folk Musicians" embodies the integration of musical, verbal, and visual artistry, has discussed the role of narrative in his life's work.

The integration of storytelling, history, music, and other arts has a long history, deriving from African cultural traditions. In an introduction to *The World of African Song,* Solomon Mbabi-Katani points out that "In most forms of African songs, words play a significant part. Indeed, it is usually the words that generate the music of the songs because most of the languages of the songs are musically accented. Both singers and audience listen for the meaning of the words of the song, which often convey a message. It is to be expected therefore that the greatest African traditional musician is also the greatest poet, historian, and storyteller in this part of the country" (Makeba, 1971, p. 21).

Such cross-modality referencing has been amply documented through the creative accomplishments of these and many other African American artists, which points to how deeply embedded these aesthetic themes are. Here, we would like to extend these observations to the structural composition of certain stories told by ordinary African American children. Obviously, African American artists compose using deliberate, conscious strategies, while children simply tell stories that sound right to them. In both cases, however, individuals draw on the aesthetic values of their culture as part of the creative process.

Given what we have said about structural differences and the extent to which these are deeply embedded in African American culture, what should educators do with this information? There has been a sensitive debate within the African American community regarding which avenue to take in the struggle to confront racism and establish equality: do you teach children to master dominant cultural linguistic forms in order to survive and succeed in the dominant society or do you recognize and encourage the use of linguistic forms prevalent in the child's own community as a means of showing such children that teachers value them and their traditions (Delpit, 1988)? This debate has been conducted primarily with reference to the phonological, semantic, and grammatical levels of language variation, which differ from the narrative level that is our focus.

As we have shown, the narrative style of African American children is linked to artistic expressions that are gaining wider acceptance in our culture. As this trend continues and increases, we begin to see that such style is not necessarily an impediment to success in certain arenas. In fact, it is an asset. Furthermore, we would like to carefully distinguish the narrative style we are documenting from the historic debate regarding use and representation of Black English Vernacular in the classroom.

Issues for Instruction

Among many other scholars, Delpit (1988) argues that Black English Vernacular (and other nonstandard dialects) needs to be recognized as valid.

However, recognizing the validity of Black English Vernacular does not necessarily mean that teachers should try to use such constructions either formally or informally unless they have participated in the African American community. Furthermore, classroom practice, Delpit argues, also should instruct children explicitly in the rules of the "culture of power." In other words, she argues that all children need to be instructed in the rules of Standard English.

Many African American adults and children engage in switching back and forth between Standard English and Black English Vernacular for many reasons (Nelson, 1990). Such linguistic code-switching reflects the duality of existing in two cultures. Instruction can proceed in the language of the "Culture of Power" because African American children have pre-existing informal exposure to the rules and practice of Standard English.

We again wish to distinguish what we have to say about narrative form from the way in which research on Black English Vernacular had an impact on educational practice. Teachers need to understand and appreciate the distinctive narrative form that some African-American children practice upon occasion. This form of narration is not an obstacle to success either aesthetically or commercially. For example, at one point in 1992, three of the ten best-selling authors on the *New York Times* book list were African American women (Toni Morrison, Alice Walker, and Terri MacMillan). In particular, Morrison and Walker demonstrate fidelity to such narrative form. African American filmmakers such as Julie Dash with her film "Daughters of the Dust" have achieved critical success with such form; her film is a fine example of intricate, parallel weaving of narrative and image. Playwrights such as August Wilson and John Edgar Wideman write plays influenced by such form, plays that are critically acclaimed and frequently performed. Journalists such as Patricia Smith, who writes for the *Boston Globe*, succeed in communicating to a wide audience using Standard English but employing elements of the distinctive narrative form we summarized above. Legal scholars such as Patricia Williams (*Alchemy of Race and Rights*, 1991) and Derrick Bell marshal African American narrative devices in their writing.

Thus, for the reason that the majority of African American children are quite capable narrators when they come to school and because such distinctive features as they display have become part of successful stories, we take the position that one should not fix what is not broken and, furthermore, what works well. Teachers could accept, explore, and encourage *the shape* of what is said—narrative form—along with instructing children in Standard English. Perhaps this combination might make the latter more effective, especially if children are not penalized for using Black English Vernacular in reported dialogue interwoven with Standard English grammar and vocabulary. Children will work hard on difficult surface issues so long as they are working to the end of what they see as genuine possible communication. Encouraging children to recognize and display clearly the form they employ has profound implications for self-esteem, as well as for appreciating others. In short, we emphasize a need for amalgamating various dialects of English, and for providing a climate where what children say is accepted first and foremost, and adjusted, "instructed" later.

Box 7: Research Into Practice

LISTENING AND TELLING

1. Invite storytellers from the African American community to come in. Ask them to talk about what makes a good story in their community. Ask them how they learned to tell such good stories.

2. Hold frequent Sharing Times. Discourage bringing in objects from home at least some of the time, as bringing in objects works against storytelling in favor of expository, descriptive, even scientific talk. Have children point out connections between their stories and those of others at the end of a group of stories. Also, talk about understanding and appreciating differences and similarities. Begin with "Have you ever felt really afraid? Embarrassed? Have you ever been hurt really bad?" Take one emotion at a time. Read stories that deal with that emotion.

3. Record children's stories at Sharing Time and write them down verbatim. Use these as reading materials for emergent literacy classrooms. Children's stories should not be overedited, but rather displayed in stanzas—accepted on their own terms—as are the oral stories in this chapter.

READING AND WRITING

1. To get a sense of African narrative heritage, read some of the widely available Spider Anansi stories, as these are often referred to in African American stories. Talk about the Spider character, as well as the explanations myths provide for natural events. Encourage your class to compose a Spider Anansi tale themselves as a group.

2. Other widely available folktales are *Why Mosquitoes Buzz in Peoples' Ears*

by Verna Aardema (Scholastic) and *The Chameleon who Couldn't Stop Changing His Mind* by Sally Nyokabi (Transafrica). These tales might be read and then dramatized by a class.

3. Read Lucille Clifton's "Tuesday All Day Rain," an Everett Anderson story that begins and ends with a theme. Have children write a narrative of their own and rewrite it to display their narratives as poetry, grouping lines on a subtopic together as a stanza.

4. Another good example of a story poem told in stanzas is *Africa Dream* by Eloise Greenfield (HarperTrophy). Have children follow this with a dream story of their own, displayed in revision as a poem in stanzas.

5. Read aloud or listen to a tape of *Flossie & the Fox*, by Patricia C. McKissack. Both tape and book are available through Scholastic Publishers. Point out both the Standard English spoken by the adult narrator in the story and the use of Black English Vernacular. Explain that both ways of talking have their own purposes and rules. Neither is better for all occasions. Head off the tendency for European North American children to hear double negatives and the like as "mistakes," explaining that Standard American English sounds funny in many ways to people from Great Britain. Emphasize that there are many kinds of English, that we can all understand each other, and that all the different dialects of English have their place and usefulness and beauty. Encourage children to write a story that prominently features quotes from their relatives in the child's home dialect, whatever that might be.

box continues

Box 7: Research Into Practice—cont'd

6. Another story that weaves Black English Vernacular and Standard English together is *Irene and the Big, Fine Nickel* by Irene Smalls-Hector, available from Little, Brown. This story, which involves teasing games played by African American children, might be a good vehicle for discussing how when you play a teasing game you don't mean to hurt someone's feelings, but you might do so anyway. Ask children to name all the teasing games they can think of and talk about times they have hurt others or been hurt by others when teasing. Have them notice the strategy the girls in the story use to make up, and discuss ways they make up with their friends when feelings have been hurt.

7. Read *The Dancing Granny* (Aladdin) and *The Cat's Purr* (Atheneum) by Ashley Bryan. Both of these stories employ onomatopoeia and recurring refrains throughout in such a way that the story becomes a sort of spoken song. Encourage the children to think of catchy nonsense refrains like Bryan's Pom-pa-lom and Pit-tap-a-la-pat and spin their own made-up stories around these refrains.

8. A story with an especially haunting refrain is *Follow the Drinking Gourd* by Jeanette Winter (Dragonfly/Knopf). The title is the refrain, and this refrain is what leads a family from slavery to freedom. This story should be prefaced with a discussion of the history of slavery in this country, as well as an explanation of the Big Dipper constellation.

9. Read *Aunt Flossie's Hats* by Elizabeth Fitzgerald Howard (Clarion) and point out how the author wove together several different stories about various experiences that happened to the grandmother by using the device of her various hats. Ask children to write stories combining several experiences, either factual or fictional, together in one story. Highlight use of refrains again, such as Howard's "Big fire/parade in Baltimore," and see if children can come up with one for their revised versions. Look for a refrain that would unite the different experiences as a sort of recurring punch line. Assume there is a link and that the children can tell you what it is.

The kind of links children use may vary considerably. Links of obviously similar experiences, links of less obviously similar experiences, or links between experiences and background information: all these are possible ways of developing a narrative through improvisation and would lead to rather different punch lines. In all these cases and with children of all backgrounds doing this exercise, encourage them to tell the story the way they feel is right on their first round. On a second round, *in conferences* make the connections between the parts of their stories more explicit. This should not come across as correction, but rather as an extension of the child's own ideas and form.

10. Read *Tar Beach* by Faith Ringgold (Crown). Point out the narrator's use of her imagination to wish for all kinds of things. Point out how the author uses metaphors such as "eyes like huge floodlights" and comparison of the lighted George Washington Bridge to a "giant diamond necklace." Ask children why

box continues

Box 7: Research Into Practice—cont'd

the author compared eyes and floodlights, lights and diamonds. Point out similarities and differences between objects compared. Also be sure to point out the way that the metaphorical terms fit in with the large issues of the book. Ask children what they think *Tar Beach* means metaphorically. Do not be afraid that children are too young to understand metaphors. Children have themselves been producing metaphors since they were about three years old, and are quite capable of talking about metaphors at least by first grade.

11. *Coconut Kind of Day: Island Poems* by Lyn Joseph (Puffin) contains many story poems displaying a number of features we have discussed: stanza format, use of Trinidad dialect, onomatopoeia, and refrains such as "Coconut" in the title poem, which in that poem introduces stanzas.

12. Read *Amazing Grace* by Mary Hoffman (Dial). Sing or listen to the famous song of the same name. Recall the Anasi the Spider stories, as well as other stories alluded to in this book. Ask the class to write a personal narrative about one time they were left out of a social situation, and to describe how they felt, how the situation was resolved, and how they wish it had been resolved. Link to Martin Luther King day a discussion of incidents in his life. Ask adults who are members of the African American community to tell about times they were discriminated against. Even preschool children can participate in this kind of exercise, but it works for much older children as well. If the person in question is well known to them,

so much the better. This type of exercise might well set the theme for a unit: *Outrage but hope.* Everyone has a place and will not be left out.

13. Coordinate with music teachers in instructing children how to sing African songs, such as Uyadela (You are arrogant), which tells a myth about the rock rabbit who has no tail (Makeba, 1971, p. 88). Another song from the Makeba collection that would be appropriate for children is Olilili (Lullaby), which also tells a story in song.

14. Listen to a recording of John Coltrane's "My Favorite Things," which exhibits the returning theme and improvisation form in musical composition. Discuss the issue of beginning and ending with a theme. For older children (fourth grade and up), link this issue to expository forms.

15. Look at African American artwork such as William H. Johnson's homecoming series, in which you can find a blend of art with a jazz aesthetic. Fourth, fifth, and sixth graders could tell stories about coming back home after a long absence, focusing on specific details that struck them most. Ask children to describe a family member's appearance (for example, your mother's hands are larger or smaller than you remember them being). Which community people were you glad to see? The mailman, grocer, librarian? When you come home, what do you think of? Who greets you? Who do you see? What is your favorite furniture, pet, cooking smell? *Children of promise* is an excellent teacher's reference for this activity.

Summary

- It has been a valued African American tradition to tell dramatic, lengthy stories that embellish facts in the interest of creative expression.
- African American children often tell stories that are structured in the classic highpoint fashion typical also of European North American children.
- Some African American children occasionally tell remarkably lengthy *performative* stories that improvise explicitly or implicitly on a theme.
- Teasing, metaphor, alliteration, rhyme, refrains, and other poetic devices are common in the written and oral narratives and stories of African American children.
- Storytelling forms used by children in the African American community are linked to various musical traditions, dance, and visual art forms also from that community, as well as to published works of fiction and nonfiction by African American writers.
- Issues pertaining to the way that educators address Black English Vernacular are separable from issues of the distinctive performative narratives described above.

References

BERLINER, P. (1990). Learning and creativity in minority communities: A case study of jazz improvisers. *The Spencer Foundation Newsletter, 5* (2), 2–3.

CAMPBELL, B.M. (1992). *Your blues ain't like mine.* New York: G.P. Putnam's Sons.

CHAMPION, T.B. (1994). "A description of narrative production and development in child speakers of African American English." Unpublished doctoral dissertation, The University of Massachusetts Amherst, Amherst, MA.

COLEMAN, LARRY G., COSBY, BILL, & POUSSAINT, ALVIN. (1989). Storytelling and comic performance. In L. Goss & M.E. Barnes (Eds.), *Talk that talk* (pp. 431–434). New York: Simon & Schuster/Touchstone.

CRADDOCK-WILLIS, K. (1990). "African American children's narrative." Unpublished manuscript, Harvard University, Cambridge, MA.

DAUBNEY-DAVIS, A. (1991, October). "Narrative structure and style in the writing of Mexican- and African-American young adolescents." Paper presented at the 16th annual Boston University Conference on Language Development, Boston, MA.

DELPIT, L.D. (1988). The silenced dialogue: Power and pedagogy in educating other people's children. *Harvard Educational Review, 58*(3), 280–298.

GATES, H.L. (1988). *The signifying monkey.* Oxford England: Oxford University Press.

GEE, J.P. (1991a). Memory and myth. In A. McCabe & C. Peterson (Eds.), *Developing narrative structure,* (pp. 1–26). Hillsdale, NJ: Erlbaum.

GEE, J.P. (1991b). A linguistic approach to narrative. *Journal of Narrative and Life History, 1* (1), 15–40.

HURSTON, Z.N. (1935–1990). *Mules and men.* New York: Harper & Row.

Hymes, D. (1982). Narrative form as a "grammar" of experience: Native Americans and a glimpse of English. *Journal of Education, 2,* 121–142.

HYON, S., & SULZBY, E. (1992). "Black kindergartners' spoken narratives: Style, structure and task." Paper presented at the Annual Meeting of the American Educational Research Association. San Francisco, CA.

LABOV, W. (1972). *Language in the Inner City.* Philadelphia, PA: University of Pennsylvania Press.

MAKEBA, M. (1970). *The world of African song.* Chicago: Quadrangle Books.

MALAN, K. (1992, October). "Structure and coherence in South African children's personal narratives." Paper presented at the 17th annual Boston University Conference on Language Development, Boston, MA.

MARSALIS, W. (July 22, 1994). Remarks made in *The Berkshire Eagle, vol. 103* (84).

MICHAELS, S., & FOSTER, M. (1985). Peer-peer learning: Evidence from a kid-run sharing time. In A. Jaggan & M. Smith-Burke (Eds.), *Kid watching: Observing the language learner* (pp. 143–158). International Reading Association, National Council of Teachers of English.

MICHAELS, S. (1991). The dismantling of narrative. In A. McCabe & C. Peterson (Eds.), *Developing narrative structure.* Hillsdale, NJ: Erlbaum.

MILLER, P.J., POTTS, R., & FUNG, H. (1989, March). *Minority perspectives on narrative development.* Paper presented at the annual meeting of the American Educational Research Association, San Francisco, CA.

MILLER, P.J., POTTS, R., FUNG, H., HOOGSTRA, L., & MINTZ, J. (1990). Narrative practices and the social construction of self. *American Ethnologist, 17* (2), 292–311.

MORRISON, T. (1977). *Song of Solomon.* New York: Knopf.

MORRISON, T. (1987). *Beloved.* New York: Knopf.

MORRISON, T. (1992). *Jazz.* New York: Knopf.

MORRISON, T. (1992). *Playing in the dark: Whiteness and the literary imagination.* Cambridge, MA: Harvard University Press.

NELSON, L. (1990). "Code-switching in the narrative discourse of African American women." Paper presented at the 15th annual Boston University Conference on Language Development, Boston, MA.

POLLIO, H.R., BARLOW, J.M., FINE, H.J., & POLLIO, M.R. (1977). *Psychology and the poetics of growth.* New York: Wiley & Sons.

RODINO, A.M., GIMBERT, C., PEREZ, C., CRADDOCK-WILLIS, K., & MCCABE, A. (1991, October). "'Getting your point across': Contrastive sequencing in low-income African-American and Latino children's personal narratives." Paper presented at the 16th annual Boston University Conference on Language Development, Boston, MA.

CHAPTER 7

Vignettes of the Continuous and Family Ties: Some Latino American Traditions

Margarita Jimenez Silva
and
Allyssa McCabe

OVERVIEW

Latino is a term used to refer to numerous groups of Spanish-speaking individuals, as well as many English-speaking individuals from Spanish backgrounds. Latinos are nonetheless a group—the fastest-growing immigrant group in America. Over the years, Latinos have not achieved sufficient success in educational settings, and we theorize that this is due in part to a mismatch of educational instruction to the skills children bring with them from home. In particular, we focus on Latino narratives, which show some important differences from the kind of narrative practiced and valued by European North Americans. Latino children from various backgrounds and in various genres of narrative tend to de-emphasize action in favor of evaluation and description. Description often centers around various extended family members. Overlapping talk, rather than distinct turn-taking, is practiced among many Latino children. Relationships to other art forms and implications for instruction are addressed.

SOME LATINO STORYTELLING TRADITIONS

The first author of this chapter is Mexican American. Both of her parents were born and raised in Mexico and immigrated to the United States before she was born. She was reared in a very traditional Mexican home, and her family spent most summer vacations visiting relatives in Mexico. Her first language was

Spanish, and to this day, her parents discourage English from being spoken in their home. Additionally, while in college, she had the opportunity to study the school systems in Mexico as part of a student exchange program. Thus, although we will address storytelling among various Latinos, we feel most qualified to speak about the Mexican and Mexican American communities. Many of the examples in this chapter come from Mexican and Mexican American individuals.

Historical Background

Although Earl Shorris wrote a book entitled *Latinos*, "the theory of it [was] that there are no Latinos, only diverse peoples struggling to remain who they are while becoming someone else (p. 12)." "Just tell them who we are and that we are not all alike" (Shorris, p. xv), says one of the people he interviews. As with other groups, there is great diversity among Latinos. Also, as with other groups, we will consider commonalities to be found amid such diversity. According to Shorris (1992), two-thirds of Latinos in the United States are of Mexican descent. While some are here temporarily, others have been here for generations.

While we have adopted the label *Latino* for the purpose of bringing coherence to our discussion, it is a label no child would identify with. Children will refer to their heritage as Mexican, Puerto Rican, Cuban, Guatemalan, El Salvadorian, Chilean. Even these labels are too broad: Children from Mexican backgrounds can identify themselves as Mexican, Mexican American, Chicano, MexiRican, and so forth. All of the ethnic groups just mentioned are very diverse groups within themselves. In other words, when we speak of Latinos, we are using an umbrella term that refers to many diverse groups, each with its own culture, history, and values.

Latinos are the fastest growing U.S. immigrant group (Marger, 1994). In less than 40 years, approximately one in five youths will be Latino (Duany & Pittman, 1990). Thus, educators will increasingly be faced with the issues of diversity posed by this group. Because so many Americans speak Spanish, we will include the original Spanish version of the narratives in this chapter.

While 83.4 percent of European North Americans and 82 percent of African Americans over the age of 25 graduated from high school by 1992, only 52.6 percent of Latinos did so. Among Latino groups, Mexicans are the most at risk for dropping out of high school: Only 45.2 percent of Mexican American individuals graduated in this time period (Marger, 1994, pp. 256, 305). While Mexican Americans have the highest secondary school dropout rates (54.7 percent) of all Latinos, Puerto Ricans (46 percent) and Cubans (37 percent) are also at risk. In addition, 17.6 percent of Latinos aged 25 and older have fewer than five years of formal education as compared to 12.7 percent of non-Latinos (Marin & Marin, 1991). Hispanics aged 14 to 19 are half as likely as non-Hispanics to complete high school (Suarez-Orozco, 1987). In the Southwest, only 60.3 percent of Mexican American youths graduate from high school, compared to 86 percent of European North Americans (Suarez-Orozco, 1987).

Dropout rates are only one symptom of the larger problem plaguing Latino students. In terms of academic achievement, Latinos trail behind not only

European North American students in the United States, but also the Asian, Jewish, and African American populations. All these grim statistics underline the importance of focusing attention on traditions such children bring to school, in order to engage them in academic tasks.

Many different theories have arisen over the years which attempt to address the problem of academic underachievement among Latinos (Erikson, 1987). Children whose first language is not English fail to succeed at school in part because poverty, which too often accompanies that status, depresses children's health, motivation, intelligence and language (Wood, 1988). Although we agree that a broad sociopolitical structure at times prevents students from reaching their full potential (Wood, 1988), we believe that one of the most important ways we can help Latino students takes place in the classroom. We propose that encouraging students to tell their stories in their own words and encouraging teachers to make use of personal narratives in their curriculum can make a difference.

Spanishes. The kind of Spanish children are comfortable with depends on which particular subgroup they are from. That is, just as there are many groups under the umbrella term of *Latino,* there are also many variations of Spanish under the umbrella term of *Spanish.* This is an issue that is not always addressed in educational settings. However, it is a discussion that must take place if we are truly interested in being culturally sensitive. The Spanish spoken in Mexico is different from the Spanish spoken in Guatemala and the Spanish spoken in Peru. Furthermore, the Spanish spoken in Mexico is different from the Spanish spoken by Chicanos in Los Angeles, California, and both are different from the Spanish spoken in Boston, Massachusetts.

The difference in dialects of Spanish results in potential misunderstanding, some humorous. For example, one South American woman was listening to a group of Spanish-speaking women from Puerto Rico talk about catching a wa-wa and boarding a wa-wa. In her variation of Spanish, a wa-wa usually refers to a baby, so she was left wondering why these women would like to catch or board a baby. Only later did she realize that Puerto Rican Spanish uses wa-wa (*guagua*) to refer to a bus. Although this misunderstanding was harmless, other instances may lead to hurt feelings or confusion. Among all of the Spanishes there are more similarities than differences, but variations do exist.

With this issue of variations of Spanish comes problems of prestige in language. Just as certain discourse styles are valued in our schools over others, it appears that certain variations of Spanish are also valued over others, even in bilingual classrooms. Therefore, we should be careful not to judge one form of Spanish as more "correct" or "better" than any other form. This too is part of the complex set of issues underlying the aforementioned staggering statistics.

Storytelling Practices in Community

One of the problems mentioned by many educators who are interested in multicultural literature is the lack of books that feature authentic Latino characters and experiences. In particular, the Mexican American community is one cultural group that has long been slighted by the world of children's book publishing (Barrera, Liguori, & Salas, 1992). However, all Latino groups seem to be underrepresented in quality multicultural literature. Despite our attempts to collect Latino literature for years in Puerto Rico, Mexico, and the United States, both authors only have small collections of authentic stories.

Many of the books that are available to both educators and the general public are merely Spanish translations of popular books in English. On a recent trip to Mexico, for example, the first author decided to browse in bookstores, hoping to find books featuring Mexican characters with authentic experiences. Unfortunately, what she found for school-aged children were Sesame Street and Ninja Turtle books.

Even more surprising was the price of the books. A simple paperback Ninja Turtle book that could be purchased in a U.S. supermarket for no more than a few dollars was priced the equivalent of seven dollars. This was the case in many bookstores in several cities. One community visited had an average household income of $200 per month. Spending money on books was seen as an unattainable luxury. According to the 1980 Census, only 6 percent of Mexicans buy books, mostly due to the expense (Oster, 1989). While observing in several schools, numerous teachers requested that the author send them any books in Spanish discarded by schools in the United States. They confirmed our conclusion that finding quality multicultural children's literature was difficult and very expensive.

Literature in general does not appear to be present in great quantities in most Latino homes in the United States. This may be due in part to the belief that books in the United States will be as expensive as books are in Mexico.

Although literature is scarce, oral storytelling plays an important role in the daily lives of Latinos, although even this shows some cultural distinction. While in other cultures exchanging personal narratives occurs at dinner time (Blum-Kulka & Snow, 1992), this does not commonly occur at Mexican American dinner tables. In many traditional working-class homes, dinner may still be served first to the men and boys in the family, while the women and girls attend to the food. Many times the women and girls will eat dinner after the men have finished or towards the end of the men's meal.

In addition, the table is often viewed as a place where children should be seen and not heard. Obviously, in such situations, conversations between adults and children about their daily experiences is not common. A frequent expression directed at children in some traditional Mexican homes is "en la mesa no se habla," which means "you should not talk at the table." We stress the word "traditional" and acknowledge that this is not the case in all Mexican homes.

Much of the storytelling in Latino homes takes place during food preparation. One of the clearest examples of this happens around Christmas-time when tamales are prepared. This is an event in which several generations of a family work together at the huge task of making tamales. Grandmothers, daughters, and granddaughters stand or sit side by side with tubs of ingredients which will take all day to prepare and assemble.

During this lengthy preparation time, many stories are exchanged. It is a time when stories about births, adventures, "the old days," dreams, and disappointments are told. During tamale-making, the first author learned about how her grandparents courted, why her parents decided to leave Mexico, and how and why her birth name was chosen. Everyone is given an opportunity to tell stories at this time—even the youngest members of the family. The following is an excerpt from a tamale-making narrative, which sheds light on the author's uncle's adventures as a child, as told by her grandmother:

> Nosotros teníamos unos vecinos que estaban bien acomodados y pues ellos tenían una televisión en blanco y negro. Luisito era niño único y pues invitaban a él Toto a jugar y a ver el programa de El Llanero Solitario que estaba de moda. Luisito tenía un rifle de municiones y muchos otros juguetes que tus tíos no tenían. Pues estaban viendo el programa de El Llanero Solitario y tu tío estaba viendo el rifle. Y cuando estaba viendo el rifle vio él la televisión que los malos iban a matar al Llanero Solitario y que el Tonto no llegaba y pues tu tío le dío al malo con el rifle y quebró la pantalla de la televisión. Nosotros no teníamos el dinero para pagarles la televisión pero si fui a pedirle discuplas a la señora.

> Translation: We had some neighbors who were well off and, well, they had a black and white television. Luisito was an only child and so they invited Toto over to play and to watch the popular Lone Ranger show. Luisito had a B.B. gun and a lot of other toys that your uncles didn't have. Well they were watching the Lone Ranger program and your uncle was looking at the gun. And when he was looking at the gun he saw on the television that the bad guys were going to kill the Lone Ranger and that Tonto had not arrived, and, well, your uncle shot at the bad guys with the rifle and broke the television screen. We didn't have money to pay for the television, but I went and apologized to the woman.

Another storytelling event centers around religious stories. Many older members of Latino families who may never have learned English have few reading materials in the home other than a Bible and religious tracts in Spanish. They may use stories from the Bible to read to children at bedtime or other times during the day. A commonly observed practice for "curing nightmares" has been to read children stories from the Bible until they fall asleep.

While Bible stories can be used to soothe fears, other stories are told to instill fear or to discipline children. Mexican parents often use short stories to warn their children about possible consequences of misbehaving (Valdez, 1994). For example, one mother stressed the importance of brushing teeth by telling the following story to her child:

> Yo conocía a una niña que nunca se lavaba los dientes y un día se levantó y se le habían caido todos los dientes y ya no le volvieron a salir. Translation: "I knew a girl who never brushed her teeth and one day she got up and all of her teeth had fallen out and they never grew out again.

Another example of using stories to warn children is the common story of "La Llorona," literally, "The Weeper." The most popular version of the story is that La Llorona is the ghost of a woman who killed her children and threw them into a river. She is now said to walk the streets at night weeping for them.

The story of the Weeper seems to be adapted to the situation at hand. One version told to a misbehaving child added that La Llorona is looking for children to replace the ones she lost and that if he continued misbehaving, the parents would give him to her. A different version told to a group of children at a park playing too close to a well was that La Llorona lives in the water and that she drowns children who are too close to the water by pulling them into the well.

The first author overheard another version told to a newly married woman who had discussed the merits of postponing children for a few years. An older woman told the younger woman that she should not forget the story of La Llorona. The reason that La Llorona wept so much was that she had had an abortion and now her conscience would never allow her peace. Adaptations of the story of La Llorona seem to be used even with adults.

Exemplary Mother-Child Interaction

In the following transcript a $3^1/_2$-year-old child is being socialized into the Halloween "trick-or-treat" routine and, in the process, is asked extensively about family relationships. Such conversation, as has been mentioned repeatedly throughout this book, is the cradle of monologues.

MONICA: Trick or treat.
MOTHER: ¿Quién va ir contigo?
    [Who is going to go with you?]
MONICA: (points at Abel, a son who is holding a camera)
MOTHER: ¿Quién es él? ¿Quién es él?
    [Who is he? Who is he?]
MONICA: (Points to Abel and mouths ñoño [= Junior])
MOTHER: ¿Que no sabes hablar?
    [Don't you know how to speak?]
MONICA: (nods yes)
MOTHER: A ver, ¿quién es él?
    [Let's see, who is he?]
MONICA: ñoño [= Junior]
MOTHER: ¿Sí? Cuántos hermanos tienes?
    [Yes? How many siblings do you have?]
MONICA: (Mouthing words)
MOTHER: No, no. Recio por que no oigo.
    [No, no. Loud because I can't hear.]
MOTHER: ¿Cuántos hermanos tienes?
    [How many siblings do you have?]
MONICA: Haci
    Like this. (holds out three fingers)
MOTHER: ¿Cómo se llaman?
    [What are their names?]

MONICA: Una Ruti, una Noma [= Norma], una Magaita [= Margarita]
    [One Ruti, one Noma [= Norma], one Magaita [= Margarita]

MOTHER: ¡Oh! ¿Cómo se llama lo que te compró Margarita?
    [Oh, what do you call what Margarita bought you?]

MOTHER: ¿Qué? ¿Una qué?
    [What? A what]

MONICA: Una cota [= cosa]
    [A thing.]

MOTHER: ¿Una calabaza?
    [A pumpkin?]

MONICA: (nods yes)

MOTHER: ¿Cómo se llama?
    [What is it called?]

MONICA: Cabayasa
    [Pumpkin]

MOTHER: Recio, no oigo.
    [Loud, I can't hear]

MONICA: Cabayasa.
    [Pumpkin]

MOTHER: Sí. Haber baila.
    [Yes. Let's see, dance.]

MOTHER: Cerquitas que se le mire su cara y su . . .
    [Close up so that we can see her face and . . .]

MOTHER: ¿Cómo vas a ir a decir en la noche?
    [What are you going to say tonight?]

MONICA: Trick or Treat.
    [Trick or Treat.]

MOTHER: ¿Sí?
    [Yes?]

MONICA: (singing)

MOTHER: ¿Cómo baila Azucena? (Azucena is a first cousin.)
    [How does Azucena dance?]

MONICA: La colita mueve.
    [She moves the behind.]

MOTHER: ¿Haber, cómo?
    [Let's see how?]

MONICA: Colita, la colita mueve.
    [The behind, the behind she moves]

MOTHER: Sí.
    [Yes.]

MOTHER: ¿Y tu Abuelita Lencha cómo baila?
    [And your grandmother Lencha dances how?]

MONICA: Baila.
    [Dances.]

MOTHER: ¿Así baila?
    [She dances like that?]

MONICA: No, baila así.
    [No, she dances like this.]

MOTHER: ¿Así baila?
    [She dances like that?]

MOTHER: ¿Y tú cómo bailas?
[And how do you dance?]
MONICA: Bailo así
[I dance like this.]
MOTHER: Así. ¿Cómo se llama tu papá?
[Like this. What is your father's name?]
MONICA: Se llama Abel.
[His name is Abel.]
MOTHER: ¿Cómo?
[What?]
MONICA: Abel.
[Abel.]
MOTHER: ¿Abel? ¿Y tu mamá?
[Abel? And your mother?]
MONICA: Se llama Abuelita Lencha.
[Her name is Grandmother Lencha.]
MOTHER: ¿Y tu otra abuelita?
[And your other grandmother?]
MONICA: Se llama Abuelita Juanita.
[Her name is Grandmother Juanita.]
MOTHER: ¿Y tu abuelito como se llama?
[And what is your grandfather's name?]
MONICA: Ah, abuelito.
[Ah, grandfather.]
MOTHER: ¿Y quién es tu amigo?
[And who is your friend?]
MONICA: ¿Román (a first cousin).
[Román.]
MOTHER: ¿Román?
[Román?]
MONICA: ¿Sí?
[Yes.]
MOTHER: ¿Sí?
[Yes.]
MONICA: Sí.
[Yes.]
MOTHER: ¿Quien vino en el sábado,? tus primas; ¿como se llaman las primas
que vinieron el sábado, las bebitas?
[Who came over Saturday, your cousins, what are the names of your
cousins that come on Saturday, the babies?]
MONICA: ¿Cuales? Liliana, Nora, Ano [= Alejandro]?
[Which? Liliana, Nora. Ano?]
MOTHER: Sí.
[Yes.]
MOTHER: ¿Te gustan las bebitas chiquitas? ¿Sí?
[Do you like the little babies? Yes?]
MONICA: (lunges forward)

As we will see, Latino children's narratives seem to highlight family relationships. In such exchanges as the one above, the child is being socialized into

the importance of relationships and their place in narratives. How specific members are related to the child appears to be the main focus of the talk, which is quite typical for this family.

Other Scholarly Treatments

Each individual possesses a diverse fund of knowledge that is used in creating and interpreting stories (Moll, Amanti, Neff and Gonzalez, 1992). This fund exists both at an individual level and at a community level, and both levels can be tapped to help students in general and Mexican American students in particular arrive at a broader and perhaps more inclusive understanding of the world. If you listen to Latino children's stories in different contexts, you will hear how this fund of knowledge is naturally exploited. In working with young children, it has often been our experience that as soon as one child tells a story, another child is anxious to share a similar story with the class.

Unfortunately, sometimes children's families have ideas about what constitutes effective language use that diverge from those practiced in schools (Dyson, 1993). As Moll et al. (1992) have written, teachers need to serve as bridges between home and school for such children. Of most relevance to the present line of argument is some evidence that Spanish-speaking children have a different sense of what constitutes a good story from English-speaking children in the United States.

Gutierrez-Clellen (Gutierrez-Clellen & Quinn, 1993) reports that Puerto Rican children's stories of personal experiences are generally a chronology of action routines with no evaluations or resolutions. These children include abstracts and evaluations only for topics they feel are worth telling about. If they are asked to retell a movie, however, Spanish-speaking children tend to give more detail than they do in recounting personal experiences (Iglesias, Gutierrez-Clellen, & Marcano, 1986, cited in Gutierrez-Clellen & Iglesias, 1992). In movie retellings, Spanish-speaking children tend to include more narrative actions and more information about mental states or goals at the age of 8 than they do during their preschool years (Gutierrez-Clellen & Iglesias, 1992).

Narratives of diverse kinds—both in terms of genre and in terms of form—need to be accepted in the academic world (Rosen, 1985). If the culture of Latino children is allowed to enter into the culture of the school, and it should be, then that culture's stories must come too, and Latino oral story-telling traditions must be acknowledged as legitimate forms of meaning making (Rosen, 1985). Traditionally there has been almost no consideration given to narrative as a linguistic form that can provide continuity between home and school uses of language (Scott, 1990), a situation this book seeks to redress.

Features of Latino Narration

Very little research addresses the characteristics of Latino narratives. Few studies have focused on Latino narratives in general, and even fewer have focused on any one group of Latinos. Nevertheless, the research which has taken place suggests that Latino narratives in general do seem to differ from the narratives of other cultural groups in some important ways.

One characteristic of Latino narratives is a de-emphasis on sequencing events (Rodino et al., 1991). Unlike children from European North American, Japanese, and African American cultures, many Latino children do not seem to follow a linear model when producing narratives. Rodino et al. (1991) found that 7-year-old Spanish-speaking children had more one-event and fewer two- and three-event narratives than English-speaking children. Spanish-speakers had lower proportions of complicating actions (for example, "I swam.") than did English-speaking children of comparable age. By some standards, the 49 percent of Latino narratives that contained no action sequences would not even be defined as narratives. For example, Labov and his colleagues (1968, p. 287) defined narrative as "one method of recapitulating past experience by matching a verbal sequence of clauses to the sequence of events which (it is inferred) actually occurred." The second author of this book and her colleagues (Rodino et al., 1990) took a different position, which was that the working definition of narrative needed to be adjusted to recognize the validity of the productions of the children they were studying. The children's productions sounded like narrative, were about past events in some general sense, involved extensive self-representation, and in these and many other ways seemed genuine narratives.

Differences in the use of particular verb tenses may exist between Spanish-dominant and English-dominant children and could account for what strikes European North American ears as a de-emphasis on sequencing. The extensive use of the progressive verb tense in Spanish narratives ("¿y en dónde estabas brincando? = and where were you jumping?") was noted by Wong Fillmore (1976). In English, a person would often use verbs of motion such as walk, run, and slide. In Spanish, however, a person would be more likely to use "andando" (walking), "corriendo" (running), and "resbalando" (sliding).

Sebastian and Slobin (1994) studied the way in which children and adults from Spain, Chile, and Argentina told a story in response to a wordless picture book. Those researchers found that 3-, 4-, and 5-year-old children oscillated between the past and present tense in this kind of narrative, but 9-year-olds and adults in all three countries nearly always *picked the present tense as the dominant tense.* That is, the present, not the past, tense seems to be the prototypical verb form for telling a story in Spanish. Those researchers also noted a tendency, especially pronounced for preschool-aged children, to use the progressive tense in this kind of narrative. The progressive tense is usually used to indicate ongoing activity (for example, "They were sleeping . . . "), but in Spanish, unlike English, less enduring actions can also be encoded as progressives by using particular auxiliaries for that purpose ("Estaban durmiendo y la rana calladita se iba escapando del frasco." Translation: "(they) were sleeping and the frog very quietly went escaping from the jar," Sebastian & Slobin, 1994, p. 248). In short, both a difference in the way verb tenses are configured in Spanish and a distinct preference for present and progressive, as opposed to simple past, tenses in narrative underlie this tendency to downplay event sequencing in Spanish storytelling.

In our own work on Latino narratives, we have observed that personal narratives in Spanish do seem to use more habitual action verbs as opposed to verbs in simple past tense. The following story was told by a 7-year-old Mexican American child. It exemplifies the prevalent use of habitual action (progressive) verbs:

> Una vez yo estaba viendo tele y vino y mí um me estaba agarrando la mano así y me dolió mucho y tenía aquí la marca y me estaba doliendo mucho. Translation: One time I *was watching* television and [he] came and my um he *was grabbing* my hand like this and it hurt a lot and I had a mark here and it *was hurting* me a lot.

In this narrative, the child used the habitual action form several times as opposed to using simple past tense verbs.

Unfortunately, this de-emphasis of sequenced events is often misinterpreted as some kind of deficiency. Teachers may have a tendency to dismiss narratives with few actions as "not really narratives." Teachers have commented that Latino children "seem to go off on tangents" when they tell a story. Moreover, such misunderstandings are not confined to children's productions. While tutoring several non-Latino students for a Latino literature course, the first author heard these students complain about all the "jumping around" in novels written by Latino authors.

Another characteristic of Latino narratives appears to be an emphasis on description. Rodino et al. (1991) and Cano (1993) found that Latino children used more orientation clauses than reported by Peterson and McCabe (1983) for European North American children. Both also reported that Spanish-dominant children included more evaluation than English-dominant Latino children, who in turn included more purely evaluative sentences than European North American children. Consider the following story about a bee sting, one that includes actions only as a backdrop, focusing instead on description and evaluation:

> Well I was going to step on a bee. Then when she saw, when the bee saw a shadow, she went flying. And she then she went EEAroh! And it hurted me a lot. Then it hurt me a lot.

Description often centers around family relations in Latino children's stories. Latino children tend to include many family members and friends as characters in their stories, no matter how slight the role assigned to a character. Teachers often see this flood of names and characters as distracting from the main story line. However, this emphasis on family may reflect a general value of the family in Latino culture, played out in part by means of many conversations like the one between Monica and her mother above. It could also reflect a need for support from extended family members in a society in which they may not feel completely accepted.

In her study of Latino children's journals, de la Luz Reyes (1991) found four common topics. In order of importance these topics were: (1) nuclear and extended family; (2) culturally specific object, event, or place; (3) personal interactions with teachers; and (4) school-related incidents. She also found that students were able to write longer, more detailed entries when the topic centered around their families or was culturally relevant. Many of the entries initiated by students related events or incidents about family members and included feelings and opinions.

While living in Cambridge from 1991 to 1993, the first author ran a mentoring program for Latina sixth-, seventh-, and eighth-graders who had been identified as "at-risk" for dropping out of school. We met once a week and discussed both cultural and academic topics. We kept dialogue journals, and the results of those journals were very similar to those found by de la Luz Reyes. Entries containing references to family members were longer and more detailed, as well as more readily shared among the girls.

In a bilingual second-grade classroom the first author recently observed in Southern California, children were asked to write and draw a picture about anything they wanted to share. Many of the stories, which were written in Spanish, incorporated family members. Because of their age, however, the stories themselves were often only three lines long. The following are examples of stories written by these students:

Story 1: Yo fuí al parque porque era el cumpleaños de mi prima y quebramos una piñata. Translation: I went to the park because it was my cousin's birthday and we broke a pinata.

Story 2: Mi papá me llevó al rio y nadé. Mis tíos vinieron tambíen. Translation: My father took me to the river and I swam. My uncles came too.

Story 3: Mi papá nos llevó a una fiesta con mi tía, y mi tía nos llevó al parque y nosotros jugamos. Translation: My father took us to a party at my aunt's, and my aunt took us to the park and we played.

Story 4: Ayer fuí al parque y jugue la pelota bien mucho. Despues fuí con mis abuelitos. Translation: Yesterday I went to the park and played a lot with the ball. Then I went to my grandparents'.

Story 5: Mi tío nos llevó Aguascalientes a mí y a mi familia en México. No echamos [= hechamos] marometas en el agua. Translation: My uncle took me and my family to Aguascalientes in Mexico. We did somersaults in the water.

In a bilingual third-grade classroom in Southern California, the prevalence in stories both of family relations and descriptive details was evident. Students in the classroom had been studying dinosaurs for several weeks. On the chalkboard were words such as "paleontologist" and "fossils," which they were asked to use in a story. In the following stories, we see that despite the constraint of having to incorporate specific and unrelated vocabulary into a story, many students nevertheless structured their stories in ways that emphasized family relations and description, especially of the fossils. (Vocabulary words, originally in Spanish, are underlined in the excerpts and translations that follow.)

Story 1: Los antiólogos [= paleontólogos] descubrieron fósiles en la tierra de la casa de mi tío proque yo me tropezé con los fósiles y mi papá escarbó y vio que era fósiles gruesos y de color amarillos y los pusimos en una caja de zapatos y los llevamos a un geólogo y a un antéologo [= paleóntologo] y yo les pregunté al geólogo y me dijo que eran fósiles de dinosaurios. Translation: The paleontologists found some fossils on the land of my uncle's house and I tripped over the fossils and my father digged and saw that the fossils were thick and yellow colored and we put them in a shoe box and we took them to a geologist and a paleontologist and I asked the geologist and he told me that they were dinosaur fossils.

Story 2: Un dia yo y mi hermano estábamos en la casa de mis abuelitos y estábamos jugando atrás de la yarda y de un derrepente nos dió ganas de escarbar y escarbamos hasta que hayamos huesos de dinosauros y el hueso era blanco y muy livianito y yo y mi hermano decidímos empacarlo y mis abuelitos nos llevaron a ver los palenteólogos [= paleontólogo] y los geólogos lo revisaron y para que el fósil lo lleve al museo. Translation: One day me and my brother were at my grandparent's house and we were playing in the yard behind and all of a sudden we felt like digging and we dug until we found dinosaur bones and the bone was white and very light and me and my brother decided to pack it and my grandparents took us to see the paleontologists and the geologists examined them so that they could take the fossil to the museum.

Latino children's emphasis on description in the oral narratives they produce reflects the preferences of adults in their communities. In the conversation between Monica and her mother about trick-or-treating, exact names and family relations were elicited, along with the characteristics of those family members. Professionals from Mexican or Mexican American backgrounds often draw on this cultural value in formal instructional practice. For example, a teacher's aide in California who had been a teacher in Mexico said that she always emphasized details in her students' writing. The example she cited was a story about a child walking down a path to see his grandmother. If the child mentioned seeing a cow on the way to the house, she said she would want details about what that cow looked like, what it was doing, and perhaps even who it belonged to in the community. We suspect that a child spending much time on detailing the condition and ownership of the cow might be interpreted by some as not "sticking to the plot."

A comment made by a Mexican parent at an American school district parents' meeting also seems to articulate conflicting values of description when telling narratives. When she had started to speak about an experience she recently had, she was constantly cut off by the board members and asked to speak only to what she knew well. She was seen as an expert in parenting and only that. She had wanted to explain her background as a nurse and her experiences of schooling in Mexico. However, she was told by several of the district leaders that she should stick to the point she wanted to make. What may seem "logical" and "straightforward" to European North Americans, for example, may be seen as "constricting" and too "narrow" to Latinos. The parent commented later that she felt American culture valued "specialities" too much.

Narratives of children from Central American and Caribbean backgrounds also foreground orientation and evaluation rather than action sequences, using family ties to provide cohesion in narratives (Rodino et al., 1991). The following is a translated excerpt from one such child, Carmen, a 7-year-old girl from El Salvador (the full narrative took about five minutes):

> Well I (was) in the hospital, in the Mass General Hospital—there where my Uncle Roberto works. That he has two children who are not twins but who are only two children because first Robertico was born, who is named after his dad, and then Christopher was born . . . But my Uncle Roberto have a dog who is one of those German ones, who is already two months old. And now, because the mom's name is Butterfly. She is with a man whose name is, who is my Uncle whose name is Juan. And by chance he gave him that dog. But look that dog, he bites Alex because he runs and bites much. HERE he bit him, and he bites him even in the face and here in the arms.

Events leading up to and from her stay in the hospital are not the ones she chooses to talk about (unlike her European North American peers). Instead Carmen prefers to fill us in on her family connections to the hospital, and even the family connections of her uncle's dog. In so doing, she anticipates the kind of questioning Monica is receiving now and which she herself undoubtedly received for years by her mother and other members of her community.

Finally, narrators often overlap in telling stories. That is, children may simultaneously talk and listen, eschewing the kind of formal sequential turn-taking favored in European North American conversational settings as well as in school.

Relationship of Narrative Features to Structure of Other Art Forms

Murals are some of the most prized visual art works in Latin America. In the United States, too, walking through the Mission District in San Francisco or East Los Angeles, one cannot help but notice the many murals painted on apartment buildings and warehouses. These murals, like the narratives of Latinos, are usually not neat, tidy, or linear. Instead, many images are presented at once, and a knowledge about the history of a people is needed to understand how the various images are related to one another. Furthermore, it is a form of art in which you have to be able to go from the big image to smaller images and then back to the big image again. Attention to detail is extremely important and, in fact, essential to the telling of a story in a mural. Shorris (1992) addresses the essence of history and interconnectedness in murals: when Yreina Cervantes stands on a scaffold under a freeway in Los Angeles painting a mural of Chicano history, she is aware of the Mexican mural artists who were her antecedents. Just as images of conquest and domination are related to images of ultimate achievement, such as that of Cesar Chavez, so is the whole mural as one piece related to other murals in other places.

In the world of music, corridos are a popular form of storytelling through music in Mexico. Corridos are songs that recount stories of individuals or groups of people. The main characters of the songs range from real historical figures to fictitious young men trying to cross the border to come up north. One of the oldest corridos in the Southwest is that of "El General Cortina." The corrido tells the story of Juan Nepomuceno Cortina, who shot U.S. Marshal Bob Shears in Brownsville, Texas, in 1859. This was done in retaliation for various injustices, which Cortina enumerated for fellow Mexicans in the form of a proclamation that is mentioned in the song (Saldivar, 1990). A more recent and popular corrido recounts the story of a couple of men who attempt to smuggle drugs across the border in the hubcaps of their car. The excursion costs them their life. (One activity in which the first author participated at home as a child was making up new lyrics to the music of popular corridos. We would substitute characters, and we smuggled bubblegum instead of drugs in the hubcaps.)

Salsa music, ubiquitous in many Latino countries, also parallels Latino narrative structures in a way. One interesting characteristic of Salsa music is that it has layered polymeters. That is, a trombone may be playing in 3/3 time while the drums play in 4/4 time. Such formal sanction of simultaneous variation in timing stands in marked contrast to the formal preference for regularity of lines (as in Japan, for example, see Chapter 5) and may perhaps provide a larger context for why we have found no regularity in terms of the lines per subtopic that Latino children narrate. At least half a dozen attempts by different individuals in our research group to analyze numerous and diverse Latino children's oral narratives using the method of displaying narratives as poetry (see Chapter 3) have met with little success.

More formal art also exhibits some characteristics similar to casual conversational narrative structure. Specifically, a libretto *(Bayoan: Quest for an Antillean Identity)* written by Dr. Juan Manuel Rivera, a Puerto Rican author, tells a narrative almost entirely in the present tense. As we have seen, this seems to be a common Spanish narrative practice.

Issues for Instruction

McDermott and Gospodinoff (1981) studied Puerto Rican Americans in classrooms and concluded that many of these children fail in school because they communicate differently and are accordingly unappreciated and misunderstood. They analyzed several moments when a child and a teacher were trying to understand each other while in face-to-face interaction during a reading lesson. They found that when they looked closely, miscommunication existed. Students were not always clear about what the teacher was asking them to do. In turn, teachers did not always understand students' responses.

Because narratives are ubiquitous in classrooms (see Chapter 1), miscommunication can often center around narrative exchanges. Not only is the content of (some) narratives and stories devalued in classrooms (Gilbert, 1993; Hymes & Cazden, 1992; Rosen, 1985), but often the form is as well. To summarize our earlier points regarding distinctive features of Latino narration: recapitulating a sequence of specific past tense events is not the point of many Latino stories. Instead, the idea is to fill listeners in on descriptive vignettes, often involving family relations of the narrator. Because there is no need to arrange ongoing activities in any specific form, Latino children are not necessarily well practiced in sequencing such statements. This difference has many implications, because existing tests of reading comprehension appear oblivious to this issue.

Current assessments of reading comprehension do not take distinctive Latino narrative traditions into account. When students in Texas were given the Texas Assessment of Basic Skills, more than 25 percent of the third-graders and nearly 33 percent of the fifth-graders failed to show mastery of the ability to place story events into the proper sequence, a "failure" that occasioned an article in *The Reading Teacher* (Baker, 1982). The article offered practical suggestions for teaching the skill of sequencing events in stories to school-aged children. Because instruction in sequencing is currently a consistent emphasis of most formal reading instruction programs, it is interesting to note that students (many of whom are Latino) actually get worse at sequencing after two more years of instruction.

Perhaps, then, a different approach to instruction and assessment is called for. Presenting sequencing as an activity valued by the European American tradition is vastly different from presenting it as a test of reading comprehension. Supplementing such assessment with requests more tailored to family vignettes would be a desirable first step. Such an approach would allow Latino students to succeed instead of placing them at a disadvantage. The annals of educational research are full of testimony that success breeds success, while failure breeds failure.

It is important to note that many I.Q. tests (for example, the W.I.S.C.-R.) have sections that require children to sequence a story in a linear fashion. The consequences of a lack of practice in sequencing in contexts such as this, which purport to assess general intelligence and general aptitude, are devastating to contemplate. Teachers may not be able to redress this issue with respect to test makers. They can, however, be conscious of it in interpreting the results of such tests as applied to Latino children.

Finally, in terms of narrative styles, structures, and language choice in those narratives, it is important to talk explicitly to students about what is expected in the classroom and in the larger world. As Delpit (1988) argued, we should be honest with our students. We are doing them a disservice by telling them that how a person talks or writes does not matter. We have to tell children from non-European backgrounds that their language and culture are unique and wonderful but that they also have to learn how to master another set of rules.

EXEMPLARY INSTRUCTION

When the first author of this chapter taught a bilingual second- and third-grade combined class in Southern California, she used several children's songs in Spanish as a way of encouraging parental involvement and storytelling. She brought in songs by a popular Mexican singer who goes by the name of "Cri-Cri." He is affectionately referred to as the "Singing Cricket," although his real name is Gabilando Francisco Soler. Most of his songs tell stories of certain animal characters such as a cowboy mouse who speaks English or a goat who rides a bicycle. One song she chose to use in her class dealt with various animals walking to school, and she integrated math and map skills into this unit by asking students to draw maps of how they walked or were driven to school every day. She also used this information to talk about drawing to scale and computing the distance from home to school.

Since many of the children's parents grew up in Mexico and were familiar with Cri-Cri's songs, Margarita encouraged these parents to help their children learn the lyrics. She also asked the parents to tell their children stories they remembered hearing as children. The children brought these stories to class and shared them. Most of the parents helped their children with these homework assignments.

To finish the unit, the class sang and acted out the song about animals walking to school, a performance the children knew would be videotaped. Surprisingly, several parents who had never come to school before came to see their children sing a Cri-Cri song. This turned out to be a very successful attempt to build bridges between home and school, both for the children and for their parents.

Box 8: Research Into Practice

1. One specific way in which the Latino culture and Latino narratives can be used in the classroom is in the form of a unit on bones. We have found that children of different backgrounds really enjoy the book *My Aunt Otilia's Spirits* by Richard Garcia (1987). The characters in the book are Puerto Rican. The story itself mixes reality and fantasy. The structure of the story seems very authentic and the text is presented both in English and Spanish.

    Another part of the unit could entail a discussion about the "Day of the Dead." The Day of the Dead is celebrated on October 30 throughout Mexico and entails several special foods and activities. One book that deals with this holiday is *Pablo Re-*

members: *The Fiesta of the Day of the Dead* by George Ancona (1993).

    In addition, the unit could encompass science and health activities relating to anatomy and the functions of bones and other parts of the body. Math activities could also be easily tied into the unit. Artwork could incorporate the theme of bones and anatomy. For older students, discussion about how death is perceived cross-culturally may prove quite interesting.

2. Another specific recommendation entails having students write narratives in different forms. Students, as Delpit (1988) has suggested, may be asked to write the same story in a "Heritage" form and in a "Formal" form. In the Heritage form, Spanish could be

---

Box 8: Research Into Practice—cont'd

---

used and features such as nonlinearity would be encouraged. In the Formal form, the use of English, topic sentences, and linearity would be expected.

3. Steinbergh (1991) argues that writing about family allows students of every cultural background, including Latinos and African Americans, to examine their relationship to parents, to extended family, and to siblings. To think about what is valued enough to pass along within a family and to accept the powerful bonds and the ambivalence inherent in family life inspires many professional, as well as nonprofessional, writers.

4. Harris-Martine (1991) talks about the importance of sharing memories, especially about family, through storytelling. In her second-grade classroom composed of African American students, who lived in Harlem, and Latino students, who were bused in from Spanish Harlem, she asked children to have their parents tell them stories about when they were babies. She also shared a story about when she herself was a baby. Students came into the classroom eager to exchange stories. She also integrated stories into her language arts program by reading stories about family relationships and remembrances. Stories such as these about families can help build bridges between school and home, which Latino students so desperately need.

5. Another related activity comes from the book, *Voices from the Fields* by S. Beth Atkin (1993), in which children of migrant farmworkers tell their stories. In the book, narratives from children and adolescents are presented along with a short biography of each individual. In addition, those who could write only in Spanish wrote in Spanish as their stories were translated and presented side by side. This would work well in a class with a diverse Latino population. Students could write about their experiences in their home country or about likes and dislikes about being in the United States. Students could also collect stories from their parents, which could build bridges between home and school.

6. The idea of stories in two forms and languages presented side by side is also exemplified in the book by Carmen Lomas Garza (1990), *Family Pictures: Cuadros de familia*. In this book, Garza presents different scenes from her youth and then tells us the story behind the picture. Each snapshot is described both in English and Spanish. Each story appears authentic, both in content and structure. Students could also be given the opportunity to share snapshots from their own lives, encouraged to present their narratives in both languages, and given the freedom to explore different narrative styles.

Summary

- The term *Latino* is a term no Spanish-speaking child would identify with; this is an umbrella term that encompasses a wide variety of cultures. Diversity even in the variety of Spanish spoken is so great that considerable misunderstandings may result between speakers of different dialects.

- Latinos are the fastest growing immigrant group in America, and the one most at risk for academic underachievement.
- Latino children de-emphasize event sequencing in their narratives. Spanish verb tense structure and use could account for these narrative preferences.
- Latino children emphasize description, giving many details about the appearance of objects.
- Latino children's description often centers around extended family members: who they are, their characteristics, and the connections they have with objects and locations.
- Latino children often overlap their narration with that of others.

References

ANCONA, G. (1993). *Pablo Remembers: The fiesta of the Day of the Dead.* NY: Lothrop, Lee and Shepard.

ATKIN, S.B. (1993). *Voices from the fields: Children of migrant farmworkers tell their stories.* Boston: MA: Little, Brown.

BAKER, D.T. (1982). What happened when?: Activities for teaching sequence skills. *The Reading Teacher,* 216–218.

BARRERA, R., LIGUORI, O. & SALAS, L. (1992). Ideas a literature can grow on: Key insights for enriching and expanding children's literature about the Mexican American experience. In B. Harris (Ed.), *Teaching multicultural literature in grades K–8* (pp. 203–240). Norwood, MA: Christopher-Gordon.

BLUM-KULKA, S., & SNOW, C.E. (1992). Developing autonomy for tellers, tales and telling in family narrative-events. *Journal of Narrative and Life History, 2*(3), 187–218.

BRUNER, J. (1986). *Actual Minds, Possible Worlds.* Cambridge, MA: Harvard University Press.

CANO, L. (1993). "Analysis of Chicano Children's Narratives." Unpublished course paper, Harvard University, Cambridge, MA.

DE LA LUZ REYES, M. (1991). A process approach to literacy using dialogue journals and literature logs with second language learners. *Research in the Teaching of English, 25,* 291–313.

DELPIT, L. (1988). The silenced dialogue: Power and pedagogy in educating other people's children. *Harvard Educational Review, 58,* 280–298.

DUANY, L., & PITTMAN, K. (1990). *Latino youths at a crossroads.* Washington, D.C.: Children's Defense Fund Adolescent Pregnancy Prevention Clearinghouse.

DYSON, A.H. (1993). *Negotiating the permeable curriculum: On the interplay between teacher's and children's worlds.* Urbana, IL: National Council of Teachers of English.

ERIKSON, F. (1987). Transformation and school success: The politics and culture of educational achievement. *Anthropology and Education Quarterly, 18,* 335–356.

GARCIA, R. (1987). *My Aunt Otilia's Spirits: Los Espiritus de mi Tia Otilia.* San Francisco, CA: Children's Book Press.

GARZA, C.L. (1990). *Family pictures: Cuadros de familia.* San Francisco, CA: Children's Book Press.

GEE, J.P. (1991). What is literacy? In C. Mitchell & K. Weiler, (Eds.), *Rewriting literacy: Culture and the discourse of the other* (pp. 3–11). New York: Bergin & Garvey.

GILBERT, P. (1993). "And they lived happily ever after": Cultural storylines and the construction of gender. In A. Dyson & C. Genishi (Eds.), *The need for story: Cultural diversity in community and classroom* (pp. 217–250). Urbana, IL: National Association of Teachers of English.

GUTIERREZ-CLELLEN, V.F., & IGLESIAS, A. (1992). *Journal of Speech and Hearing Research, 35,* 363–372.

GUTIERREZ-CLELLEN, V.F., & QUINN, R. (1993). Assessing narratives of children from diverse cultural/linguistic groups. *Language, Speech, and Hearing Services, 24,* 2–9.

HARRIS-MARTINE, D. (1991). Reading, writing, and literature in a Harlem second grade. In J. Freely, D. Strickland, & S. Wepner (Eds.), *Process reading and writing: A literature-based approach* (pp. 32–41). New York: Teachers College.

HEATH, S.B. (1983). *Ways with words.* Cambridge, England; Cambridge University Press.

HYMES, D., & CAZDEN, C. (1992). Narrative thinking and story-telling rights: Differential treatment of narrative experience. In C. Cazden (Ed.), *Whole Language Plus: Essays on literacy in the United States and New Zealand* (pp. 170–185). New York: Teachers College.

LABOV, W., COHEN, P., ROBINS, C., & LEWIS, J. (1968). *A study of the non-standard English of Negro and Puerto Rican speakers in New York City,* (Vol. 2) (Cooperative Research Project No. 3288). Washington, DC: Office of Education.

MARGER, M.N. (1994). *Race and ethnic relations: American and global perspectives* (3rd ed.). Belmont, CA: Wadsworth.

MARIN, G., & MARIN, B. (1991). *Research with Hispanic Population.* Newbury Park: Sage Publications.

MCDERMOTT, R.P. & GOSPODINOFF, K. (1981). Social contexts for ethnic borders and school failure. In H. Trueba, G. Guthrie, & K. Hu-Pei Au (Eds.), *Culture and the bilingual classroom: Studies in classroom ethnography* (pp. 212–230). Rowley, MA: Newbury House.

MICHAELS, S. (1981). "Sharing time": Children's narrative styles and differential access to literacy. *Language in Society, 10,* 423–442.

MICHAELS, S., & COOK-GUMPERZ, J. (1979). *A study of sharing time with first grade students: Discourse narrative in the classroom.* Proceedings of the Fifth Annual Meeting of the Berkeley Linguistics Society, (5), 647–660.

MILLER, P. (1991, April). "Narrative practices and their role in childhood education." Paper presented at AERA. (Location unknown.)

MILLER, P., MINTZ, J., HOOGSTRA, L., FUNG, H., & POTTS, R. (1992). The narrated self: Young children's construction of self in relation to others in conversational stories of personal experience. *Merrill-Palmer Quarterly, 38,* 45–67.

MINAMI, M., & MCCABE, A. (1991). Haiku as a discourse regulation mechanism: A stanza analysis of Japanese children's personal narratives. *Language in Society, 20,* 577–599.

MOLL, L., AMANTI, C., NEFF, D., & GONZALEZ, N. (1992). Funds of knowledge for teaching: Using a qualitative approach to connect homes and classrooms. *Theory into practice, 31,* 132–141.

OSTER, P. (1989). *The Mexicans: A personal portrait of a people.* New York: Harper & Row.

PETERSON, C., & MCCABE, A. (1983). *Developmental psycholinguistics: Three ways of looking at a child's narrative.* New York: Plenum.

RODINO, A., GIMBERT, C., PEREZ, C., CRADDOCK-WILLIS, K., & MCCABE, A. (1991, October). *"Getting your point across: Contrastive sequencing in low-income African-American and Latino children's personal narrative."* Paper presented at the 16th Annual Conference on Language Development, Boston University, Boston, Massachusetts.

ROSEN, H. (1985). *Stories and meaning.* Upper Montclair, NJ: W.W. Norton.

SALDIVAR, R. (1990). *Chicano narrative: The dialects of difference.* Madison, WI: University of Wisconsin.

SCOTT, J.C. (1990). The silent sounds of language variation. In S. Hynds and D. Rubin (Eds.), *Perspectives on talk and learning* (pp. 285–298). Urbana, IL: National Council of Teachers of English.

SEBASTIAN, E., & SLOBIN, D.I. (1994). Development of linguistic forms: Spanish. In R.A. Berman & D.I. Slobin (Eds.), *Relating events in narrative: A crosslinguistic developmental study* (pp. 239–284). Hillsdale, NJ: Erlbaum.

SHORRIS, E. (1992). *Latinos.* New York: W.W. Norton.

SNOW, C. (1991). Literacy and language: Relationships during the preschool years. In A. Minami and B. Kennedy (Eds.), *Language Issues in Literacy and Bilingual/Multicultural Education* (pp. 207–234). Cambridge, MA: Harvard Educational Review.

SNOW, C., & DICKINSON, D. (1990). Social sources of narrative skills at home and at school. *First Language, 10,* 87–103.

STEINBERGH, J.W. (1992). To arrive in another world: Poetry, language development, and culture. *Harvard Educational Review, 61,* 51–70.

SUAREZ-OROZCO, M. (1987). Towards a psychosocial understanding of Hispanic adaptation to American schooling. In H.T. Trueba, (Ed.), *Success or Failure Learning and the language minority student* (pp. 156–168). Rowley, MA: Newbury House.

VALDEZ, G. (1994, February). "Who will teach the children: How prepared are parents, teachers, and the American society for a multicultural, bilingual, 21st Century?" Paper presented at the Annual Meeting of the National Association of Bilingual Education, Los Angeles, CA.

WATSON, K.A. (1975). Transferable communicative routines: Strategies in group identity in two speech events. *Language in Society, 4,* 53–72.

WONG FILLMORE, L. (1976). "The second time around: Cognitive and social strategies in second language acquisition." Unpublished doctoral dissertation, Stanford University, Stanford, CA.

WOOD, D. (1988). *How children think and learn: The social contexts of cognitive development.* Oxford England: Basil Blackwell.

CHAPTER 8

Context and Structure: Some North American Indian and Aboriginal Traditions

Diane Pesco
Martha B. Crago
and
Allyssa McCabe

OVERVIEW

Many aspects of history account for the enormous diversity among Native and Aboriginal peoples. This chapter focuses on Algonquin storytelling traditions. Genres of narratives adults tell include historical narratives, personal experiences, traditional stories and legends, and oral bedtime stories. Among various Native American groups, linguists have noted a pronounced regularity in terms of stanza structure, although the number of lines per stanza varies from group to group. In other words, the poetic aspect of narration in American Indian groups is striking. Algonquin narratives also contain highpoint elements (description, action, and evaluation) that were noted for other cultures, but seldom are they combined into a classic European story form. There is considerable variation in the form of narratives told by Algonquin children, although many contain repetition sequences or multiple episodes linked thematically. Issues for instruction are addressed at the end of the chapter.

SOME NATIVE NORTH AMERICAN STORYTELLING TRADITIONS

Issues of Context

Every story has a setting or a context (Johnstone, 1990). This chapter, too, has a particular context. The narratives of Algonquin children that form a central part of this chapter were gathered as part of a larger set of studies, spanning a number of Canadian Aboriginal communities. These studies concern the teaching and learning conversations that take place in Aboriginal classrooms. They were designed to contribute to the creation of a culturally relevant knowledge base for a Canadian Aboriginal teacher education program. Two of the authors of this chapter have been researchers working on this set of studies. We are not Aboriginal women. One of us has, however, taught extensively in Aboriginal teacher education programs and spent several years doing research with a variety of Aboriginal communities. The contents of this chapter have been approved by members of the community from which they were derived. Without this approval, the material would not appear in publication.

Historical Background: Diverse Dimensions of Context

From our work in four different Canadian Aboriginal settings, we have identified a number of dimensions and complex issues that create considerable diversity among American Indian and Canadian Aboriginal communities. We feel it is important to discuss these issues before introducing the properties of narratives from a particular group of Canadian Algonquin children.

Cultural Differences. Although many American Indian and Canadian Aboriginal groups were historically hunting and gathering societies, each group has its own individual set of traditional practices and beliefs and its own language. Some cultural practices are conscious and overt, such as celebrations associated with spiritual belief systems. Different groups also have less conscious or more subtle traditional practices. For instance, child rearing practices vary across Native and Aboriginal groups and reflect differing cultural belief systems about the role and status of children. These include ways of interacting with children, instructing them, and integrating them into their communities (Crago, 1992; Heath, 1989; Schieffelin & Ochs, 1986).

Culture Contact. Another major dimension of diversity among Native and Aboriginal groups is the history of contact with dominant society. In part, this relates to geographic isolation. However, geographic factors are not the only determinants of cultural contact. The degree of self-determination and the history of domination are very powerful aspects of variability among Native and Aboriginal groups. The influence of the church and Christianity have also had profound effects on traditional practices, education, language, and literacy in certain communities.

Educational History. The educational history of a community is another dimension of Native and Aboriginal life that is responsible for diversity among communities. It has particular pertinence to this chapter. One of the central issues in educational history is that of language retention (Taylor, Crago, & McAlpine, 1993). Language retention is influenced by who controls the schools. In situations where the church or the federal government has historically controlled schools, most Native and Aboriginal children have lost their first language. In many communities that have their own educational authority, native languages have been maintained or re-introduced. Language maintenance and culturally based educational programs often are accompanied by the introduction and creation of instructional materials in both the native language and in the second language. These include readers and storybooks.

In many of these same communities, there are a number of Native or Aboriginal teachers and even community-controlled teacher education programs, some of which are conducted in the native language. Some Canadian Aboriginal teachers teach in their native language. Some teach in the dominant language, which may or may not be their second language. Furthermore, the communities we have worked in have a combination of Aboriginal and non-Aboriginal teachers. These variations in cultural heritage and in language lead to a marked diversity of teachers in Native American and Canadian Aboriginal schools.

Variation in teaching experience is also an important issue in these schools. Remote Aboriginal schools in Canada, for example, typically have a large number of inexperienced non-Aboriginal teachers and only a few longtime residents of the communities who teach.

For all of these reasons, Native American and Canadian Aboriginal children are exposed, in their homes and schools, to a range of cultural patterns, first and second languages, as well as written and oral narratives. These contextual factors, in turn, can be expected to influence the narratives produced by children from these communities.

Storytelling Practices in an Algonquin Community

The Context of Algonquin Children's Narratives. The Algonquin community where we have conducted our research is situated on a very small parcel of land in the middle of a large recreational wildlife reserve. It has a population of approximately 350 and was established in 1961. Previous to that time, the people of the community lived in the "bush," moving with the seasons to hunt for a living. Now, the children of the community live with their families on the reservation which they refer to as "town." There is no television reception, no store, and only three telephones in "town." For the most part, the community members are not integrated into the mainstream Canadian economy. On the weekends and during school holidays, many families leave the reservation and return to the "bush" lands, where they continue to live a traditional life-style.

The people of the community are Algonquin speakers. Their language remains primarily an oral one. However, an orthographic system for writing the language was introduced by French missionaries in the seventeenth century. Written materials in Algonquin are primarily limited to the Bible and books of prayer (Collis, 1992). Children come to school as fluent speakers of Algonquin and receive instruction in their native language in nursery school and kindergarten. At the time that our research was carried out, the school employed three Aboriginal and five non-Aboriginal teachers. After seventh grade, the children must leave the community to complete their high school studies.

In this chapter we discuss narratives from eighteen Algonquin children between the ages of 10 and 13. These stories were recounted in English, the children's second language. Developmental information on narratives is not available in this study. At earlier ages, most of the children's English was not well enough developed to make storytelling and story analysis in that language possible. Unfortunately, we were not able to research the children's stories in Algonquin since neither of us is a speaker of that language.

Community Stories. Before we describe the children's stories, we will discuss the stories from the community that we heard and that children are likely to hear. Our interaction in the family with whom we lodged enriched our understanding of local narrative practices.

Historical Narratives. We heard, on rare occasions, narratives that recounted past events of historical importance. One dealt with the conflict between Iroquois and Algonquin peoples and told of a decisive moment in the struggle between the two groups. The narrative recounts how an Algonquin woman traveling by canoe sighted and escaped notice by the Iroquois. Forewarned of an imminent attack, the Algonquin "attacked and took an Iroquois man and cut his ears off and sent him back to his people. Then the Iroquois stopped fighting us." This Algonquin narrative is similar in form and content to a Cree historical narrative described as containing a "bare minimum of setting, no characterization, and a statement of events leading straight to the goal of the narrative. There is no dating" (Ellis, 1988, p. 22).

Stories of more recent history are sometimes told at gatherings or pow-wows in this Algonquin community. One Algonquin teacher explained that elders might tell about "how the things were in the past . . . some of the disappointments, mistakes they made that we don't have to make. That we can change." Narratives "sometimes have to do with government, with the way our leadership should act . . . parents, children's responsibilities. [Stories] cover a wide variety of subjects, different by different people." Drawing on community experience to make their points, storytellers "give different examples" but are careful not to single out particular individuals or families in doing so.

Personal Experience Narratives. Like events experienced by the entire community, experiences of particular individuals are an important source of teaching and learning. For example, when an 11-year-old girl cut her finger on a knife while preparing strips of bark for basket-making, two of the Algonquin adults present reacted primarily by telling about injuries they had endured in childhood or as adults. One man recounted, "When I was 9, my grandfather gave me a curved knife. I learned so much from that knife. I learned about medicine when I cut myself. I learned how to cut many things, too."

Personal experience narratives also serve as expressions of individual and group identity. One older woman told us a series of stories about times when she or others in her family had successfully repaired skidoos, cars, and other items through creative problem-solving. The theme of these anecdotes was the resourcefulness and self-reliance of the individuals involved, and of Aboriginal people in general. This theme recurred in some of the traditional tales discussed below in which the main characters manage trying circumstances by being clever and imaginative.

Traditional Stories and Legends. The traditional stories we heard often included activities such as hunting, trapping, fishing, and related information about the local physical environment. In some cases, the verbal content of narratives was combined with physical displays such as fish bones or animal furs. Through these stories and presentations children learn about the spiritual importance and distinguishing physical characteristics of animals and fish common to the region. Given a traditional and continued reliance on animals and fish as food sources, such information is important from a practical point of view as well.

Traditional stories also function to communicate cultural values and themes. One storyteller distinguished the theme from the topic of a story. Linking one story to another she had told, she said, "See, that story is like the pike and the sturgeon [story]. It's about thinking ahead, seeing ahead. Everything has a purpose."

Sometimes we heard the same story told by different people for different purposes. For example, we heard the story of "The Pike, The Mink, and The Walleye" on three separate occasions. One teller was an adolescent who gave a particularly detailed and careful rendition of the story, demonstrating his pride in maintaining traditional ways and his emerging competence in a primarily adult domain. We quote his entire story because it is characterized by features common to many of the narratives we heard. These features include animals and fish as main characters, dialogue and indirect reported speech, humor, trickery, surprise endings, and morals. In this particular example, the narrator briefly introduces the topic, begins each narrative section with a leitmotif of the mink running back and forth between the two fish, and completes the story with "that's it," a formulaic ending used by many of the children. Note also that the narrative is displayed as if it were poetry (see Chapter 3).

> It's the story about the pike, the mink, and the walleye.
>
> A long time ago there was this mink who was hungry.
> He had nothing to eat so he was walking around,
> thinking of what to kill to find something to eat.
> So an idea comes up to him 'cause he saw a pike in the water.
>
> And he goes, he goes to the pike
> and tells him that the walleye says "You have big eyes."
> And uh the mink ran back and the pike told him that he has a big mouth.
> And the pike told that to the mink.
>
> And the mink runs back to the walleye
> and tells the walleye that the pike said to him that he has a big mouth.
> And uh the walleye didn't mind, didn't mind, didn't say anything.
> But he said to the mink that the pike has a big head.
>
> The mink ran back
> and told the pike.
> And the pike got angry.

The pike told the mink that the walleye is fat and round.

And uh the mink ran back, ran back to the walleye
and told the walleye that the pike said that you're fat and round.
So the walleye got angry at him too.
So the walleye told him, "I'll meet you by the rock over there."
"There, we'll get things straightened out here", the walleye said.

So the mink ran back to the pike
and told him what the walleye had said.
And the pike it was okay,
he said "It's okay."

When sunset came both of them were at the rock.
And uh "So, you've been calling me names, eh?," the pike says.
"So was you, that's why I've been calling you names," the walleye says.

So they started fighting.
The mink's there, watching, laughing.
Soon both the fish got tired, got tired and killed each other
and both of the fish floated up the surface.

The mink was all happy.
He got the two fishes.
Brought 'em to shore.

Just about when he was about to eat,
two men came, two men came and look around
and he saw two fish on the ground laying.

They didn't know it was the mink's fishes.
Then the man told to his friend, "Here's some fresh fish,
At least we can have something to eat instead of going to the woods and hunt."

They got their knives,
made fire,
and ate the fish.

Later on the mink didn't have anything to eat again.
So he tried another plan
but it seemed it didn't work.
That's it.

Certain traditional narratives feature the reappearance of human or super-natural characters in different situations. One such character is the "Wihtigo." In an anthology of works by non-Aboriginal and Aboriginal people about the Windigo (a nominal variant of Wihtigo), Colombo (1982) called it "a creature of the Algonkian* imagination and experience . . . [T]he personification of both physical and spiritual famine" (p. 1).

Darnell (1989), describing Wihtigo as "a man who becomes a cannibal," points out that "most native people do not like to talk about wihtigo spirits because they know they are disbelieved [by outsiders]" (pp. 319–320), whereas

---

*The term Algonkian refers to a family of languages to which the Algonquin language belongs.

the Algonquin people consider them to be real. Darnell also claims that Wihtigo stories are sometimes used by adults to threaten children.

The characterization of Wihtigo as a cannibal and the potential role of Wihtigo stories in controlling the behavior of children who might otherwise disobey orders is suggested in the following excerpt from a narrative by one of the children in the community. Once again, we have displayed it as if it were poetry:

My grandmother told me this story.

A guy same age like me keepin' a little kid.
When that guy, the boy, says "Hey be quiet."
"I hear somebody outside."
The kid says "Ah, you're crazy!"

Then, then after,
"Hurry up, be quiet."
"I hear somebody."
That guy goes . . . (Peer gives vocabulary: "Ah, you make me mad")
So he says "Ah you make me . . . "

That guy Whitigo, the big monster, comes inside.
Then that guy [the boy] runs out.
And he runs to the boat.
And he run as fast as he can.

Then he went to his father's house.
"Dad, Dad, they ate all my brothers and sisters."
"They were foolin' around."
"I'm tryin' to stop them,
and they kept on playin' them."

Next day the father went over there.
And the next day that guy was, the kid was dead.
All bloods.
And that guy, that monster, made a fire outside.
And then he went home.

Bedtime Stories. Bedtime stories in North American middle-class homes are often in the form of bookreading by parents to children. In this Algonquin community, oral bedtime stories were a traditional practice. Some children in the community still have the pleasure of hearing them, primarily from grandparents. One girl recounted "I went to sleep by my grandfather and he told a story about a long time ago, what Indians there used to make." Another girl began her retelling of a narrative this way: "I told my mom, 'Can I go sleep over at my grandfather's?' and she said yes. Then we went to bed . . . He told us the story 12:00." The narrator continued the story primarily in Algonquin, and told how she laughed when her grandfather demonstrated the way the characters in the story danced. We also had the opportunity of hearing a story at bedtime. A woman told it to us and her adult children as we went to sleep in a large, common bedroom. We did not understand the story as it was told in Algonquin, but recall the narrator's quiet voice, and her steady, soothing tone. Much to our surprise, one of the adult listeners told us the next day he'd been unable to sleep much of the night because of fears aroused by the story. Bedtime stories, then, are intended to entertain, but apparently may frighten, as well as amuse, the listeners.

Narrative Structure in Other Native or Aboriginal Communities

Myths and legends have been the main focus of studies by folklorists, anthropologists, and linguists working in Native American and Canadian Aboriginal communities. Because adults are usually the tellers of traditional stories and children do not normally tell stories to audiences, there is less information about the kinds of narratives children tell and how they structure them. We will discuss some of what is known about the structure of traditional stories by adults and other types of narratives by children.

Other Scholarly Treatments of Narratives by Adults

One of the methods of analysis that has been used to analyze the structure of adults' traditional stories is verse or stanza analysis (see Chapter 3). As readers will recall, stanza analysis involves grouping together narrative lines and series of lines based on prosody, content, and linguistic features. Regularities in the number and patterning of narrative units (that is, lines per verse, verses per stanza, and so forth) have been found in the narratives told by members of different Native American groups (Bright, 1982; Hymes, 1982). In particular, patterns of four or five have been identified in oral narratives told by Native Americans speaking different languages (Hymes, 1987).

Features of Narration by Children and Adolescents

The studies outlined below were each carried out in a different Canadian Aboriginal or Native American community. The ways of examining structure and the ages of the children varied greatly, making it difficult to compare the results directly. However, the studies give an idea of the aspects of a narrative that contribute to its overall form.

Scollon and Scollon (1984) analyzed a story retelling by an Athabascan adolescent, using the kind of stanza analysis we have discussed. Like the traditional stories, this recount of actual events had a stanza structure, with a patterned number of four lines in each stanza and four stanzas in all.

Lindsay (1992) found that intonation was used to establish cohesion in the narratives of first- and second-graders from another Canadian Aboriginal group. She also found that most of the narratives she collected concentrated on a single topic that was developed with a nonlinear structure (that is, no clearcut beginning, middle, and end) and no shifts in time or place.

Manuel-Dupont, Strong, and Fields (1990) studied narratives by Northern Ute children 8 to 11 years old. They looked at the kinds of information children provided in their narratives, using a method called story-grammar analysis. They found that these children included many actions in their narratives, as well as events leading up to and resulting from those actions. Information about place and time were rare, as were descriptions of the characters, and information about the characters' plans, motivations, and reactions to the events of the narrative.

Narrative themes have also been a subject of research. Of Pueblo, Hopi, Zuni, and Navaho adolescents, those from more remote and traditional communities were found to include more cultural themes than did adolescents from urban areas. Such themes included continuity between generations, harmony, visions, charms, and communication with spirits (John-Steiner & Panofsky, 1992). These same authors have also described narrative structure in terms of how much description or action they contain. Using this approach, they found that story retellings by Navaho children were "quieter and more contemplative" (p. 225) than Sioux children's action-filled versions of the same story.

As the studies indicate, the structure of children's narratives is shaped by the kinds and amounts of information provided, the number, type, and relationship of themes, the ways the narrator makes her or his meaning clear (for example, with words or with intonation and gesture), and the way different parts of the narrative relate to other parts.

The Structure of Algonquin Children's Narratives

We analyzed one narrative of personal experience told by each of eighteen students in either a combined fourth and fifth or sixth grade. We looked first at the kinds of proportions of narrative components or elements that children included in their narratives. According to the model we used, which is described in detail in Chapter 3, the main elements of a story about past events are (a) description or orientation (Who, when, what, where?), (b) complicating actions (What happened?), (c) resolving actions (What finally happened?), and (d) evaluation. Boundary markers like abstracts and codas—optional parts—respectively signal a narrative's beginning and ending.

We attempted to determine whether the narrative conforms to a "classic" European pattern where "the narrative builds up to a high point, evaluatively dwells on it, and then resolves it" (Peterson & McCabe, 1983, p. 37). Recall that this type of pattern has been found to be common among European North American children, but less so among other groups such as Japanese and Latin American children (Minami & McCabe, 1991). If only some of the narrative elements are present, or if they are sequenced in different ways, then the narrative may take a different form, such as a straight chronology of events or a story that reaches a high point and then just ends (Peterson & McCabe, 1983).

High Point Features. We found that nearly all of the Algonquin narratives included the elements of orientation, action, and evaluation. A few of the narratives resembled the classic European form, some ended at the high point, and others did not fit the model at all. The children varied in how much they concentrated on different kinds of information and where in the narrative they gave this information. The most common forms of orientation in all the narratives were introductions to participants, ongoing events ("We went riding"), and features of the scene of action. Some narrators provided lots of description and concentrated it at the beginning of the narrative, while others embedded it throughout the narrative, or counted on the audience to fill in such details based on their familiarity with the people and places involved in the story.

One narrator (the sole student in the study who spoke English as a first language) opened her narrative with a general setting, the people present, and the ongoing events, and then focused on a dramatic event experienced by her cousin. Following that, she gave the detailed description that appears below. This description of the room where the events took place was followed with a recapitulation of her story:

> Like I was on a little couch in the bedroom.
> Not even this big, about here (demonstrates size).
> Anyways, that big.
> I was laying there in the bedroom.
> Here's N's bed (demonstrates location).
> And the couch was right here (demonstrates location).
> And it was wall there.
> But the door was right here in I's room (demonstrates location).
> And I was sleeping there.
> And N was sleeping in there with Y.
> And all of a sudden it came out of the closet right here.
> And it grabbed N.
> It started shaking her.
> I got on my knees.
> Tried to open the light.
> But he saw me.
> and he threw N back on the bed and ran into the closet.

While the initial descriptive lines of many narratives set the stage for listeners, the ones above also seemed to serve a different function. By providing such a detailed description of her couch and bedroom the narrator seemed to be stressing the importance of the events from her point of view, and asserting her reliability as a witness and reporter of those events.

Narrators also differed in the amount, type, and position of evaluation. In the narrative excerpt below a girl's sick grandmother falls to the floor. The narrator evaluated the events through recounting her actions and through explicit statements of her emotional response to the situation:

> But I got scared.
> I just, I got scared.
> And my grandmother was breathing' yet.
> And I went back out.
> I went to my aunt's where my dad was.
> And my dad was coming back.
> and I saw S and all those kids there outside.
> I was running fast.
> and S said, "What's wrong?"
> I didn't say nothin'.
> I just ran over there.
> And I got to M's, my aunt's over there.

And I stood there.
And I got real scared.
I stood there keeping my cousins.
And they called the ambulance, my father over there.
I got scared she was gonna die.

The narrator's actions, the words themselves, and the repetition and build-up (from "I got scared" to "I got real scared" to "I got scared she was gonna die") leaves little doubt in the mind of the listener as to the narrator's point in telling the story. Note that she begins and ends with that refrain.

In other cases, evaluation was less explicit. For example, in the following excerpt, the narrator reacts to seeing a particular spirit and evaluates the events with reflection on the reasons why it might have appeared, really drawing a moral from the experience:

Mamazagameshish.
When you walk around late you see it.
He's dressed green, white.
I saw that.
When K's baby died it was on my sister's birthday.
Then somebody busted the window at my sister the first time.
Then I just run out of the house.
And I saw somebody at the generator.
It had long coat.
He was green, though.
I told my father.
And we look for it.
We couldn't find it.
K's baby was dead that day.
It was my sister's birthday.
My parents were out drinking.
My parents asked me where he ran.
Maybe because they drink and somebody died.
Maybe that's why it happened.
Somebody was dead and drinking.

Other Features. Although evaluation provides much of the meaning of narratives, the inclusion of multiple events with the same theme was also a significant feature of several of the narratives by children in this community. One narrator, for example, recounted with humor how he and his friend were fooled three times while fishing:

Me and W were going fishing over there in M's boat.
And uh W thought he caught a fish.
And it was a chub, a big chub there, big.
And he said, "I caught a big bite," he said.
He thought it was a big bite.
And it was a small chub.

And (laughs) after when he caught that there came a big pike.
And he dropped his fishing line.

Dropped his fishing rod.
And uh when we got over there we fell in the water.
And we got out of the water and went back up.

This time we used my fishing rod and uh caught uh two walleyes.
William caught two.
I didn't catch any.
And then William caught a pike and brought it up.
Brought it up and caught it.
And uh big splash like that.

And we brought it in the boat.
And when we left there, when we went home, the pike was gone.
It wasn't there.
He got off.

That's it.

Another narrative with repetition sequences was told by a girl about a trip to the bush. In their home, the narrator and her family discovered a porcupine who had eaten a hole in the door and a leg of a bed. The second part of the story echoed and developed the theme of the first part, and recounted how the girl's grandmother's friend saw a damaged tree near the outdoor toilet and also discovered the culprit:

. . . She says "Holy cow, who do this?"
And after she went in the back because there was noise.
She saw the bear.
The bear was sleeping.
And after the bear was coming close to her.
And after she says "A bear!", she says.
She came running.
Her pants was up to here (indicates knees).

As this last narrative excerpt and other examples we have given indicate, many of the narratives we heard included the speech of others. According to Hymes (1982), such verbal exchanges are a frequent feature of Native American narratives. Tannen (1989) proposed that much of what people report as the speech of others involves creative rewording and even invention. For this reason she calls reported speech "constructed dialogue" (p. 25). Speakers use this strategy to engross their listeners in what they are saying.

In the following narrative, the teller uses dialogue skillfully to involve the listener, report and evaluate actions, characterize the participants, and shift perspective from one character to another. After the conclusion of his narrative the narrator repeated with laughter his favorite narrative line "Run for your life!" The boy might well have been borrowing the line from a story read in the fifth-grade class, suggesting that good lines of fiction are well appreciated and appropriated in talking about personal experiences. The very last lines of this narrative and other children's comments reminded us that peers are, in this community and probably in many others, an intended and favorite audience for narratives.

Me and J were riding around with the four wheeler.
and J, J say "D, you wanna get on with B?"
"Yeah," I says.

We went riding.
That there generator over there.
First road.
There's down.
We went down.
After it turns.

And B, B says "J, go fast here!"
"It's fun here!"
J goes fast.
Ooh!
After we went slow up that big hill.
Tipped over.

And J says "Run for your life!"
And J says "Holy moley, see that crash!"
"The gas is leaking," I said.
Told 'em "Back up."

And then "Oh man."
And B, "Oh hide!" (laughs)
"The four wheeler's gonna blow up!" (laughs)
We went all the way up to the bushes.
Wait for a minute.
Went down.

"I don't see nothing," I said.
And I check the four wheeler.
Start it up (gives sound effect of engine starting).
And J says "Oh scary cats."
She says to B "Thought it was gonna blow up!" (laughs)

After that we went home,
we went home told the whole story to our friends.

As our examples have shown, there is diversity among the children in this community in how they organize their narratives, and each narrative form has different strengths. There is also diversity in narrative length: Some children told many and long narratives, others told short ones or few. Many liked to perform their narratives and did so effectively using gesture, facial expressions, demonstrations, sound effects, and dialogue. Some children had favorite topics, but together the children spoke about a wide range of subjects, including the pleasures and surprises of fishing, hunting, and being in the bush; conflict and harmony with parents and friends; brushes with danger in the form of accidents, illness, and death; and perplexing, scary, or intriguing events such as dreams and meetings with spirits. This variety reflects the range of experiences that comprise the lives of children in this community.

Conclusion

In addition to the diversity of Native and Aboriginal groups, other factors such as the variety of structural components investigated in research, the diversity of narrative genres discussed, and the possibility of second language effects on narrative make it impossible to conclude this section with a unitary description of Aboriginal or even Algonquin children's narrative structure. Our inability to claim such a structure has not, however, made our investigation of narratives less meaningful to us, nor diminished our pleasure as listeners. Rather, we hope that an acknowledgment of both similarities and diversity has made us a better and more attentive audience.

Issues for Instruction: The Oral-Literate Connection

We feel somewhat uneasy about connecting the oral narrative tradition of American Native and Canadian Aboriginal children to literacy activities. There is a nexus of complex issues surrounding this connection important to consider. Recounting a particular episode that occurred in an Algonquin bush camp may help the reader understand our dilemma. Two of the authors were staying at the camp of the family of a young Aboriginal teacher. They commented to him how difficult they found it to write field notes in the context of the camp. The very act of writing did not seem to fit. He laughed and said, "Now you know how uncomfortable I felt in school, when all they asked me to do was to read and write."

Historically, Native American and Canadian Aboriginal communities had no tradition of literacy. Writing was brought to these communities as a by-product of Christianity. Alphabets were created by priests and missionaries for the express purpose of translating the Bible.

Later, anthropologists recorded legends and wrote them down, often not in the language in which they were first told and often not for the readership of the people from whom they were derived. More recently, literacy has been developed in Native and Aboriginal languages as a part of native language retention programs. Stories have been written so that children can acquire literacy in their own language. These written stories do not always follow in the pathway of the oral narrative tradition that preceded them. Some stories are written as instructional materials centered on the teaching of reading, rather than on rendering the oral narrative tradition into print. Furthermore, stories written in English that have Native or Aboriginal content represent a dissociation between a culture's own language and its ways of life. Such issues as these create a sense of tension for us around the transformation of oral stories into a written form.

On the other hand, dual strength in both modernism and traditionalism is important for today's Native American and Canadian Aboriginal children. Many live straddling and integrating two worlds. Literacy instruction to these children will need to involve very direct, self-conscious teaching and interpretation. The explicit discussion of Native or Aboriginal ways of storytelling and the explicit comparisons between those ways and the ways of other cultures need to become a part of classroom discussion. Teachers, Native and non-Native alike, must help children in Native communities continue to value their oral tradition while they also find meaningful new ways of incorporating its traditional features into modern literacy programs.

Box 9: Research Into Practice

LISTENING AND TELLING ACTIVITIES

1. The important skills developed in Native and Aboriginal children by listening to stories can be incorporated into school activities. Children can be taken to visit elders in their communities to hear them tell stories of their adventures or to hear them recount legends. Stories by adult community members can also be recorded and tied into appropriate lessons in the classroom.

2. Storytelling skills can be practiced in classrooms during sharing times. The use of objects to demonstrate and punctuate the story should be permitted. Patterns of interaction for such things as how the speaker is chosen, as well as who can talk and add to the story, should be determined according to local norms.

3. In keeping with the practice of using recurring themes and characters, children could be helped to identify certain characters and themes and tell multiple versions of stories about them.

4. Teachers could also encourage children to retell stories that they have heard in the community.

5. With children in upper elementary school and high school, class discussions on their communities' ways of telling stories can help them to understand and value their tradition. For instance, they might discuss who generally tells stories to whom, the usual content and style of stories told in their community, and how one might adapt a story to particular audiences. These discussions can also include how traditions are changing and what new patterns of storytelling are emerging.

6. In general, the more natural and culturally consistent the storytelling situation the better. For instance, older children might find it more meaningful to tell stories to younger children or peers rather than to an adult audience.

READING AND WRITING

7. Features of the local community's oral narrative patterns might be developed in writing. In the Algonquin community we have described, features of children's stories that could be encouraged would include reported speech, inclusion of traditional legends and characters even in personal experiences, a primary theme that gets developed and redeveloped, and the weaving of multiple perspectives into a story.

8. Students could be encouraged to write in different genres, such as adventure stories, personal experience stories, and legends, as well as to contrast such genres across cultural groups. This will help children develop a sense of themselves and their people.

9. Issues of audience need to be discussed so that children can develop writing skills that will suit people

---

Box 9: Research Into Practice—cont'd

who do not share their cultural and community-based frame of reference. Moreover, material written for circulation in a Native or Aboriginal child's own community is likely to require a different style than material designed for readership by a non-Aboriginal audience.

10. Books for children could also be written in both the native and the dominant language using narrative features identified in this chapter. There are books with Aboriginal content and characters that should be available for children to read. The following are some of the books that teachers in the Algonquin community reported to us as the favorites of their upper elementary school students. One teacher remarked that teachers' enthusiasm for a story and their animation in reading stories aloud has an important effect on children's responses to stories.

The favorite stories are: *Harpoon of the Hunter* (Markoosie, 1970), *Julie of the Wolves* (George, 1972), *Frozen Fire* (Houston, 1977), *Lost in the Barrens* (Mowat, 1956), *Water Sky* (George, 1987), *Island of the Blue Dolphins* (O'Dell, 1960), *April Raintree* (Culleton, 1983), *Spirit of the White Bison* (Culleton, 1985).

Traditional native legends are compiled in the following two sources:

Native Stories from Keepers of the Earth, by J. Bruchac (1991), (available from Fifth House Publishers, 620 Duchess Street, Saskatoon, Sakatchewan, S7K 0R1).

Four Worlds Development Project (video compilation of legends, available from the University of Lethbridge, 4401 University Drive, Lethbridge, Alberta, T1K 3M4).

Summary

- Native and Aboriginal peoples in Canada and the United States differ from each other for many historical reasons.
- Adults in Algonquin communities tell historical narratives, personal experience narratives, traditional stories and legends, and bedtime stories. Often these are told to children to educate or control them.
- The poetic structure of many Native American groups is quite regular in terms of the number of lines per stanza, though the specific number per stanza changes from group to group.
- While Algonquin narratives contain description, action, evaluation, and reported speech—just like all other cultural groups, including European North Americans—these elements are seldom arranged in classic European form even when narratives are given in English.
- Some Algonquin narratives link multiple episodes thematically or by use of repetition sequences.

References

BRIGHT, W. (1982). Poetic structure in oral narrative. In D. Tannen (Ed.), *Spoken and written language: Exploring orality and literacy* (pp. 171–184). Norwood, NJ: Ablex.

COLLIS, D.R.F. (1992). Le Statut des langues autochtones et leurs domaines d'utilisation au Québec. In J. Maurais (Ed.), *Les langues autochtones du Québec* (pp. 115–149). Québec: Publications du Québec.

COLOMBO, J.R. (1982). *Windigo: An anthology of fact and fantastic fiction.* Saskatoon, Saskatchewan: Western Producer Prairie Books.

CRAGO, M.B. (1992). Communicative interaction and second language acquisition: An Inuit example. *TESOL Quarterly, 26*(3), 487–505.

CULLETON, B. (1983). *In search of April Raintree.* Winnipeg: Pemmican Publishing.

CULLETON, B. (1985). *Spirit of the white bison.* Winnipeg: Pemmican Publishing.

DARNELL, R. (1989). Correlates of Cree narrative performance. In R. Bauman, & J. Sherzer (Eds.), *Explorations in the ethnography of speaking* (pp. 315–336). Cambridge, England: Cambridge University Press.

ELLIS, D.C. (1988, March). "Now then, still another story": Literature of the Western James Bay Cree content and structure." Paper presented at the Belcourt Lectures, University of Winnipeg: Manitoba.

GEORGE, J. (1972). *Julie of the wolves.* New York: Harper & Row.

GOODWIN, M.H. (1990). *He-said-she-said: Talk as social organization among black children.* Bloomington: Indiana University Press.

HEATH, S.B. (1989). The learner as cultural member. In M.L. Rice & R.L. Schiefelbusch (Eds.), *The teachability of language* (pp. 333–350). Baltimore, MD: Paul H. Brookes.

HOUSTON, J. (1977). *Frozen fire.* Toronto: McClelland and Stewart.

HYMES, D. (1982). Narrative form as a "grammar" of experience: Native Americans and a glimpse of English. *Journal of Education, 2,* 121–142.

HYMES, V. (1987). Warm Springs Sahaptin narrative analysis. In J. Sherzer & A. Woodbury (Eds.), *Native American discourse: Poetics and rhetoric* (pp. 62–102) Cambridge, England: Cambridge University Press.

JOHN-STEINER, V. & Panofsky, C. (1992). Narrative competence: Cross-cultural comparisons. *Journal of Narrative and Life History, 2*(3), 219–233.

JOHNSTONE, B. (1990). *Stories, community, and place: Narratives from Middle America.* Bloomington: Indiana University Press.

LINDSAY, A. (1992). Oral narrative discourse style of First Nations children and the language of schooling. *Reflections on Canadian Literacy, 10*(4), 205–209.

MANUEL-DUPONT, S., STRONG, C., & FIELDS, T. (1990). "Spoken narrative assessment: Language-impaired and Native American school-aged children." Paper presented at the American Speech-Language and Hearing Association conference, Seattle.

MINAMI, M., & McCABE, A. (1991). Haiku as a discourse regulation device: A stanza analysis of Japanese children's personal narratives. *Language in Society, 20,* 577–599.

MARKOOSIE. (1970). *Harpoon of the hunter.* Montreal: McGill Queens University Press.

MOWAT, F. (1956). *Lost in the barrens.* Boston: Little, Brown.

O'DELL, S. (1960). *Island of the blue dolphins.* Boston: Houghton Mifflin.

PETERSON, C., & McCABE, A. (1983). *Developmental psycholinguistics: Three ways of looking at a child's narrative.* New York: Plenum.

RODINO, A.M., GIMBERT, C., PEREZ, C., CRADDOCK-WILLIS, K., & McCABE, A. (1991, October). "Getting your point across: Contrasting sequencing in low income African American and Latino children's personal narratives." Paper presented at the 16th annual Boston University Conference on Language Development, Boston.

SCHIEFFELIN, B.B., & OCHS, E. (1986). *Language socialization across cultures.* Cambridge, England: Cambridge University Press.

SCOLLON, R., & SCOLLON, S.B.K. (1984). Cooking it up and boiling it down: Abstracts in Athabaskan Children's story retellings. In D. Tannen (Ed.). *Coherence in spoken and written discourse.* (pp. 173–200) Norwood, NJ: Ablex.

TANNEN, D. (1989). *Talking voices: Repetition, dialogue, and imagery in conversational discourse.* In J. Gumperz (Ed.), Studies in Interactional Sociolinguistics (Vol. 6). Cambridge, England: Cambridge University Press.

TAYLOR, D.M., CRAGO, M.B., & MCALPINE, L. (1993). Education in Aboriginal communities: Dilemmas around empowerment. *Canadian Journal of Native Education, 20*(1), 176–183.

CHAPTER 9

Chameleon Writers?: Narrative Styles in Written Story Books

Barbara S. Burt
and
Allyssa McCabe

OVERVIEW

The preceding chapters have presented a convincing argument for the need to be aware and appreciative of the different ways children from a variety of cultures tell their own stories. We have touched on a few of the implications for these differences when it comes to teaching reading, and we will pursue that topic in more detail in this chapter. Specifically, we will analyze the narrative structure of some available multicultural stories to see whether that structure resembles the structure of oral narratives produced by children from the cultures represented.

NARRATIVE STYLES IN WRITTEN STORY BOOKS

Mapping the Path to Literacy

During the last half century, research into reading has focused on skills that can be broken down into small, easily described and measured units, well-suited to experimental study in laboratory settings. This "decoding process" lured researchers with its promise of "scientifically verifiable results," and much progress was made in understanding the cognitive processes employed in learning to read. But none of us learn to read for the joys of decoding, unless we're planning a career as a cryptographer. The impetus for becoming literate is certainly as much psychosocial as it is cognitive. We may be curious about the world. We may need some particular bit of information to complete a task. We may wish to understand another's experience. We may have an urge to tell our own stories and are searching for some models. Or perhaps we may feel the need to escape our daily cares through fantasy. In any case, the drive to write and to read is a part of the human urge to communicate. The desire to hear and tell stories has been a significant motivator of communication for as long as recorded history. Written narrative is the literate expression of this desire.

Finding decoding an insufficient explanation for the acquisition of literacy, a number of researchers searched for the antecedents to literacy by examining the environment surrounding the child. Gordon Wells (1986), Shirley Brice Heath (1982), Catherine Snow (Snow & Ninio, 1986), G.J. Whitehurst et al. (1988) and many others have looked at the influence of home attitudes and activities on the subsequent success of the child in achieving literacy. These accounts all demonstrate that the home environment does indeed play a large part in the child's acquisition of literacy. Parents' reading habits, the number of books in the home, the presentation of books to children—these and other factors have been identified as predictive of children's eventual literacy.

Comprehension: Acknowledging the Reader's Contribution

Even so, the basic question remains unanswered. How do we come to understand print, anyway? What does a reader do in "comprehending"? In a sense, this is a rhetorical question, a conundrum with no simple answer. The more carefully we think about reading, the less we know what we mean by "understanding."

Some have advanced the hypothesis (Rosenblatt, 1978, Cairney, 1991) that comprehension is a third entity of meaning created by the interaction of the writer's text with the reader's private store of remembered experiences. This notion is nicely corroborated by the work of cognitive psychologists on memory in general. Indeed, investigations into reading comprehension by Walter Kintsch (1987), Robert Pritchard (1990), and others (for example, Hamann, Schultz, Smith & White, 1991) have borne out the importance of the reader's previous knowledge and understanding in creating meaning from the printed text.

Margaret Meek (1982) also reminds us to consider something that forms a large part of a child's store of prior knowledge—the "thriving unself-conscious culture which is unnoticed by the sophisticated world" (p. 286). She refers here to the childhood culture of rhymes, songs, games, and sayings, all of which share many of the formal characteristics of literature. Meek goes on to state that "when it [an aspect of childhood culture] is learned, it is acquired holistically, as form and content, signifier and signified, metaphor and meaning." Of course, the rhymes, songs, games, and aphorisms of childhood exist within a larger culture of which the child is a member, and reflect the forms and inflections employed by that particular culture. What is acquired holistically goes far beyond the rhymes and games of childhood; it is the overarching attitude toward the purpose of language, the mode of shaping stories, and the conception of the role of the listener.

An Informal Experiment

Eager to explore the role of cultural schema in shaping our ability to comprehend and retain information, the first author of this chapter conducted a small experiment (with acknowledgement to Bartlett, 1932) with a group of thirty-two European North American adults (predominantly female) who were attending a lecture on children's books at a public library in Maine. She read two selections of equal length aloud to the audience: the first was a description of preparations for cooking lobsters, a procedure with which most adults in Maine are quite familiar; the second was a story called "Making Tamales" from *Family Pictures: Cuadros de familia* by Carmen Lomas Garza (1990). She asked them to listen carefully but gave no further instructions. After reading each selection, Barbara spoke about a completely unrelated topic for approximately ten minutes. Then she stopped and asked the audience to write down as much as they could recall of the two stories. When everyone was finished writing, Barbara had them count the number of words they had written about each story. Upon being asked who had written more about "Making Tamales," three people raised their hands. Twenty-two people had written more about preparing to cook lobsters, and the remaining seven people estimated that they had written a similar amount for each. (One woman mentioned that during most of the reading of "Making Tamales," she assumed the author was referring to the green liver of the lobster which is known by the name "tomalley"!) This type of experiment can be easily replicated with any group and is a vivid demonstration of the extent to which the amount of information we can take away from a text is dependent upon what we bring to that text. In this case, cultural knowledge seemed to help 69 percent of the audience absorb and retain more information from the narrative written by a person of similar narrative tradition, while only 9 percent were able to recall more of the narrative written in an unfamiliar style about an unfamiliar topic, even though the original narratives were of equal length.

What Form Has the Reader's Contribution Been Assumed to Take?

Most first books for children either tacitly or intuitively subscribe to this description of understanding as the intersection between the writer's intentions, expressed by the text, and the reader's personal experience. Carolyn Baker and Peter Freebody report in their book *Children's First School Books* (1989) that the vast preponderance of children's books "deal with children's ordinary lives" (p. 23). They go on to tell us that "the first school reading books appear to attempt to make school reading 'relevant' to the child's daily experience." Baker and Freebody point out that this definition of relevance and the attempt to create it are both inherently misguided. By way of example, they claim that "it is hard to imagine adults reading books about people apparently very like themselves going about their unremarkable, everyday lives." But even more important, when you reflect that most editors and writers of children's school books are European North American, you can see the difficulty they may encounter in trying to portray a child's daily experience as if it were a universal condition, no matter how noble their intentions might be.

Another way in which writers of early childhood books, particularly the writers of basal series readers, attempt to engage the child's personal store of knowledge is by the heavy use of direct reported speech (for example, "Clean your room," said Mrs. Smith.) in the course of the story. This is seen as a transition from the oral language of children, in which contextualized dialogue plays a major part, to a more decontextualized, "literary" style, as is found in writing for older children and adults. In literary language, dialogue is often described indirectly (Mrs. Smith told Joe to clean his room), unless some specific purpose, such as character development, is furthered by the use of direct reported speech.

One odd result from this use of direct reported speech in early books is that it is difficult for experienced readers to follow precisely because it doesn't conform to literary convention. The voice of the author is almost nonexistent; descriptive and evaluative information is truncated or left out entirely. The following example from a pre-primer (Clymer et al., 1985) serves to illustrate this effect:

The Work Van
"Here's the van!
Here's the work van!"
"Can you work?"
Sara said, "I can work!"
Ken said, "And I can work!"
Sara said, "Jim can come and work.
Beth can come and work."
Ken said, "And Ana can come and work."
She said, "Look at it!
Here's the work.
And here's a can.
Dig in!"
Sara said, "Look, Ken!
Run and get it."
Ken said, "I can get it!"
He said, "I can work!"
"Here's a can in a can," Jim said.
"It is good to work," said Beth.
"Look at Ken work!" said Ana.
"Is the work good?" Sara said.
"It is good!
It is good work.
You can work!"

It is extremely difficult for a skilled reader to make sense of the preceding passage, even with access to the accompanying photographs. (We wonder if novice readers fare any better!) Upon examination, though, some interesting assumptions are revealed by additional information supplied in the pictures. The main characters, Sara and Ken, are European North American (Sara even has long, blond ponytails) and apparently middle-class. Jim appears to be Asian American, Beth is African American, and Ana (we assume by both the spelling of her name and her long dark hair) is meant to be Hispanic. Did you notice how passive these latter three characters are in the "story"? They are bystanders who are asked by Ken and Sara to come and work. Their contribution to the story is to remark about things they see, or, in Ana's case, on Ken's hard work. Is this what is meant by multicultural awareness?

Now let's recast the story in more literary style:

The Work Van Comes

Ken was excited to see the work van arrive at the park, where he and his friend Sara had been eagerly waiting for it. They were planning to help clean up the park.

A woman in a park uniform got out of the van. She seemed to be in charge. Taking a rake and some large trash barrels out of the work van, she walked over to Ken and Sara and asked them if they wanted to work. They both enthusiastically replied that they did.

Then Sara noticed her friends Jim and Beth. She said that they could come and help, too. Ken pointed to his friend Ana and added that she could also help.

The woman drew the children's attention to the litter in the park. She told them to get started. Sara pointed to a spilled bag of trash. She told Ken to run and get it. Ken was willing. He said he was a good worker.

Jim put a can in one of the barrels and made a joke about putting a "can in a can." Beth commented generally that it was good to work, and Ana remarked on how hard Ken was working.

Then the woman came over to where the children had been working. Sara asked if the work was done well. The woman told her it was good work. "You can work," she said to Sara.

While this rewritten version is no literary masterpiece, it is now clear what is happening in the story, although ethnic and racial indicators are not present. Many readers probably would assume that all of the characters are European North American children. One of the reasons for our being able to comprehend the story more easily is that the first author rewrote it following the conventions of Western culture regarding written narrative. It conforms to European North American expectations, which have been formed by previous experiences with many similar examples. Could our feeling of disquiet upon reading the first version be akin to the reactions of children who are called upon to read a form not familiar to them? How much more jarring that discordance must be for a child not yet comfortable navigating the world of print, for whom any familiar sight is a vital landmark.

In fact, this point has been made more formally. That is, researchers rewrote basal reader stories to conform to European story grammar conventions (Beck, McKeown, Omanson, & Pople, 1984; Feldman, 1985). Even first-grade readers recalled these revised stories more readily than they did basal reader stories, despite the fact that the revisions supposedly increased the level of difficulty of the text.

The Importance of Stories to Pre-readers

Stories are generally accepted as accessible and suitable venues for introducing children to print. Most of what is published under the heading of children's literature consists of stories; most of the contents of early reading textbooks for children are some sort of story, as we pointed out in Chapter 1.

Even before children come to school, storyreading has been found to be important. The Bristol Study (Wells, 1986) followed thirty-two children from the age of 15 months to 10 years. A tape recorder was strapped on toddlers' backs and activated at various intervals throughout the day. This kind of surveillance yielded a fairly complete picture of the talk in normal family life for these children. Dimensions of this talk, among many other variables, were correlated with each child's subsequent performance in school. Of all the possible predictors of achievement (such as parents' socioeconomic class, parents' educational attainment, the quantity of conversation between parent and child, and the child's early linguistic facility), only one factor was found to be consistently associated with higher literacy test scores—having stories read aloud at home. (All of the families were European North American and resided in England.) In other words, while reading may be more common in middle-class than in lower-class homes (Heath, 1982), poor families who read to their children can overcome the general educational disadvantages they face to some extent.

Suppose for a moment that written narratives conform to cultural variations similar to the cultural variations we have found among oral narratives. What happens to those parents who can't find books that sound right to their ears to read to their children, books that reflect their cultural intonations? Most likely, these parents will find it difficult to use reading aloud as a means of fostering pre-literacy skills. If they don't feel comfortable reading to their child and only manage to do so twice monthly, by the time that child reaches kindergarten he or she may have heard fewer than a hundred books. Contrast that number to the quantity of books read to a child whose parents feel entirely comfortable with the structure of Western children's books. If that child has heard one book a night, by the age of 5 he or she will have heard over 1,800 stories. In actuality, the gap is greater, for some parents never read aloud at all, while others read more than one book every night starting at birth or even before it. While quantity doesn't necessarily equal quality, such an enormous gap is likely to have significant results.

If we were to assume that children coming from a culture less attentive to the world of print need not be inculcated into that world, this disparity wouldn't be so worrisome. But the fact is, no matter what our origins, we live in a world that is highly driven by conventions of literacy. The ability to participate fully in the United States educational system, business community, legal system, artistic community, and governmental system requires a high degree of literacy. Our goal as teachers is to make that level of literacy accessible to every child in our classroom.

In California today, the majority (over 60 percent) of students are considered "minority" students. While California is not emblematic of the country as a whole, it is an indication of the country's future. Already, nationally, Spanish-speaking or Spanish background children account for 10 percent of the public school population. Yet, European North American writers create the vast majority of learning materials and published stories these children use for learning.

The Publishers' Dilemma

Unfortunately, change in the publishing world happens slowly. As one highly regarded editor at a prominent children's trade book publishing house said, "By the time we recognize a trend, we're jumping on the bandwagon." Primarily well-intentioned, editors can't help but be cognizant that most librarians and booksellers are also European North American and middle-class. Each of those groups can exert a tremendous amount of influence on the success or failure of a book. They are the buying public.

But as minority representation in our population grows, so does the possibility of a far larger audience awaiting the publishers' attention. In the last few years, major trade publishers have rushed to compile lists of what they term their "multicultural titles." However, for someone hoping to find in these books the voices of non-Western, nonmainstream culture, the reaction may be disappointment. You do find stories with a "rainbow" of characters, sometimes even placed within fairly realistic settings. Unfortunately, many of these books lack authenticity, particularly when examined in light of the findings presented in *Chameleon Readers*.

The Problem of the "Good Story"

"Our first criterion is that it be a 'good story,'" an editor once explained to the first author of this chapter, a comment that echoes the remarks made by the American Society for Curriculum Development quoted in the preface to this book. Aristotle (translated by Bywater, 1973) argued that a good story had to have a clear beginning, middle, and end, a definition that continues to circulate today. Good stories also must involve sequenced actions in his view: "Tragedy is essentially an imitation not of persons but of action and life, of happiness and misery. All human happiness or misery takes the form of action." Sequencing events is a staple focus of many reading programs through elementary school levels (for example, Macmillan Publishing Company, 1992; Silver, Burdett & Ginn, 1992). Ever since the late seventies, educators have also been encouraged to instruct children in the problem-solving structures emphasized by story grammar (Pearson & Fielding, 1991). Recall that story grammar itself was based on Propp's (1968) analysis of Russian folktales. All these definitions of good stories, then, are derived directly from the European tradition.

We also looked more broadly for definitions of "good" children's literature, turning to books giving advice about choosing books for children. Zena Sutherland (1980) introduces *The Best in Children's Books: The University of Chicago Guide to Children's Literature 1973–1978* by arguing that children's books should be critically evaluated in much the same way that we evaluate literature for adults:

> A well-constructed plot; sound characterization with no stereotypes; dialogue that flows naturally and is appropriate to the speaker's age, education, and milieu; and a pervasive theme are equally important in children's and adults' fiction (p. viii).

In his textbook *Children and Literature,* John Warren Stewig (1988, pp. 18–19) mentions nine elements he considers important for what he calls "internal evaluation" of a children's book: characterization, dialogue, setting, plot, conflict, resolution, theme, style, and mood:

> **Plot.**   Is the plot an exciting one that carries us along? . . . Do we want to continue reading to find out what happens? Is what happens logical, even if the story is a fantasy?
>
> **Conflict.**   The driving force that makes things happen is the conflict . . . Whatever the type of conflict, it must be convincing; the reason for the disagreement must ring true.
>
> **Resolution.**   . . . To evaluate a story's resolution, we need to ask if the ending could have happened. Given what the author establishes in the book, is what happens a logical consequence? Does the resolution bring naturally to an end what the author set in motion?
>
> **Theme.**   . . . Many experts have written about theme. Cohen (1985) took the single most pervasive theme in literature—the quest—and analyzed its components (problem, struggle, realization, and achieving the goal), demonstrating her categories in the context of three popular books.

"The theme never overwhelms the plot," categorically state Joan Glazer and Gurney Williams III (1979, p. 30), in their textbook *Introduction to Children's Literature.*

Reflecting on what we now know about differing cultural styles of oral narrative, these statements and definitions seem particularly inappropriate for evaluating stories from Latino and African American culture. Yet these textbooks attempt in other ways to be sensitive to the needs of minority children. Are we stretching the concept of cultural variation too far when we apply it to written narrative? Perhaps there does exist a universal definition of the "good story" when it comes to literature. On the other hand, perhaps not. Perhaps instead we should expand our definition of what makes a good story.

Delineating the Differences

We turn now to some examples of children's books from the four cultures discussed in chapters 4 through 8 in order to pin down the qualities that both define the books as being from a particular culture and differentiate them from works of three other cultures. We stress that this is *not* an exercise in literary criticism, but an attempt to identify the attributes within each book that implicitly point to the book's ethnicity.

After experimenting with various methods of narrative analysis, the first author of this chapter found three to be the most enlightening for examining written narrative. These are: (1) stanza analysis (Gee, 1986; Hymes, 1982, described in Chapter 3); (2) highpoint analysis (Labov, 1972; Peterson & McCabe, 1983, also described in Chapter 3); and (3) episodic analysis (a version of story grammar described in Peterson & McCabe, 1983).

There were several criteria for choosing the books for this chapter. First, these books are all trade books, and we can assume the authors had no ostensible pedagogical purpose in writing them. The second criterion was that they had to be written in the form of personal narratives and be stories about a specific event that took place sometime in the past. This left out certain genres such as nursery rhymes, alphabet books, counting books, folktales (too many antecedent tellings to be considered original), and informational books written in expository form. The books chosen are all picture books intended for young children who are either pre-readers or beginning readers. Finally, the books are accepted as "good books" within their culture, although this was sometimes difficult to determine.

There are two points to bear in mind while examining the data derived from our examination of trade books. First of all, with some cultures there are very few books from which to select a representative sample. Finding Latino books presented a particularly difficult challenge. We should also remember that all of these books have been published by trade publishers in the United States. These books have gone through the editing and production phases in companies staffed predominantly by European North American, upper middle-class people. We do not know what transformations the original manuscripts might have undergone during the editing process.

Japanese English Picture Books

Four Japanese English picture books were analyzed: *Umbrella*, by Taro Yashima (1986); *Faithful Elephants*, by Yukio Tsuchiya (1988), translated by Tomoko Tsuchiya Dykes; *I Wish I Had a Big, Big Tree*, by Satoru Sato (1989), translated by Hitomi Jitodai and Carol Eisman; and *Tree of Cranes*, by Allen Say (1991). All of these authors are native Japanese speakers, although Yashima and Say have resided in the United States for most of their adult lives.

General Observations. The number three worked its way into these stories in numerous ways. There were three little bushes in Kaoru's yard (Sato 1989); Momo's umbrella was a gift for her third birthday (Yashima 1986); and there were three faithful elephants (Tsuchiya 1988).

Latino Picture Books

The four Latino picture books analyzed are: *Tonight Is Carnaval*, by Arthur Dorros (1991b); *Family Pictures: Cuadros de familia*, by Carmen Lomas Garza (1990); *Abuela*, by Arthur Dorros (1991a); and *My Aunt Otilia's Spirits*, by Richard Garcia (1987).

General Observations. Most significantly, all four books are about family life, and family relationships are an important aspect of the stories. Finding out "what happened" would not be a strong reason for reading these books; who was there and what their relationship is to the narrator takes center stage. Unlike many of the other books analyzed for this chapter, if you were to take the family relationships out of the Latino picture books, there would be no story.

African American Picture Books

The four titles grouped under this heading include: *Some of the Days of Everett Anderson* by Lucille Clifton (1970); *Africa Dream*, by Eloise Greenfield (1992); *The Black Snowman*, by Phil Mendez (1989); and *Aunt Flossie's Hats (and Crab Cakes Later)*, by Elizabeth Fitzgerald Howard (1991).

General Observations. Three of the four African American picture books were written as a series of scenes with connecting links. In *Aunt Flossie's Hats*, two girls encourage their great-great aunt to reminisce by pulling out different old hats to remind her of the accompanying stories. The theme of crab cakes runs through the book as a kind of descant refrain or "B" theme. *Some of the Days of Everett Anderson* is a series of vignettes involving a 6-year-old boy, in which the connecting link is the days of the week. In *The Black Snowman*, the theme moves back and forth through time and is embodied in an ancient piece of Kente cloth that brings magical powers to the wearer. These three stories exhibit the kind of form we called performative narrative structure in Chapter 6.

European North American Picture Books

The books chosen to represent this group were: *Where the Wild Things Are*, by Maurice Sendak (1963); *On the Day You Were Born*, by Debra Frasier (1991); *The Polar Express*, by Chris Van Allsburg (1985); and *Miss Rumphius*, by Barbara Cooney (1982).

General Observations. All four of the main characters in the European North American picture books are on some sort of quest. Even though the main character of *On the Day You Were Born* is "you," "you" are experiencing the first major quest of life—being born—and the world is preparing the way for your birth and making much of your arrival. In other words, "you" are the center of the universe!

The Polar Express, Miss Rumphius, and *Where the Wild Things Are* employ the theme of coming home at the end of a series of adventures; and certainly *On the*

TABLE 2. A Comparative Look at Written Stories from Four Cultures

	African American	Japanese American	Latino	European N. American
Number of lines/stanza	2	3	varies	varies
Percent of sentences that are:				
Evaluation	52%	69%	50%	55%
Actions	38%	26%	24%	47%
Description	6%	7%	10%	5%
Habitual action	2%	<1%	10%	<1%

Note that these percentages do not add to 100 percent due to the presence of some comments that did not fit into any of these categories and the existence of some comments that belonged in more than one category.

Day You Were Born could also be construed as being about "coming home." In this respect, they employ the earliest kind of resolution children use in their oral personal narratives.

Stanza Analysis

The two groups for whom regular stanza structure was found for oral narratives—Japanese American and African American—also have regular stanza structure in their written stories. Japanese stories, like the oral narratives of Japanese children, displayed a remarkably consistent pattern of three-line stanzas, roughly comparable to paragraphs in the written texts. Furthermore, African American written stories, just like the narratives of children in that culture, also show regular stanza structure. Here, however, there tend to be two lines per topic, or stanza, whereas there are often four lines per stanza in oral narratives. This is a phenomenon noted in the context of Native American narration: cultures that have a regular stanza structure also have a regular, shorter variant (Hymes, 1982).

Another similarity here is that the two groups for whom no regular stanza structure was found for oral narratives—Latinos and European North Americans—also have no regular stanza structure in written stories.

Highpoint Analysis

How do the results of analysis of written stories (Table 2) compare with the findings regarding oral narrative discussed in earlier chapters and displayed in Table 1? First of all, African American stories for children are almost as action-packed as the oral narratives of African American children. Relatively little emphasis on description occurs in both stories and narratives from this tradition. Also, as in the oral narratives, there is virtually no use of habitual action in these written stories.

Latino stories for children place more emphasis on description than do the stories of any other group and are quite similar in that regard to the oral and written productions of Latino children, which are also filled with more description than the oral narratives of other groups. There is striking and unique focus on habitual actions in printed stories, just as in the oral, personal ones by Latino children. Specific past tense action in stories, as in narratives, is de-emphasized.

European North American stories—more than those of any other group—focus on specific past tense action. The oral personal narratives of children from this tradition were also the ones most focused on actions—more than any other group and more than any other component. There is virtually no focus on habitual actions in stories or narratives.

There are differences as well. Most notable, perhaps, is the remarkable focus on evaluation in Japanese stories, an element that is not particularly evident in oral personal narratives. However, overall, there is a congruence of emphasis on the components of narration that one finds in published stories and oral personal anecdotes in all four cultures examined.

Episodic Analysis (Story Grammar Structure)

We have referred to this analysis previously and it is well-known in educational circles. Story grammar identifies a number of alternative structures (Glenn & Stein, 1980, described in McCabe & Peterson, 1984). Note that the first four are viewed as primitive, inferior to the complete episode and its more complex variations.

1. **Descriptive Sequence:** a description of a character and his or her surroundings and habitual actions.
2. **Action Sequence:** a focus on behavior, with a series of causally unrelated actions, as well as external and internal states of the characters involved.
3. **Reactive Sequence:** a focus on changes in the environment described where one change generally causes other changes; something happens that causes something else to happen, although there is no evidence of goals.
4. **Abbreviated Episode:** This describes aims of a protagonist, but planning generally must be inferred. Two components are required: (a) some motive for action, either an event in the environment or an internal motivating state, must exist and lead to (b) a specified consequence that achieves or fails to achieve the protagonist's goal, which may or may not be specified.
5. **Complete Episode:** This describes purposeful behavior, with more evidence of planning on the part of participants. A complete episode must include at least three of the following: (a) motivating states, (b) attempts to achieve a goal, and (c) consequences of those attempts. If consequences are omitted, the episode is incomplete. Complete episodes may also include settings, reactions of participants, and judgments.
6. **Complex Episode:** Some complex episodes involve reactive sequences or complete episodes embedded in more complicated structures. Others involve some kind of complication in a protagonist's pursuit of a goal.
7. **Interactive Episode:** two characters have goals and influence each other.

Not all good stories are scored as having good story grammar structure, and the cultural groups fared differently in the extent to which stories matched the kind of structures valued in this approach. Three of the four Japanese stories were scored as Interactive Episodes. There was also a strong emphasis on plot in European North American stories: three were scored as Complex Episodes. The fourth, *On the Day You Were Born* was scored as a Reactive Sequence. There was no predominate type of episode in African American stories. One was scored as an Action Sequence, one a Descriptive Sequence, one a Reactive Sequence and one a Complex Episode. Two of the four Latino stories were scored as Action Sequences, one was a Descriptive Sequence, and one an Abbreviated Sequence. In short, teachers should exercise caution in applying story grammar, an analysis derived from Russian folktales, to the stories written by non-European authors.

The Treatment of Fantasy Sequences

Stories for children often embed fantasy sequences in the middle of fictional reality, and the stories differ somewhat in the way this is handled. There was one fantasy sequence in the Japanese books, and that fantasy in *I Wish I Had a Big, Big Tree* was clearly marked by the format of the book: you have to turn it sideways to read that section. Two of the African American authors employed fantasy, and in both cases it was clearly marked for readers. In *Africa Dream*, the title denotes the fantasy subject; in *The Black Snowman*, the fantasy is introduced first in italic type and then tied to the talisman, the Kente cloth. Two European North American stories, *The Polar Express* and *Where the Wild Things Are*, contained fantasy journeys; the former's fantasy is less clearly marked than the latter's (no children's book author would dare imply that Santa Claus exists only in imagination!).

Of greatest interest, however, is the treatment of fantasy in the Latino stories, two of which involved fantasy to a large extent. In both *Abuela* and *My Aunt Otilia's Spirits*, the narrator's fantasy (told in the first person) is the major driving force of the book. In *Abuela*, the fantasy takes place as the answer to a "what if" question posed by the narrator, which is then spun out through the rest of the book. In *My Aunt Otilia's Spirits*, the fantasy is unmarked to the reader and appears to fulfill the narrator's wish. That fantasy is not marked off from supposed, objective (albeit fictional) reality in the novel the way it is in stories from the other cultures. In this respect, fantasy in *My Aunt Otilia's Spirits* functions more like the magic realism to be found in many Latin American novels (Aldama, 1995).

Another Quick Test: "What's It About?"

In written narratives, as in oral narratives, a major difference in the various cultural styles hinges on the importance of plot. "What is this story about?" is a quick and fairly reliable way to recognize cultural variation. In a European North American story, a particular event (or a causally connected series of events) is foregrounded. "What happened in this story?" will elicit a synopsis of the event or events. For example, *The Polar Express* can be summarized using action verbs: the main character rides a mysterious train to the North Pole; he meets Santa Claus; Santa gives him a silver bell; he loses the bell; he returns home; he gets the bell back; he realizes the bell's magical property.

In a Japanese story, too, we can ask what happened and receive a plot summary in response. So, for a European North American reading a Japanese English story, the feeling of discombobulation is not strong. Some differences lie in the source of the conflict that is providing the plot, the three-line stanza form that is so prevalent in the Japanese English stories, and the nature of the resolutions. For example, in *Umbrella*, the main character, Momo, is a little girl who wants to try out her new umbrella. But the weather is either sunny or windy, and her mother won't let her take the umbrella out until there is rain. Finally, of course, the rain comes, and Momo gets her wish. Momo, on the other hand, after waiting for her wish to come true, is so engrossed in her umbrella that she walks alone for the first time, "without holding either her mother's or her father's hand." In effect, at the end of this book, Momo is beginning the process of leaving home. This resolution contrasts with the returning home conclusion so popular in European North American stories (such as *Where the Wild Things Are*).

When we ask "What happened?" about an African American story, we may find there is no simple answer. "What's it about?" may elicit more information about characters and setting than it does about events. *Some of the Days of Everett Anderson* is about the daily life of a 6-year-old African American boy who lives in the city. What happens? Lots of things happen to this lively character; he is the link between the happenings. *Miss Rumphius*, another story nominally about the main character's life, is really about that character's quest to fulfill three objectives: to travel, to live by the sea, and most of all, to make the world more beautiful. *Africa Dream* is about a young girl's dream of going to Africa and is full of her description of the people and things she sees there. The central character in *Africa Dream* also does various activities (she shops for pearls and perfume, she rides a donkey through the crowds), but the most important part of the story is her description of people and places and the relationships she forms with them. Significant, also, is the fact that she doesn't return home at the end of her dream.

"What's the story about?" in a Latino picture book seems primarily to concern vignettes of the continuous, especially focusing on family and friendships. *Abuela* is about a young girl, Rosalba, who imagines flying in the sky over New York with her grandmother, her *abuela*. What happens? They fly around, visiting various family members. The main point of the story is to describe the loving relationship between Rosalba and her grandmother, as well as the other family members. There is no plot-advancing conflict. *Tonight Is Carnaval* is about a family's preparations for a major fiesta, without conflict except for the main character's impatience for the time to come. The warm feelings among family members and among friends are the most important aspects of this story, along with a detailed description of the Andean Mountain area where they reside. On the other hand, *My Aunt Otilia's Spirits* is about a problem: a young boy doesn't like having to share his bed with his crotchety aunt when she comes to visit. It is, in fact, about a breakdown in family relationships. But the solution to his problem comes via a fantasy in which her spirit leaves the house, her bones become jumbled up, and she is nowhere to be found in the morning. Ostensibly, he has done nothing to effect her departure; he didn't need to directly confront her.

If we go back to the criteria posed by several authorities (pp. 161-162) as suitable for judging good stories—a well-constructed plot, conflict, resolution, and theme (the quest)—we can see that these categories are inappropriate for appreciating narratives written by Latino and African American authors. To employ them would imply that these stories are somehow deficient, while letting the stories' central themes go unappreciated. Recall how one pair of authors stated, "The theme never overwhelms the plot." To apply that criterion to all stories would be akin to criticizing a woman for not having large muscles, a low voice, and a beard: in short, for not being a man.

Narratives Influence Stories and Vice Versa

In various ways, then, we find congruity between the structure of children's oral personal narratives and that of fictional stories written by adult authors from various cultures. Lifelong habits of telling personal narratives undoubtedly influence authors who write children's literature. But, too, the influence of stories upon narratives should not be discounted. Throughout this book we refer to oral storytelling traditions, and we have examined instances where those stories crept into children's personal narratives (for example, Chapter 8). To the extent that they are common in a young child's life, written tales read to children also shape the way children tell stories (Purcell-Gates, 1988).

Turning Theory into Practice

In a study published in 1985, McConaughy found that children who are perceived as poor readers "are capable of high quality story comprehension when they are presented with text material which is from a familiar genre and which has a predictable underlying structure" (p. 230). Although she was not specifically considering narrative style, we can assume that the impact of cultural variations among narrative styles is as great as that of differences among genres. To a Latino child, the "predictable underlying structure" is likely to mean something quite different than what it means to a European North American child.

Hybrid Stories: Chameleon Writers?

Can we become "chameleon writers" as well as "chameleon readers"? What a happy solution that would be. Not only could we teach children to assume various styles, but writers could move from one style to another with dexterity. Unfortunately, it does not seem to be easy to do. If we examine books written by one group (with all good intentions) about another group, we find that the original cultural narrative style of the author remains dominant. For example, in *I Speak English for My Mother*, by Muriel Stanek (1989), a young Hispanic child tells of her experience in acting as translator for her mother. The story is appealing, and the main character is portrayed in a strong way. Why, the story is even about "family!" But as we analyze it more closely, we come to see that the plot is a Complex Episode and the high point analysis turns up very few orientative clauses. When we ask, "What's it about?" we find it's about the daughter's efforts to enroll her mother in English classes. In fact, the group *I Speak English for My Mother* belongs in structurally is European North American.

A great many books that are included in various curricula as multicultural selections are books that involve characters and sometimes practices from various ethnic backgrounds but that are written by European North American authors. Ezra Jack Keats is one such popular author. In sections of libraries devoted to folktales from around the world, one finds many collections by European North American writers.

Bear in mind that the authors of this chapter are themselves of European North American heritage. We applaud efforts to advance cross-cultural understanding. However, we must bear Paula Gunn Allen's comments in mind (Chapter 2), extend them to folktales collected from other cultures, and be cautious about thinking that these translations are truly authentic. Some authors admit they discarded stories that did not make sense to them when they went back and listened to tape-recordings of indigenous storytellers (for example, see Diane Wolkstein's, 1978, comments in *The Magic Orange Tree and Other Haitian Folktales*). Apparent universals in storytelling form may be artifacts: European structures imposed upon stories that were originally distinctly different in form.

Authenticity is a huge, much-disputed issue, though to date it has focused on the life experiences of authors rather than the form of storytelling that is our focus in this chapter. The case of Forrest Carter, who wrote *The Education of Little Tree*, caused renewed and emotional scrutiny of authors who write about members of cultures not their own. The book purported to be a biography of Little Tree, an orphaned child of 10 who learns Indian ways from his Cherokee grandparents. This book sold widely, received critical praise, and was touted as an exemplary multicultural work. Unfortunately, "Forrest Carter" turned out to be a pseudonym for the late Asa Earl Carter, described as a Ku Klux Klan terrorist, fascist, and secret author of the infamous 1963 speech by Governor George Wallace: "Segregation now . . . Segregation tomorrow . . . Segregation forever" (see Gates, 1991).

Henry Louis Gates (1991) addresses many of the components of this complex controversy, more than we can reiterate or do justice to here. Some people assume that the works of any author from a background underrepresented in world literature "convey the authentic, unmediated experience of their social identities" (Gates, 1991, p. 26). He points out that literature has always been about imagination as much as it has been about any kind of social reality. "Subtract from the reality column, add to the art column," Gates (1991, p. 29) argues, giving credit to authors who successfully represent social realities of individuals who do not match them in gender, class, ethnicity, age, and so forth. We agree with Gates (1991, p. 29) that "The distasteful truth will out: like it or not, all writers are 'cultural impersonators.'"

Nonetheless, it may be easier for authors to weave the details of perspectives, feelings, yearnings, and the like, of members from different cultures into their own form of storytelling than it would be to emulate forms of storytelling that they have not been socialized into from earliest childhood. As experienced readers, we can learn to appreciate cultural styles different from our own, but we may have a devil of a time trying to replicate them. Yet we ask some children to do it every day in school, both in writing and in reading.

Thus, this is not a call to censure writers, but rather to expand our definitions of what constitutes "good writing." As publishers, critics, librarians, teachers, and readers, we must embrace the diverse forms that grace our literary landscape, and seek out that variety that adds to our understanding of all literature. We must assume that form is present, even when it is not immediately apparent to us. We must encourage its recognition and appreciation, and allow new forms to be judged on their own terms. We cannot be content to admire and teach stories about other groups that are written in styles and by authors that are exclusively of European extraction. Put simply, Ezra Jack Keats is not enough.

And finally, we must look at reality through the stories of and for all our children. Then, and only then, will we truly be "chameleon readers."

Box 10: Research into Practice

1. Teachers are encouraged to analyze the stories they include as multicultural selections. Use the various methods of analysis we used in this chapter (some described in more detail in Chapter 3). How well do the stories match the form of storytelling valued in the various cultures described?

2. Ask advanced students to talk about the form of the stories they read. For instance, give them some examples of Performative Stories (such as *Aunt Flossie's Hats (and Crab Cakes Later)*) with thematically linked episodes. Discuss that kind of story. Then give students some new stories that are of this sort and let them name the form.

Summary

- Children learn to read not for the joy of decoding but for the joy of having their narrative curiosity satisfied, for the sake of communication.
- Many cultural schemata are evoked, appropriately or inappropriately, when we hear or read stories.
- Rewriting stories that were "scientifically designed" for children's readers can actually improve their comprehensibility; despite the fact that the language used is more complicated, the story makes more sense to children.
- Reading stories is very important during children's preschool years. Parents whose sense of story differs from that found in the largely European stock of stories available to them in bookstores and libraries may avoid reading these to their children for that reason alone.
- Definitions of what makes a story good are derived almost exclusively from European traditions.
- Using a variety of analyses, we found that children's stories written by Japanese, African American, Latino, and European North American authors were structured like the oral narratives of children from those backgrounds. The traditions were not identical.
- When European North American authors write stories about children from different cultures, they typically use European story form. We speculate that it may be easier to represent the social reality of other kinds of people—by no means an easy task in itself—than it is to emulate the form of storytelling practiced by individuals in those cultures. In any case, story form should be a part of the raging authenticity debates.

References

ALDAMA, F.L. (1995). The structural configuration of Magic Realism in Gabriel Garcia Marquez, Leslie Marmon Silko, Charles Johnson, and Julie Dash. *Journal of Narrative and Life History, 5.*

ARISTOTLE. (1973). *Poetics*. Trans. Ingram Bywater. In R. McKeon (Ed.), *Introduction to Aristotle*. Chicago: University of Chicago Press.

BAKER, C., & FREEBODY, P. (1989). *Children's first school books: Introductions to the culture of literacy*. Oxford, England: Basil Blackwell.

BARTLETT, F.C. (1932). *Remembering*. Cambridge, England: Cambridge University Press.

BECK, I.L., MCKEOWN, M.G., OMANSON, R.C., & POPLE, M.T. (1984). Improving the comprehensibility of stories: The effects of revisions that improve coherence. *Reading Research Quarterly, XIX* (3), 263–277.

CAIRNEY, T.H. (1991). *Other worlds: The endless possibilities of literature*. Portsmouth, NH: Heinemann Educational Books.

CLIFTON, L. (1970). *Some of the days of Everett Anderson*. New York: Henry Holt.

CLYMER, T., INDRISANO, R., JOHNSON, D., & VENEZKY, R. (1985). *Little dog laughed*. Lexington, MA: Ginn.

COHEN, C.L. (1985). The quest in children's literature. *School Library Journal, 31,* 28–29.

COONEY, B. (1982). *Miss Rumphius*. New York: Viking.

DORROS, A. (1991a). *Abuela*. New York: Dutton.

DORROS, A. (1991b). *Tonight is carnaval*. New York: Dutton.

FELDMAN, M.J. (1985). Evaluating pre-primer basal readers using story grammar. *American Educational Research Journal, 22* (4), 527–547.

FRASIER, D. (1991). *On the day you were born*. San Diego, CA: Harcourt Brace Jovanovich.

GARCIA, R. (1987). *My Aunt Otilia's spirits*. San Francisco: Children's Book Press.

GARZA, C.L. (1990). *Family pictures: Cuadros de familia*. San Francisco: Children's Book Press.

GATES, H.L. (1991, November 24). 'Authenticity,' or the Lesson of Little Tree. *The New York Times Book Review,* 1, 26–30.

GEE, J.P. (1986). Units in the production of narrative discourse. *Discourse Processes, 9,* 391–422.

GLAZER, J.I., & WILLIAMS, G. III (1979). *Introduction to children's literature*. New York: McGraw Hill.

GREENFIELD, E. (1992). *Africa Dream*. New York: Harper/Trophy.

HAMANN, L., SCHULTZ, L., SMITH, M., & WHITE, B. (1991). Making connections: The power of autobiographical writing before reading. *Journal of Reading, 35*(1), 24–28.

HEATH, S.B. (1982). What no bedtime stories means: Narrative skills at home and school. *Language in Society, 2,* 49–76.

HOWARD, E.F. (1991). *Aunt Flossie's hats (and crab cakes later)*. New York: Clarion Books.

HYMES, D. (1982). Narrative form as a "grammar" of experience: Native Americans and a glimpse of English. *Journal of Education, 2,* 121–142.

KINTSCH, W. (1987). Contributions from cognitive psychology. In R. Tierney, P. Anders, & J.N. Mitchell (Eds.), *Understanding readers' understanding: Theory and practice* (pp. 5–14). Hillsdale, NJ: Lawrence Erlbaum.

LABOV, W. (1972). *Language in the inner city*. Philadelphia: University of Pennsylvania Press.

MCCABE, A., & PETERSON, C. (1984). What makes a good story? *Journal of Psycholinguistic Research, 13* (6), 457–480.

MCCONAUGHY, S.H. (1985). Good and poor readers' comprehension of story structure. *Reading Research Quarterly, XX*(2), 219–232.

MEEK, M. (1982). What counts as evidence in theories of children's literature? *Theory into Practice, 21,* 284–292.

MENDEZ, P. (1989). *The black snowman*. New York: Scholastic.

PEARSON, P.D., & FIELDING, L. (1991). Comprehension instruction. In R. Barr, M.L. Kamil, P.B. Mosenthal, & P.D. Pearson (Eds.), *Handbook of reading research* (Vol. II, pp. 815–860). NY: Longman.

PETERSON, C., & McCABE, A. (1983). *Developmental psycholinguistics: Three ways of looking at a child's narrative.* New York: Plenum.

PRITCHARD, R. (1990). The effects of cultural schemata on reading processing strategies. *Reading Research Quarterly, 25*(4), 273–295.

PROPP, W. (1968). *Morphology of the folktale.* Austin, TX: University of Texas Press. (Originally published, 1928).

PURCELL-GATES, V. (1988). Lexical and syntactic knowledge of written narrative held by well-read-to kindergartners and second graders. *Research in the Teaching of English, 22* (2), 128–160.

ROSENBLATT, L.M. (1978). *The reader, the text, the poem: The transactional theory of the literary work.* Carbondale, IL: Southern Illinois University Press.

SATO, S. (1989). *I wish I had a big, big tree.* New York: Lothrop, Lee & Shepard.

SAY, A. (1991). *Tree of cranes.* Boston: Houghton Mifflin.

SENDAK, M. (1963). *Where the wild things are.* New York: Harper & Row.

SNOW, C.E., & NINIO, A. (1986). The contracts of literacy: What children learn from learning to read books. In W.H. Teale & E. Sulzby (Eds.), *Emergent literacy: Writing and reading* (pp. 116–138). Norwood, NJ: Ablex.

STANEK, M. (1989). *I speak English for my mom.* Niles, IL: Albert Whitman.

STEWIG, J.W. (1988). *Children and literature* (2nd ed.). Boston: Houghton Mifflin.

SUTHERLAND, Z. (1980). *The best in children's books: The University of Chicago guide to children's literature, 1973–1978.* Chicago: University of Chicago Press.

TSUCHIYA, Y. (1988). *Faithful elephants.* Trans. T. Dykes. Boston: Houghton Mifflin. (Original work published in 1951).

VAN ALLSBURG, C. (1985). *The polar express.* Boston: Houghton Mifflin.

WELLS, G. (1986). *The meaning makers: Children learning language and using language to learn.* Portsmouth, NH: Heinemann Educational Books.

WHITEHURST, G.J., FALCO, F.L., LONIGAN, C.J., FISCHEL, J.E., DeBARYSHE, D.B., VALDEZ-MENCHACA, M.C., & CAULFIELD, M. (1987). Accelerating language development through picture book reading. *Developmental Psychology, 24,* 552–559.

WOLKSTEIN, D. (1978). *The magic orange tree and other Haitian folktales.* New York: Knopf.

YASHIMA, T. (1986). *Umbrella.* New York: Puffin Books.

CHAPTER 10

Chameleon Readers: Notes toward an Authentic Multicultural Literacy Program

Allyssa McCabe

OVERVIEW

Whatever method is used to teach reading, a careful consideration of diverse cultural traditions of storytelling is called for. This chapter focuses on the implications this diversity has for reading materials, assessments, and writing programs. Reading materials should more adequately include all kinds of good stories. Assessments of story comprehension should be tailored to suit various kinds of stories and students. Educators should rethink efforts to switch all children into a European storytelling style. Writing instruction will be more effective if a variety of storytelling forms is valued. We address implications of diverse storytelling styles for social interactions between teachers and students and among students themselves. Educators are asked to assume that each child is well versed in a storytelling style and to work with that child's skill, instead of labeling the style deficient from a European point of view. We also address possible objections to multicultural literature programs in general and to the kind of program envisioned in this book. Finally, evidence is provided that the curriculum strategies recommended here can be very effective in a variety of ways.

WHAT DO ALL THESE IDEAS MEAN FOR CLASSROOM PRACTICE?

The field of reading is historically and currently the site of hard-fought battles over method. A focus on developing a well-thought-out multicultural literacy curriculum can easily slip from central consideration in the face of such battles. The debate between traditional and whole language approaches has not directed attention specifically to cultural issues, such as those faced by African American students (Ladson-Billings, 1992). Ladson-Billings articulates the need for a culturally relevant approach to teaching that recognizes and celebrates African and African American culture in order to foster and sustain students' desire to choose academic success in the face of competing options. In this chapter, we suggest some ways of expanding on this notion in order to address the diverse needs of the many kinds of children now in American schools.

Implications for Materials, Assessment, and Writing

Reading

Stories Read to and by Children. For children on the cusp of literacy, instruction in reading should from the outset be a deeply meaningful process. For children who display a narrative structure not familiar to a teacher, it would be a good idea to read stories that conform to that structure.

Educators may want to engage in extended celebrations of various cultures—one at a time and in enough depth to get a real feeling for each one—through art, music, dance, and, of course, stories, pointing out aesthetic values that transcend specific forms. It is only through repeated exposure to different examples of a particular form of story that the form itself becomes apparent. A single-shot exposure without provision of background information about the culture that gave rise to the story is likely to backfire, leading to dismissal of the form rather than acceptance and enjoyment.

In Chapter 9, our survey of existing texts touted as being multicultural reveals a varied assortment. There are numerous European North American stories with illustrations of children from diverse ethnic backgrounds. There are also stories with strange mixes of basal reader language and supposedly ethnic values. Some "hybrid" stories have genuine cultural themes but are written with unmistakably traditional story grammar structure by European North American authors. Finally, there are a few authentically structured tales from various cultures and countries, but these are often presented with no background information that would facilitate understanding for those who do not share the cultural background giving rise to the story.

Harris (1991), who reviewed African American children's literature within an historical perspective, recommends adoption of those texts that constitute an authentic body of literature written about and for African American children. Almost without exception, such books, Harris notes, are written by African American authors, although they need not be (Gates, 1991).

A well-considered multicultural literacy curriculum mindful of cultural differences in narrative structure would include *numerous* stories written by African American, Asian American, Native American, European North American, and Latino authors. These stories should be read to and by all children in all grades. Enough of each kind should be available so that children could come to appreciate the form of stories told by cultures not their own. Why not devote a full fifth of each school year to stories of each of these major groups? Such an approach would allow all children sufficient exposure to stories and cultures that they do not share, while ensuring that all children would share a home background in narrative that is recognized as valid in school for part of the school year.

Educators should think in terms of three goals in selecting stories to be read to and by children:

1. Match each child's particular sense of storytelling at least some of the time.
2. Challenge European North American children by extensive exposure to traditions other than the European one, and do this by going into the cultural backdrop of these other traditions in some depth.
3. Challenge children from backgrounds other than the European North American one by exposing them to that tradition in such a way that they come to understand and appreciate it.

Mindful of these goals, educators who decide to include numerous stories about African Americans, Latinos, Asians and Asian Americans, and American Indians will find an invaluable resource in *Journeys to Self-Esteem: Children's Books with Themes of Cultural and Social Empowerment* by Ewa Pytowska and Gail Pettiford Willett (available by contacting Savannah Books, 1132 Massachusetts Avenue, Cambridge, Massachusetts 02138). The authors have collected numerous books from those cultural traditions and sorted them by appropriate grade level. Another similar reference work is *Our Family, Our Friends, Our World: An Annotated Guide to Significant Multicultural Books for Children and Teenagers* by Miller-Lachmann (1992) (available from R.R. Bowker, New Providence, New Jersey).

Discussing Stories Read to and by Children. By and large, U.S. schools operate under the assumption that the kind of story that resembles European fairy tales is the only literate kind of story there is. Such an emphasis is in accord with recent research on reading comprehension (for example, Pearson & Fielding, 1991). This research concludes that "ideas that are identified as important in a story grammar or central story content analysis, especially if they are implied but not stated, should receive instructional focus" (p. 826), although efforts should be made to see whether such instruction, applied to texts written expressly for such purposes, transfers to real short stories and novels, which often do not conform to story grammar sequences. As should be clear by now, this kind of focus on story grammar structure will work for many stories from the European North American tradition, but may not work well for stories from other traditions. Alternative kinds of story structures should also receive instructional focus. See Chapter 3 in particular for ways to provide alternative frameworks for discussion.

Talking to children about different forms of stories will provide them with the rich metalinguistic vocabulary they need to work with their own stories, while enabling them to understand those from different cultures. An exchange of information with children and parents of various cultures represented in the classroom would enrich everyone's understanding of stories from these cultures (see Delpit, 1986, 1988). Talking about the kind of tradition that gave rise to specific stories is imperative for understanding stories from cultures not your own. Delpit's (1986, 1988) argument that children from non-European North American backgrounds need to have the rules of that tradition made explicit for them needs to be extended. All children need explicit instruction in diverse communicative approaches in order to be prepared for reading the important world literature of our time.

Assessing Story Comprehension. Assessments should reflect an awareness of the kind of information a child is likely to extract. At present, schoolchildren are often asked to reconstruct sequences of events as a means of assessing comprehension of stories (Baker, 1982). Reconstructing a sequence of events is also often used in basal reading systems as a means of ostensibly "increasing reading ability" (Harris & Sipay, 1990). However, in light of what we know about Latino children's narrative structure, for example, heavy reliance on this kind of assessment needs to be reconsidered.

The movement in literary criticism to recognize the role of readers in responding to literature (for example, Beach & Hynds, 1991) may need to be invoked here. That is, comprehension of a story can be construed as a kind of response to a story, as can recalling it. Simply because children of different cultures *recall* the same story in different ways (John & Berney, 1968) does not by definition mean that some have "correctly" understood that story while others have not.

The Problem with Switching Children's Oral Storytelling Style. Some educators may feel that it would be simpler just to switch children into the European North American storytelling style that so dominates American society today than it would be to do the kinds of modifications of curriculum we are proposing. Unfortunately, such an approach would not seem congruent with currently available research findings.

First of all, consider developmental research. Children acquire basic narrative structure at home with their parents during their infancy and preschool years (see, McCabe & Peterson, 1990, 1991). Parents in all cultures engage in discussions of past events with their children or in front of their children (Miller et al., 1990; Schieffelin & Eisenberg, 1984).

Second, consider research on attempts to change narrative structure. Carole Peterson and I conducted two experiments that attempted to facilitate narrative development in a variety of ways, most employing adults to talk with preschool and kindergarten children one at a time for six weeks to a year, for hours, about past events. Not only were these efforts unrealistic in terms of potential curriculum efforts, they were unsuccessful. These two intervention projects failed to advance the children's narrative structure in any of the many ways we have available to assess that structure (McCabe, 1989). We learned from these projects that "teaching oral narrative structure at school" was a tremendously daunting and perhaps fundamentally misguided task. Moreover, Grover Whitehurst and his colleagues have been remarkably successful at facilitating vocabulary and syntax, but not narrative (Whitehurst, Angell, Crone, & Fischel, 1994).

With children living in America watching as much television as they do, one might expect all children to tell stories in a similar way, even if the original culture of their parents diverged from mainstream American culture. Surprisingly, such is not the case, as we saw in preceding chapters. Evidently, television is not a source for oral storytelling structure, at least when children talk about events that have really happened to them.

Writing: Expanding the Child-centered Approach

Having children dictate or write their own stories would seem an ideal forum for coming up with stories that have a structure the child comprehends. Unfortunately, numerous research efforts have documented cases where children who do not come from European North American families are misunderstood in, for example, process writing conferences (Michaels, 1991). Teachers may not know what questions to ask to help children extend their stories, tripping them up or cutting them off instead of helping.

In essence, teachers need to accept and appreciate a great variety of children's early productions. Try to figure out what kind of story they are telling, dictating, or writing rather than judge them deficient because their sense of storytelling does not match your own. In early elementary school years, children's struggle with the mechanics of print—decoding, letter formation, spelling, and so forth—is sufficiently daunting that they need the pull of communicating to go to the trouble of learning all those mechanics. I will revise whatever I write many times, so long as I feel that I am doing so in order better to convey what I have to say to an appreciative audience.

Process writing programs (see Graves, 1983) advocate having children write personal narratives of real experiences. After twenty years of listening to and reading both factual and fictional children's stories, I can understand and sympathize with this position. Children's factual stories, as I noted earlier in Chapter 4, are more compelling because their own particular experience of reality forces them to be original. In contrast, children's fictional productions are typically rehashes of stories they have heard or watched. Such a phenomenon is not limited to the verbal narrative realm; when children draw pictures while observing real things they are often strikingly original. When they draw pictures from memory, however, young children tend to be schematic. Nevertheless, when children are telling stories about things that really happened to them, it seems to me that particular care must be taken not to usurp their authority.

Trying to write literary forms not indigenous to one's own culture is tremendously difficult. For example, unless one appreciates the fact that Japanese parents routinely train their children to engage in empathic extension of what they hear and, when speaking, to avoid garrulousness that would be insulting and offensive to empathic listeners (Minami & McCabe, 1991), one would not completely understand the communicative compression that is the essence of *haiku*. Although the form of *haiku* is often taught in American classrooms, examination of the results of such instruction reveals that European American students tend to see this simply as short sentences consisting of the prerequisite number of syllables, not condensed expression. Consider the following *haiku* I collected from fifth-graders in Vermont:

American:

I can feel the wind.
I smell smoke walking in woods.
I hear birds in trees.

Swimming

You get very wet.
You can have a lot of fun.
You get very cold.

Contrast those samples with the following *haiku* by Japanese children (translations into English from Gakken, 1989, by Masahiko Minami, 1990, focus on meaning rather than syllable counts):

Japanese second-grader:

A foot-race
My heart is throbbing;
Next is my turn. (Kumon, 1989)

Japanese fourth-grader:

Although it is cold,
The Statue of Liberty
Stretches herself.

Both of the Japanese samples distill a story into a short but true poem, and the reader is invited to imaginatively extend their provocative pieces, whereas the European North American efforts simply describe general experiences, with many filler syllables (such as *I, you, can, get*).

Thus, without provision of information about communicative values underlying various literary forms, efforts to emulate the literary forms of cultures not one's own may not succeed even when those forms are as short as and have as clearly prescribed rules as does *haiku,* with its requirement of three lines consisting of 5, 7, and 5 syllables each.

A promising route of instruction would be to encourage children to tell their own stories the way they want to in view of the fact that such stories are so critically a matter of *self-presentation* and *sense-making.* To convey to children that somehow they are not getting their own stories straight would seem to lead to alienation.

We often take our own culture, whatever that may be, for granted and expect others to do the same. Teachers from the European North American tradition may find it strange to think of explaining that this tradition values making things very explicit, talking about one thing at a time, giving lots of actions in a sequence. Yet this kind of explicit instruction may be just what is needed for children who have not been in circumstances that gave them the opportunity to figure out those rules more or less unconsciously.

The current educational focus on sequencing actions and representing problem-solving in narrative instruction needs to be supplemented with other kinds of foci in writing instruction. For example, the development of connections among characters and the use of metaphors should be seen as at least as important to narrative as the arrangement of events in a sequence. Other kinds of suggestions for alternative foci in writing instruction appear at the end of each of the chapters detailing specific traditions.

Implications for Social Interactions

This book has tried to show that experience can be packaged in very different ways by different cultures. Cultural differences in how to tell a story are as much a part of "accent" as are differences in pronunciation, vocabulary, and syntax. Yet few people hear differences in storytelling style as something imported from another language. Instead, they sometimes dismiss stories from different cultures as "not making sense," as if that property were an objective, culture-free one.

Most of the time such dismissal results in a failure to communicate between two peers. However, when such failures to communicate occur in circumstances such as in a school (Michaels, 1991), courtroom (Barry, 1991), or clinical assessment (Perez, McCabe, & Tager-Flussberg, in preparation), the impact of being misunderstood is more profound due to the disproportionate power of teachers, lawyers, and psychologists over children. For example, clinical psychologists rated Latino narratives such as the one on page 129 as significantly more "illogical" and "incomprehensible" than European North American narratives, and were inclined to make a diagnosis of developmental delay on the basis of such narratives (Perez, 1992). Thus it is vital that adults who work with children come to recognize and appreciate cultural differences in storytelling style.

Sarah Michaels (1991) has recorded numerous interchanges between European North American teachers and European North American students and between African American teachers and African American students in which teachers pick up narrators' intentions, ask appropriate questions, and help students round out and organize their narrative accounts. Unfortunately, she also has documented incidents in which European North American educators who have been accustomed to discourse with discrete topics tend to misunderstand children whose culture allows them to use a narrative discourse consisting of a series of implicitly associated personal anecdotes, dismissing these as "rambling," or "not talking about one important thing" (Michaels, 1991). Minami (1990) found that the beautifully ordered simplicitly of Japanese children's narratives struck some American educators as "boring" or "unimaginative."

Furthermore, many studies (for example, Finkelstein & Haskins, 1983; Newman, Liss & Sherman, 1983; Singleton & Asher, 1979) document the troubling fact that simply placing children of different cultural backgrounds in the same classroom is no guarantee that they will interact with each other at all, let alone interact positively. Various programs (for example, Slavin, 1985; Weigel, Wiser, & Cook, 1975) that encourage cooperative learning have been devised to promote such cross-cultural exchanges. However, unless educators themselves understand that there are diverse ways of communicating and in some way inform their students about such differences, there may very well remain barriers to cross-cultural communication among children even in these contexts. That is, children often form impressions of personality characteristics on the basis of other children's discourse style (Hemphill & Siperstein, 1990). In observations of a diverse classroom of 6-year-olds, Rebecca Keebler (personal communication, March 4, 1993) recorded one African American girl commenting on how frustrating it was when her European North American classmates continually criticized her, her family, and her friends for their performances in Sharing Time Narratives.

> DORA: But some people say, "It's [the stories told by herself and her friends] not true. It's not true." It made me feel bad.
>
> REBECCA (observer): Kids say something's true and everybody says, "That couldn't be true." "How about this?" or "Why about that?" "Right (said sarcastically)."
>
> DORA: And, "How come this is true? It can't be true!" Like on Carl's story, Sally said, "Well how come your cousin never brushes his teeth?" And Charles said, "Well, BECAUSE. He never brushes his teeth. He brushed his teeth with a toothbrush and shaving cream." So he didn't know what toothpaste was. Sally said, "That's not true, that's not true."
>
> REBECCA: Why do you think that makes you feel bad, when people ask you if it's true and then don't believe you?
>
> DORA: Because it hurts a lot of people's feelings when they say that . . . like my sister. She told a story when she was 4 years old in her class. The whole class except for her teacher. She told a story about a cat and everybody said, "That's not true. You're joking. You're not telling the truth." And that made my sister cry.

The reaction of teachers is also critical. One African American man in his thirties can still recall enthusiastically recounting a story for his third-grade classmates with great audience success. All the children loved it. He used many embellishing devices including metaphor, humor, vocal tone, gestures, imitations of players in the story. At the end, his European North American teacher said, "I know you enjoyed it, Class, but remember that wasn't all true. He was pretending." Later on, in private, the teacher more directly scolded him for his embellishment.

Another example of cultural misunderstanding occurs in the following narrative I collected from a 9-year-old European North American girl, Alice, who was drawing her favorite animal, a cat. The story concerns her interactions with her African American art partner:

> He was teasing about CATS. He was saying like I'm going to bomb all the cats and I'm going to make a picture of a pool with a cat in it and the pool will explode. He said the worst things—like airplanes dropping bombs on kitties and

bad things like that. I just go, well nothing [like that] happens in real life so you can't make ME sad. Stuff like that.

Such small incidents of miscommunication occur often in numerous classrooms. Without some sort of information to the contrary, Dora and her friends and family were left with the impression that the European North American children were being mean rather than simply repeating the rules for storytelling that they most probably had heard from their parents. The young man felt his story had been completely misunderstood. Alice was left with the impression that her partner was trying to be mean rather than attempting to have fun conversing with her.

Educators may want to serve as translators for children from different traditions, and discussions centered on books would be one opportunity to do so. Teachers could discuss the fact that African American storytelling traditions place great emphasis on the value of telling dramatic stories. As was mentioned in Chapter 6, Zora Neale Hurston (1935/1990, p. 8) and Henry Louis Gates, Jr. (1988, p. 56) bring to our attention the fact that "lies" is a traditional African American word for figurative discourse, tales, or stories. Similarly, teasing in general is a common language game among African Americans, and is frequently either the point of a story or part of what is recapitulated (Labov, 1972). For example, *Irene and the Big, Fine Nickel* by Irene Smalls-Hector is a story that involves teasing games played by African American children and could serve as a vehicle for discussing such games. Children could be encouraged to notice the strategy the girls in the story use to make up with each other after the teasing goes too far for one of them, as we suggested in Chapter 6.

Listen to Each Child; Assume Form but Little Else

Issues of assimilation to mainstream culture at the expense of or while maintaining ethnic identity are quite complex. Some groups, some families, and some individuals seek assimilation with European North American culture more vigorously than others, and that will always be the case. Sensitivity to the fact that some children prefer to stress cultural heritage more than do others is critical.

Second, not all children from any one background will bring the same kind of oral narrative structure to school with them. Teachers must recognize that individual differences abound within any one culture, and must assess children on a case by case basis.

New Immigrants from Cultures about which Little Is Written

There are many cultures in the world and here in America about which there is little formal information regarding story form or traditions. Characterizing cultural differences takes time and a knowledge of linguistic methodology. This would be a very important task for university personnel to undertake. It would not be reasonable to expect teachers to do so while they are simultaneously performing their myriad other duties. Meantime, teachers can do the following with children from other cultures:

1. Assume that children's narrative productions have narrative form instead of the lack of it.
2. Use writing instruction as a means of getting the child's story on paper in such a fashion that you can reflect on it and see form and sense-making that was not apparent in the fast pace of oral conversation.
3. Try to give beginning readers stories that will make sense to them by drawing on local libraries. Ask librarians to order tales from the cultures of children in your classrooms. If even librarians cannot locate such stories, set up an exchange of information with children, parents, and community leaders of various cultures represented in the classroom. Transcribe what stories they recall as favorites in the country of origin.
4. In some communities, there are local individuals famous for their storytelling abilities. Invite these individuals into the classrooms and ask permission to record their performances. Set up a station where children can listen to these stories. Perhaps, also with permission, you could provide written versions of the stories for children to follow along with.
5. Try to organize a celebration of cultures underrepresented in current curriculum materials by asking children to bring in art, music, dance, food, and stories from home. Ask parents or community leaders to point out aesthetic values.

Possible Objections from Teachers Who Already Include Multicultural Materials in Their Classrooms

1. "These stories would make sense to anyone. They are good stories. It is just that in these books the children are rainbow colored." We hope the preceding chapters have convinced readers that authentic children's literature from any one culture will challenge children who have not grown up with extensive experience speaking the form of discourse from which the stories derive. Recall Paula Gunn Allen's comments in Chapter 2 that stories that are authentic translations of Indian tales should not easily make sense to European North American readers. It is only by listening and reading many such stories that understanding may begin.
2. "I bring in adults from different cultures and ask them to tell us stories, but I don't have to worry about their form because I just use them as conversation starters." We would see this as a lost opportunity. Moreover, even more directly than complete exclusion from the classrooms, such marginalization of stories from their own culture would seem to convey the message that they do not really count. In a world as interconnected as the world of the twenty-first century will be, all cultures will in fact count a great deal. Moreover, valuing all kinds of stories in American classrooms would seem one way of making it clear that all kinds of students are valued as well.
3. "Kindergarten and first-grade children need to be taught narrative. They have a particular need for instruction in sequencing." Again, we would

point out that in the case of cultures, such as the European North American one, for which we have extensive developmental information available, the form of oral story valued by the culture is something the child has been using for a couple of years prior to entering school. We would remind readers that we know of many failed attempts to change oral narrative structure and no successful ones. Moreover, we have considerable reservations about the wisdom of switching children because we believe that all traditions have compelling stories. Our country could be very rich indeed if we drew on the accumulated forms of wisdom of all the traditions represented in our classrooms today.

4. "Translations of Western European or American stories into Spanish (or Cambodian or Portuguese) will work, and at least I understand those stories." Maybe teachers understand the stories, but the most critical thing is that the children understand the stories enough to see the point of decoding. Comprehension of the narrative thrust of the material would seem to entice children to go to the extraordinary trouble they have to take to master decoding.

Possible Objections from Those Who Have Reservations about Multicultural Literature

In anticipating or answering some of the questions to be faced in discussing the ideas of this book, I found myself adapting various arguments for and against bilingual education (see Snow, 1990) with particular attention to the narrative level of language, which has not been addressed in prior arguments on the topic. Note that I do not propose to debate bilingual education itself here; in fact, English-only programs could easily be modified to address the concerns I am expressing.

1. "Won't reading stories to children that match their sense of story result in a kind of ghettoization of them as readers?" A true reader can and, more importantly, will read anything, and the goal is to get all children reading and enjoying what they read. Children will learn whatever it takes to find out the end of stories that engage them. Moreover, while we recommend starting children out by reading stories that match their sense of what a story should be, we also advocate eventual instruction of all ethnic groups in stories from other ethnic groups.

   Furthermore, the exchange of stories should not be one-way, as it is now, for the most part. European North American children will miss a great many excellent stories if they confine themselves to the Western tradition. In order truly to understand literature from other cultures, however, it is essential to understand general cultural differences, and to have practice reading stories from those cultures over the years.

2. Other people might argue that "prior immigrant groups were given mainstream stories to read and they did just fine." However, prior immigrant

groups (such as German, Italian, Irish, and Jewish) shared a Western tradition. Collections of fairy tales from these various European backgrounds show remarkable similarity in content as well as form. For example, in many European countries there is some version of a story about a worthy sibling (one of three, the other two of which are unworthy) who marries an animal. The animal is then restored to its prior (and temporarily eclipsed) royal status. In France, there is "Beauty and the Beast." In Germany, there is "The Three Daughters and the Frog King." In Italy there is "The Prince who married a Frog." The overlap is that specific. Moreover, Catherine Snow (1990) also makes the point that many immigrants in the early part of this century failed to achieve the high levels of literacy required in today's marketplace.

3. Some individuals might argue that it is a hopeless cause to maintain instruction in stories from different cultures because assimilation to mainstream values has traditionally been quite extensive after only two or three generations. However, American Indians and African Americans have been in this country for hundreds of years and yet they have maintained a distinctive sense of storytelling, so this argument is not completely true. Moreover, forcing ethnic groups to assimilate more than they wish to verges on the unethical. Forced, albeit more-or-less unconscious, assimilation to mainstream storytelling also has been remarkably ineffective. That is, most educators know very well the grim statistics documenting the fact that many American Indian, Latino, and African American children fail to achieve literacy.

4. Of course, most readers will be familiar with the zero-sum arguments that today's students will learn about other cultures at the expense of knowledge of the Western European canon. That debate is not a dominant concern of this book. However, it is a mistake to think of instruction in reading and literature as a product (that is, mastery of a fixed set of literary works), instead of induction into the process of lifelong appreciation of literature. Furthermore, studies have documented that on the school-aged level, many of the stories that would be "bumped" are a distinctive basal reader genre that does not conform even to the standard European North American story grammar structure (see, Beck et al., 1984).

5. Related to this argument is the idea that if the goal of instruction is to train children in the white Western literary canon, then they might as well spend their time reading stories of that form. To this criticism, we would argue that learning to make sense of experience in many different ways is a valuable exercise in developing thought. One of the best ways of training children to understand each other is to get them to read things from truly different perspectives and to identify with heros and heroines of many different cultures and kinds of experiences. Finally, we repeat that European North American children will miss many good stories on all levels from various cultures if they do not ever have the opportunity to encounter these stories or the ability to understand them if they do.

What Evidence Exists that Such Curricular Interventions Will Succeed?

Instruction about Story Structure

First of all, numerous studies have found that explicit instruction in aspects of story structure effectively increases children's comprehension (see Pearson & Fielding, 1991, for review). Children in kindergarten and elementary school show improved comprehension of the stories discussed, as well as generally improved comprehension of other stories. However, these efforts have virtually all pertained to instruction in story grammar—the precipitation and resolution of protagonists' goals. We are encouraged by the effectiveness of these past interventions but would like to see such efforts extended to the less European aspects of story structure discussed throughout this book.

We also wish to stress that in literature rules are made to be broken. Children play with all sorts of rules in the process of acquiring them. Teenagers, especially gifted ones, consciously flaunt conventions of storytelling in their story writing (Freedman, 1987). Published fiction writers are known for their deliberate, masterful violation of many so-called rules of writing. We urge instruction in all the many European and non-European rules of storytelling to be mindful of this paradox.

Culturally Relevant Instruction

Past work (for example, Vogt, Jordan, & Tharp, 1987) has documented increased effectiveness in reading instruction that is tailored to be culturally compatible with children in terms of educational process (administration of praise, means of discussing stories, and so forth). But perhaps one of the best documentations of the potential for including stories from a child's own culture in their reading assignments comes not from educational research, but from a clinical psychology treatment program termed "Cuento therapy" (Constantino, Malgady, & Rogler, 1984, 1986). In that project, the authors used Puerto Rican folktales *(cuentos)* to reduce anxiety and aggression among high risk Puerto Rican children, aged 5 through 8 years. Stories selected were those that best expressed thoughts, feelings, values, and behaviors representative of Puerto Rican culture, and they stressed themes such as social judgment, control of aggression, and delay of gratification. Although prior studies had found it difficult to involve Latinos in therapeutic services, this program did not. In the successful treatment conditions, therapists and mothers read either original or modernized versions of the stories bilingually to children. They all subsequently discussed the stories and dramatized parts of them. The clinical effectiveness of this twenty-week program was evident at its completion: children in cuentos therapy had significantly lower scores on the State-Trait Anxiety Inventory, fewer reports of aggression by teachers, and significantly higher comprehension scores (using the Wechsler Intelligence Scale for Children-Revised Comprehension subtests). The effect of lowered anxiety was also evident at a follow-up assessment done a year later. The authors did not stress the benefits of such a program on children's literacy skills, although the benefits of parental bookreading are quite well-known (see, Wells, 1985).

It is also worthwhile noting that Nielsen rating of the Top Ten primetime shows among African American viewers are completely different from the Top Ten overall. The most popular shows in African American households not only feature African American characters, but are what have been called "black lifestyle shows" centered around life and activities in African American households (Doug Alligood, The Boston Globe, May 3, 1994).

Oral storytelling skills that minority students bring from their homes to school can and should serve as a foundation for the development of their academic and literacy skills. This kind of additive program has been implemented by the Kamehameha Early Education Program (KEEP) in Hawaii, a primary grades program that aims at producing normal school achievement for urban Hawaiian children of low socioeconomic status. KEEP is comprised of a language arts program and a behavior/classroom management component that facilitates the smooth operation of the language arts component. The program acts on the premise that teachers from European North American backgrounds need to understand and appreciate minority children's early socialization patterns and home narrative discourse practices. Furthermore, teachers are expected to help those children learn without molding them into the patterns of European North American children (Au, 1993; Au & Jordan, 1981; Jordan, 1984). In KEEP, educators facilitate students' academic success by combining new areas of linguistic knowledge with the communicative skills that they already have acquired in their homes and local communities. That is, KEEP teachers use an instructional method similar to that found in "talk story," an important speech event for Hawaiian children in their local speech communities. By establishing culturally compatible classroom practices through culturally responsive instruction, therefore, narrative discourse practices children acquire at home can facilitate their effective participation in school activities. (See Minami & Ovando, 1994, for further discussion of these issues.)

Teaching Tolerance

Finally, and of most direct relevance to the issue of promoting communication among children of different cultures, is a project done by Phyllis Katz and Sue Zalk (1978). They selected urban and suburban second- and fifth-grade European North American children who were determined to be highly prejudiced against other races and asked them to participate in one of four short-term intervention techniques, all of which attempted to modify their racial attitudes: (a) One condition involved increased positive racial contact; two African American and two European North American children solved a puzzle cooperatively. (b) One group involved training children to differentiate minority group faces. (c) A third group involved reinforcement of the color black. (d) The fourth condition was a storybook reading one—children were asked to listen to a fifteen-minute story, which was accompanied by slides, and then answer a few questions about it. In the critical condition, white children were shown slides of African American characters who triumph over adversity to take a sick grandmother to the hospital, whereas in the control condition the children heard the same story but saw slides of European North American characters.

Of critical importance for a number of arguments we have been making is their finding that the condition in which children read *one fifteen-minute story* with African American characters and the one in which they were taught to differentiate minority group faces were considerably more effective in lowering negative racial attitudes than were the group interaction and reinforcement conditions. Again, just putting children of different backgrounds into the same room or even into cooperative learning environments is not sufficient to ensure understanding, let alone appreciation. But even one very short story—probably not an authentic one—is sufficient to produce measurable results. Remarkably, the results of this single-shot story condition were still measurable *four months later*. Moreover, second-graders in this condition reported more African American friends four months later in addition to showing reduced general prejudice.

The Issue of Initial Resistance. Katz and Zalk (1978) reported another important finding that educators will need to consider in implementing a genuine multicultural literacy curriculum. Twice as many of the white children who saw slides of African American characters exhibited restlessness as did those who saw European American characters. This kind of initial resistance to stories from different cultures is one that Xiaofang Xu (1993) also found when she read stories from four cultures to predominantly European North American preschool children. However, Xu found that if she not only did not stop reading such stories to the children, but even read more of them, the children came to appreciate them far more. In other words, as Xu paraphrased a Chinese proverb, "Familiarity breeds proficiency."

The kind of resistance documented in this research is resistance of children who by and large find European North American stories at home and at school and are, perhaps for the first time, reading stories about people from cultures other than their own. The resistance of children who are not European North American to stories from that tradition has not been documented so far as we know. But it is likely to occur and to be of a different sort than the one deriving from the unfamiliarity previously described. It is not hard to imagine such children given a steady diet of books from the dominant culture becoming familiar, even proficient, with that story form but drawing the conclusion that books in general had little to do with their lives.

An even more powerful emotional impediment to a serious multicultural literature program is the fact that direct discussion of race, racism, and prejudice disturbs many teachers and parents, as well as students (Amster, 1994). However, within the parameters of the kind of program we have been advocating so far lies considerable leeway for the directness with which these issues are faced. Some educators may feel comfortable selecting books that talk directly about these explosive issues. Others may prefer to select books that emphasize positive aspects of the lives of people in many cultures, both abroad and within the United States. The most important point to keep in mind is that in powerful stories written by authors from various backgrounds, characters are distinct individuals easily recognized as such and individuals with whom readers will empathize. Teachers may want to inform or even involve parents in selecting materials for a multicultural literature program.

Two strategies for overcoming resistance to story forms unfamiliar to children are (1) consistently dramatizing stories, and (2) bringing in accomplished storytellers from the communities under consideration, particularly parents who are good at this activity. The former strategy would involve each child in informal dramas done regularly so that each child would literally be included in the stories in question. The second strategy would stimulate parent-school connections with communities that may, for a variety of reasons, mistrust the schools. Thus, children who may not feel at home at school could be encouraged to do so by this means of including their parents and / or stories from their community. For children unfamiliar with the story forms in question, the drama of a live storyteller can be considerable, and very engaging.

Conclusion

Despite having worked on the research on which this book is based more-or-less nonstop for years now, and despite the fact that I as main author have attempted to include in this book all information I know of about cultural differences in storytelling traditions, it seems likely that I have only scratched the surface of the rich set of storytelling traditions represented in the United States, not to mention the world, at the present time. Even though I have talked to hundreds, maybe thousands, of individuals about the ideas discussed here, I keep encountering new "treasure troves" of stories from a particular culture sitting in someone's basement or in someone's memory, loved but forgotten for years. I hope readers will send me word of these omissions so that someday this book can be twice the size it is now. Many things need to change to improve relations among various cultural groups in our vast country, but I truly believe that if our school curricula included the best stories from all our traditions we would have wiser, more communicatively competent individuals running the country in a few years' time.

EXEMPLARY INSTRUCTION

Janet McClurg (Abouzeid & McClurg, under review) works with high school-age students in a rural Virginia school district. She works with twenty boys and ten girls who have been sent to this alternative school because of unacceptable behavior in the regular public school. The children are African American and European North American, ranging in age from 14 to 18 years. In the fall of 1994, Ms. McClurg decided to experiment with the narrative genre and the access to literacy it might provide her students. The teacher began by encouraging them to tell personal stories. Many of the initial efforts were elaborate scary stories, more fiction than fact. Ms. McClurg brought in a tape recorder and recorded personal stories from each student, which she later transcribed. The students seemed "enamored with reading their own words" (Abouzeid & McClurg, under review, p. 3), and these stories seemed far more grounded in real personal experiences. One young man was inspired to draft his ideas in outline form before taping the next version. Students went on to use the computer for some personal transcriptions. They were given the assignment to collect holiday stories from relatives, which they were actually excited about. One student suggested that the class "should all sit in a group and tell stories," which the teacher agreed to do. In other words, daily exchanges of real personal narratives became the core of Ms. McClurg's curriculum.

Did it work? One student commented, "This is the most work I've done in five years," a self-appraisal that was confirmed by prior teachers. Ms. McClurg reports newfound enthusiasm from students who literally had been so alienated from school that they had been thrown out of it prior to coming to her class. More important, when the students were given a choice of whether or not to keep their personal narratives (written and transcribed), they chose to keep almost all of them. Narratives—the personal stories of ordinary children—mean a lot to them. The importance of narratives continues beyond elementary school and can be tapped, as it was here, by ingenious teachers of even the most demanding students.

Summary

- Cultural differences in storytelling traditions and forms have many implications for classroom instruction.
- The stories read to and by all children should match their sense of storytelling some of the time, and challenge it at other times.
- Assessments of narrative ability must take diversity in storytelling form into account. Children should not simply be asked to switch into European North American form in oral or written stories.
- Writing instruction could be improved if teachers accepted a wider variety of narrative and story forms as good ones.
- Cultural differences in storytelling traditions and forms also have many implications for social interactions in the classroom. Teachers and students alike make assumptions about the personality of children on the basis of their narratives and stories, and these assumptions can be quite mistaken when individuals do not come from the same cultural background.
- Educators are asked to assume form, instead of the lack of it, in children's oral storytelling.
- Possible objections to multicultural literature programs in general and the kind advocated in this book in particular are addressed. There is evidence that this kind of program works in many important ways.

References

ABOUZEID, M.P., & MCCLURG, J. (under review). "We ought to be talking to each other": High school students map out a narrative strategy.

AMSTER, S. (1994). Making the invisible visible: Anti-racist education goes beyond "Let's appreciate diversity." *Harvard Education Letter, X* (1), 5–8.

AU, K.H. (1993). *Literacy instruction in multicultural settings.* Fort Worth, TX: Harcourt Brace Jovanovich.

AU, K.H., & JORDAN, C. (1981). Teaching reading to Hawaiian children: Finding a culturally appropriate solution. In H. Trueba, G.P. Guthrie, & K.H. Au (Eds.), *Culture in the bilingual classroom: Studies in classroom ethnography,* (pp. 139–152). Rowley, MA: Newbury House.

BAKER, D.T. (1982). What happened when? Activities for teaching sequence skills. *The Reading Teacher,* November: 216–218.

BARRY, A. K. (1991). Narrative style and witness testimony. *Journal of Narrative and Life History, 1(4),* 281-294.

BEACH, R., & HYNDS, S. (1991). Research on response to literature. In R. Barr, M.L. Kamil, P.B. Mosenthal, & P.D. Pearson (Eds.), *Handbook of reading research* (Vol. 2, pp. 453–489). New York: Longman.

BECK, I.L., MCKEOWN, M.G., OMANSON, R.C., & POPLE, M.T. (1984). Improving the comprehensibility of stories: The effects of revisions that improve coherence. *Reading Research Quarterly, XIX* (3), 263–277.

CONSTANTINO, G., MALGADY, R.G., & ROGLER, L.H. (1984). Cuentos Folkloricos as a therapeutic modality with Puerto Rican children. *Hispanic Journal of Behavioral Sciences, 6*(2), 169–178.

CONSTANTINO, G., MALGADY, R.G., & ROGLER, L.H. (1986). Cuento therapy: A culturally sensitive modality for Puerto Rican children. *Journal of Consulting & Clinical Psychology, 54*(5), 639–645.

DELPIT, L.D. (1988). The silenced dialogue: Power and pedagogy in educating other people's children. *Harvard Educational Review, 58*(3), 280–298.

DELPIT, L.D. (1986). Skills and other dilemmas of a progressive Black educator. *Harvard Educational Review, 56*(4), 379–385.

FINKELSTEIN, N.W., & HASKINS, R. (1983). Kindergarten children prefer same-color peers. *Child Development 54:* 502–508.

FREEDMAN, A. (1987). Development in story writing. *Applied Psycholinguistics 8:* 153–170.

GATES, H.L. (1988). *The signifying monkey.* Oxford: Oxford University Press.

GATES, H.L. (1991, November 24). "Authenticity" or the lesson of Little Tree. *The New York Times Book Review,* pp. 1, 26.

GRAVES, D.H. (1983). *Writing: Teachers and children at work.* Exeter, NH: Heinemann.

HARRIS, A.J., & SIPAY, E.R. (1990). *How to increase reading ability.* New York: Longman.

HARRIS, V.J. (1991). Multicultural curriculum: African American children's literature. *Young Children, 46*(2), 37–44.

HEMPHILL, L., & SIPERSTEIN, G. (1990). Conversational competence and peer response to mildly retarded children. *Journal of Educational Psychology, 82,* 128–134.

HURSTON, Z.N. (1935/1990). *Mules and men.* New York: Harper & Row.

JOHN, V.P. & BERNEY, J.D. (1968). Analysis of story retelling as a measure of the effects of ethnic content in stories. In J. Helmuth (Ed.), *The disadvantaged child: Head Start and early intervention* (Vol. 2, pp. 259–287). New York: Brunner/Mazel.

JORDAN, C. (1984). Cultural compatibility and the education of Hawaiian children: Implications for mainland educators. *Education Research Quarterly, 8* (4), 59–71.

KATZ, P.A., & ZALK, S.R. (1978). Modification of children's racial attitudes. *Developmental Psychology, 14* (5), 447–461.

Kumon Education Institute (1988). Kongetsu no haiku [The *haiku* of this month]. *Tanoshii vochien: Sukusuku room [Happy kindergarten: Growing-up room], 12*(2).

LABOV, W. (1972). *Language in the inner city.* Philadelphia, PA: University of Pennsylvania Press.

LADSON-BILLINGS, G. (1992). Reading between the lines and beyond the pages: A culturally relevant approach to literacy teaching. *Theory into Practice, XXXI* (4), 312–320.

McCABE, A. (1989, March). "Strategies for developing narrative structure in a pre-school
setting." Paper presented at the annual meeting of the American Educational Research Association, San Francisco, CA.

McCABE, A., & PETERSON, C. (1990). What makes a story memorable? *Applied Psycholinguistics, 11*(1), 73–82.

McCABE, A., & PETERSON, C. (1991). Getting the story: A longitudinal study of parental
styles in eliciting narratives and child narrative skill. In A. McCabe, & C. Peterson
(Eds.), *Developing narrative structure* (pp. 217–254). Hillsdale, NJ: Lawrence Erlbaum.

MICHAELS, S. (1991). The dismantling of narrative. In A. McCabe, & C. Peterson (Eds.),
Developing narrative structure (pp. 303–352). Hillsdale, NJ: Lawrence Erlbaum.

MILLER-LACHMANN, L. (1992). *Our family, our friends, our world: An annotated guide to significant multicultural books for children and teenagers.* New Providence, NJ: R.R.
Bowker.

MILLER, P.J., POTTS, R., FUNG, H., HOOGSTRA, L., & MINTZ, J. (1990). Narrative practices
and the social construction of self. *American Ethnologist, 17*(2), 292–311.

MINAMI, M. (1990). "Children's narrative structure. How do Japanese children talk about
their own stories?" Unpublished qualifying paper, Harvard University, Cambridge,
MA.

MINAMI, M., & McCABE, A. (1991). *Haiku* as a discourse regulation mechanism: A stanza
analysis of Japanese children's personal narratives. *Language in Society, 20,* 577–599.

MINAMI, M., & OVANDO, C.J. (1994). Language issues in multicultural contexts. In
J. Banks & C. McGee Banks (Eds.), *Handbook of research on multicultural education.*
New York: Macmillan.

NEWMAN, M.A., LISS, M.B., & SHERMAN, F. (1983). Ethnic awareness in children: Not a
unitary concept. *The Journal of Genetic Psychology, 143,* 103–112.

OMANSON, R.C. (1982a). An analysis of narratives: Identifying central, supportive, and
distracting content. *Discourse Processes, 5,* 195–224.

OMANSON, R.C. (1982b). The relation between centrality and story category variation.
Journal of Verbal Learning and Verbal Behavior, 21, 326–337.

PEARSON, P.D., & FIELDING, L. (1991). Comprehension instruction. In R. Barr, M.L. Kamil,
P.B. Mosenthal, & P.D. Pearson (Eds.), *Handbook of reading research* (Vol. 2, pp.
815–860). New York: Longman.

PEREZ, C. (1992). "Clinicians' perceptions of children's oral personal narratives." Unpublished master's thesis, University of Massachusetts, Boston.

PEREZ, C., McCABE, A., & TAGER-FLUSBERG, H. (in preparation). Clinicians' perceptions of
children's oral personal narratives.

SCHIEFFELIN, B.B., & EISENBERG, A.R. (1984). Cultural variation in children's conversations. In R.L. Schiefelbusch & J. Pickar (Eds.), *The acquisition of communicative competence* (pp. 378–420). Baltimore, MD: University Park Press.

SINGLETON, L.C., & ASHER, S.R. (1979). Racial integration and children's peer preferences:
An investigation of developmental and cohort differences. *Child Development, 50,*
936–941.

SLAVIN, R.E. (1985). Cooperative learning: Applying contact theory in desegregated
schools. *Journal of Social Issues, 41*(3), 45–62.

SMALLS-HECTOR, I. (1991). *Irene and the Big, Fine Nickel.* Boston, MA: Little, Brown.

SNOW, C.E. (1990). Rationales for native language instruction in the education of language minority children: Evidence from research. In A. Padilla, H. Fairchild, & Con-
cepcion Valadez (Eds.), *Bilingual education: Issues and strategies* (pp. 60–74). NY: Sage.

VOGT, L.A., JORDAN, C., & THARP, R.G. (1987). Explaining school failure, producing school success: Two cases. *Anthropology & Education Quarterly, 18,* 276–286.

WEIGEL, R.H., WISER, P.L., & COOK, S.W. (1975). The impact of cooperative learning experiences on cross-ethnic relations and attitudes. *Journal of Social Issues, 31*(1), 219–244.

WELLS, G. (1985). Preschool literacy-related activities and success in school. In D.R. Olson, N. Torrance, & A. Hildyard (Eds.), *Literacy, language and learning* (pp. 229–256). New York: Cambridge University Press.

WHITEHURST, G.J., ANGELL, A., CRONE, D., & FISCHEL, J. (1994). "Effects of time budgets and interactional styles of teachers on the development of language and emergent literacy skills of children in Head Start." Paper presented at the annual meeting of the American Educational Research Association, New Orleans, LA.

XU, X. (1993). "Familiar and strange: A comparison of children's literature in four cultures." Unpublished master's thesis, Tufts University, Medford, MA.

Subject Index

Author Index